Architecture Re-assembled

Beginning from the rise of modern history in the eighteenth century, this book examines how changing ideas in the discipline of history itself have affected architecture from the beginnings of modernity up to the present day.

It reflects upon history, tradition and memory, in order to encourage and assist the reader in finding well-founded principles for architectural design.

This is not simply another history of architecture, nor a 'history of histories'. Setting buildings in their contemporaneous ideas about history, it spans from Fischer von Erlach to Venturi and Rossi, and beyond to architects working in the fallout from both the Modern Movement – Aalto, Louis Kahn and Aldo van Eyck – and post-modernism – such as Rafael Moneo and Peter Zumthor. It shows how Soane, Schinkel and Stirling, amongst others, made a meaningful use of history, and contrasts this with how a misreading of Hegel has led to an abuse of history and an uncritical flight to the future. This is not an armchair history but a lively discussion of our place between past and future that promotes thinking for making.

Trevor Garnham is an architect and former Principal Lecturer at Kingston University School of Architecture, UK.

First published 2013
by Routledge

2 Park Square, Milton Park, Abingdon, Oxon OX14 4RN
Simultaneously published in the USA and Canada
by Routledge

711 Third Avenue, New York, NY 10017

Routledge is an imprint of the Taylor
& Francis Group, an informa business

British Library Cataloguing in Publication Data
A catalogue record for this book is available from the British Library

Library of Congress Cataloging in Publication Data
Garnham, Trevor
Architecture re-assembled: the use (and abuse) of history / Trevor Garnham
pages cm
includes bibliographical references and index.
1. Architecture and history. 2. Architecture, Modern. I. Title.
NA2543.H55g37 2013
720.1'04–DC23
2012042353
ISBN: 978-0-415-52244-1 (hbk)
ISBN: 978-0-415-52245-8 (pbk)
ISBN: 978-0-203-52829-7 (ebk)

Typeset in 10pt Adobe Garamond Pro and 8pt Myriad Pro
by zerotwonine design

Printed and bound in Great Britain by
TJ International Ltd, Padstow, Cornwall

Architecture Re-assembled

The Use (and Abuse) of History

Trevor Garnham

ACKNOWLEDGEMENTS

I would like to thank Fran Ford first of all, for her support throughout the complicated circumstances that coincided with the writing and the design of this book. Fran's suggestion that I direct my proposal to explore the relationship between historiography and architecture proved to be decisive in determining its final form. I am extremely grateful to Timothy Garnham for the time spent designing the book. In addition thanks for the five weeks he spent touring Europe taking the photographs that make up the majority of illustrations. Special thanks to Bill Ungless for reading, re-reading, editing, improving the text, and for many judicious comments along the way. Thanks to Brendan Woods for crucial interventions that covered some oversights.

I would like to take this opportunity to thank some former colleagues with whom I taught closely in design and seminar courses and whose insights have found their way into my own thinking: Daphne Beckett, Andy Humphries, Bryn Riches, Randall Thomas and Jeremy Till.

Thanks to Linda Downes of Kingston University Library for invaluable assistance in borrowing books, well beyond the call of duty. Thanks to Richard and Fiona of McDaniel Woolf for letting us use their office space when designing the book. Several friends and former colleagues were generous in supplying photographs: Kris Ellam, Tim Gough, Tony Ingram, Peter Kohane, Werner Kreis, Tim Wilcockson and Brendan Woods.

Last but not least, many thanks to Lorna for typing up the drafts and in particular for all her help and support through the final difficult stages of the book's completion.

I would like to dedicate this book to the memory of my mother, Joyce Garnham, who died a week before it was completed.

Contents:

Introduction

Friedrich Nietzsche begins *The Use and Abuse of History* by quoting Goethe: 'I hate everything that merely instructs me without increasing or directly quickening my activity.'[1] This book begins by quoting Nietzsche quoting Goethe: are we to be condemned to work over and over again the words of our predecessors? Is history the great dead weight of the past? Or is it the deep and fertile soil from which a healthy culture grows? And do we need to know our architectural history in order to practice? Nietzsche uses Goethe as a springboard for his observations on 'the worth and worthlessness of history'. History had come to arrest the natural development of his own age, he argued. An 'excess of history' and piling up of facts was the 'enemy of the life of a time', destroying the vitality required to create a living culture.[2]

Posterity has judged Nietzsche to be one of the most radical and influential thinkers of modern times. His call at the end of the nineteenth century for a 'revaluation of all values' is taken to mean a total rejection of existing culture and that inherited from the past. Despite this received opinion, he in fact concludes the essay by stating that we do need history, but only if it is considered in the right spirit. 'We do need history', he says, 'we need it for life and action.'[3] By this he means not passively deferring to the past, but looking there actively and creatively for lessons to help forge a living culture, a culture of the present and appropriate to the times. Nietzsche attacked Christian morality for its denial of the 'will to life', and specifically, the Reformation, which he charged with cutting short the Renaissance rediscovery of classical mythology with its 'life-affirmative values', which would again underpin the living culture he aspired to.[4]

This book has two aims: firstly to explore the proposition that history might be necessary 'for life and action' and, secondly, to provide a reading of modern architecture and its history in the conviction that history is important to architectural design today. It is often said that we live in an age of such unprecedented change that lessons from the past are irrelevant. But, as the historian John Tosh says, 'in all spheres of life, from personal relationships to political judgements, we constantly interpret our experience in time perspective. The mere fact of living alongside people older than ourselves makes us conscious of the past.'[5] How we deal with this fact in the design of the built environment, made up of so many traces of the past, will be a leading question addressed here. However, this should not be taken to imply that we pursue a conservation project nor resort to historical copying. As Nietzsche warned, this would be destructive 'of the life' of our time.

Architectural histories tend to follow the empirical template described in David Watkin's book *The Rise of Architectural History* (1980), essentially outlining how and when one style succeeded another with various explanations: aesthetic, technological, political, economic, etc.[6] In *The Idea of History* the philosopher R.G. Collingwood describes this legacy of positivism as a 'dry-as-dust attitude'.[7] The idea of history itself is rarely discussed in architectural histories. Architectural history has been taken to be merely the accumulation of significant buildings. History itself has been taken as 'an indefinite given category' in the past twenty years or so, says Adrian Forty, rather as 'nature' was in the eighteenth century: 'in general late twentieth century architects showed a remarkable lack of curiosity about what had been going on in the discipline of history itself.'[8] He alludes here to how post-modernists, post-structuralists and deconstructivists have challenged the possibility of establishing secure knowledge, including the problem of objectivity in history. A conservative architectural historian such as Watkin, for example, presents what he considers to be an objective account in his *A History of Western Architecture* (1986), whereas a post-structuralist would argue that subjectivity is inevitably involved. A deconstructivist in turn would claim that Watkin's repeated insistence on 'taste' and the way he links this to classical architecture is evidence of his unacknowledged subjectivity. Post-structuralists assert that 'there is no reality against which the truth or accuracy of language can be measured.'[9] Extreme post-structuralism leads to what has been called a 'vitiating relativism' which encourages pure subjectivity. These developments in historiography have been paralleled in architecture, for example, by the shift from the Modern Movement's aim for objectivity to the extreme subjectivity seen in the novel forms of more recent 'icon' buildings. This intellectual sea-change is generally known under the umbrella term, post-modernism, a movement that flourished in the 1980s and 1990s. The ambition of these new, challenging ideas was in turn contested by architect-critics influenced by phenomenology, a contest played out in schools of architecture during this period. Their opposing views of history help explain the diversity of contemporary architecture.

Any historian writing in the knowledge of these intellectual currents, cannot but be aware that he or she is writing a specific narrative that reflects their choice of subject and selection of supporting facts. The reader will have noticed that I have selected a statement of Nietzsche's that emphasises his connecting history with the 'life' of a culture, a view that runs counter to prevailing interpretations. How architecture has turned away from ideas of 'life', and turned towards mechanical or technological conceptions, will be an underlying thread of the historical narrative presented here. My intention is to discuss the idea of history together with selected relevant buildings in the conviction that this will help aid reflection upon the practice of architectural design. Significant landmarks in the rise of modern philosophy of history will be discussed in relation to the way certain architects responded, both in their writings and buildings. It follows that this will not be a comprehensive or seamless survey: this will allow me to give a more detailed discussion of how buildings themselves were shaped by changing ideas of history. Consequently the book takes the form of a series of vignettes that compare principles with practice, tradition versus innovation, with historiography providing a connecting thread. This will not be an 'armchair' history nor a work of pure theory, but aims to promote thinking for making.

Where Nietzsche presented a snapshot of nineteenth century culture, I want to present a broader view. For behind his critique of emerging modernity he points to the impact of the Enlightenment. The early eighteenth century, therefore, makes for an appropriate place to begin this study because Giambattista Vico's *Scienza nuova* (1725) is often referred to as the first modern history (more properly, a philosophy of history) and its publication more-or-less coincided with the first comparative history of architecture, Johann Fischer von Erlach's *Entwurff einer Historischen Architektur* (1721).[10] Before Fischer, a renaissance architectural treatise was essentially normative and prescriptive, setting down precepts for practice drawn from the Roman architect/engineer Vitruvius. The opening of the modern era in history sprang from Vico pointing out that the nature of anything is 'its coming to be and passing away'.[11] Time and change became central and man became 'historical man'. Vico's cyclical conception of history shows his roots in the Renaissance, but, as I will discuss, in the Enlightenment this was replaced by a linear view which became linked to the idea of 'progress'.

This suggested a chronological presentation of two broad divisions. The first part looks at eighteenth century responses to the challenges made to Vitruvian authority by science and history, followed by a nineteenth century ensnared in historicism and the attempts to overcome this, including Nietzsche urging the 'eternal recurrence', what I have called 'a history beyond history'. This establishes the background to the crucial chapter, 'Approaches to Modernism'. Shaped by historians such as Nikolaus Pevsner, a narrative was constructed whereby the Modern Movement defined itself against history. Here, in contrast, turn-of-the-century 'pioneer' architects are considered from the perspective of the traditions of practice in which they were trained rather than emphasising the traits of an inevitable white International Style, which Pevsner and others argued they foresaw. 'Pioneers' were more interested in history than is portrayed. In *The Historiography of Modern Architecture* (1999), Panayotis Tournikiotis describes this 1930s phase as 'operative' histories. He proceeds to consider how the Modern Movement came to be considered a failure, which led to the return of history to architectural design discourse in the late 1960s. In the second half of this study, I look more specifically at how misgivings about the rational and technological bias of modernism led to a new engagement with the humanities more generally, which played a significant part in leading architects back to history. By one of those curious coincidences of history, Robert Venturi's *Complexity and Contradiction in Architecture* (1966), which launched post-modern architecture, was published in the same year as Aldo Rossi's *The Architecture of the City* (1966). The two books had entirely different aims but between them they established the significance of history, tradition and memory to architectural design in the latter part of the twentieth century.

History might be thought of as akin to memory. To be human is to be poised between memory and anticipation. This moment, every moment, has its past and its future. Our sense of time 'involves some feeling or awareness of duration' and we 'experience a feeling of duration whenever the present situation is related by us either to our past experiences or to our future expectations and desires'.[12] Child development studies demonstrate that our sense of expectation develops before our consciousness of memory. And a child's awareness of time only emerges when memory develops. Without memory we could do almost nothing but, at worst, like goldfish, we would drift aimlessly from here to there, or at best only satisfy immediate desires like an overgrown and spoilt child. In *The Landscape of History*, John Lewis Gaddis argues that history helps people form 'a sense of identity that parallels the process of growing up'. He defines 'historical consciousness as the projection of that maturity through time.'[13] Compared with an individual's sense of the past, which is produced spontaneously, for a society, says Tosh, 'History is collective memory, the storehouse of experience through which people develop a sense of their social identity and their future prospects.'[14] Just as memory plays an important part in our becoming a fully fledged adult, so perhaps a mature society needs a cultural memory. Forty has pointed to the paradox that memory was ignored by modernist architects yet in literature 'it was paramount'.[15] Proust's *Remembrance of Things Past* is the most well-known example. Forty notes how 'memory full' was the twentieth century with its plethora of museums, archives and the rise of a heritage industry. But he wonders whether the notion of memory is 'inherently alien to architecture.'[16] The relationship between architecture and memory will be explored in the final two chapters, and distinctions between history, tradition and memory clarified.

If Nietzsche felt that his time was stifled by history, it could be said of our own age that the reverse is true.[17] Relativism has over-played the element of subjectivity in design and played a part in the current obsession with novelty of form, such that the meaning of an architectural experience is often defined simply by a name-tag of its shape, as, for example, the 'Gherkin' or 'Shard'. Our age seems ever more like an uncritical flight to the future driven by progress, science and technology. Ignoring history, misusing or abusing history makes for a situation where the deepest needs and desires of humanity are easily overlooked. Given the significance of memory, a genuine dialogue between past and present would seem to be vital.

In *The Ethical Function of Architecture* (1997), Karsten Harries acknowledged the lack of consensus following 'three decades of post-modern, poststructuralist, and deconstructivist experimentation', but insists nevertheless that architecture has an obligation to 'help us find our place in an ever more distracting world'.[18] Architecture is not simply a style, an aspect of the history of art of a period or an expression of the spirit-of-the-age, but makes the habitable world of humans. Modern disciplines – the philosophy of phenomenology, psychology, anthropology, the history of religions – suggest that there might be some fundamental structure to human being that allows cross-cultural comparisons to be made and some universal lessons to be drawn, although always given a particular cultural inflection.

History has essentially two ways by which it tries to explain the past, namely by the acts of individuals or social processes. All design is the outcome of intention it could be argued, whether conscious, subconscious, individually willed or culturally impelled. Alternatively, historians see specific contexts – social patterns, politics, technology, economic forces, etc. – determining events or forms. Neither one nor the other can satisfactorily explain in itself history. As the eminent historian E.H. Carr has written, history is the interplay of these two conditions. The aim here is to offer a reading of architecture, focusing on ideas, that involves the interplay of two specific factors – architects' intentions and the impact of historiography – in the period from Vico to the most recent past.

Precepts for practice must be appropriate to our own time, and remain true to the essential roles of architecture as seen through time. Without that design is mere belief: belief in one's individual right to self expression or in an enduring faith in technology and progress seen uncritically as the 'spirit of the age'. In the flight to the future characteristic of 'progress' and 'modernisation', we stress the different condition in which humanity finds itself today rather than the fundamental needs and hopes that persist. The dominating ideas of evolution and progress have become intertwined with a teleological conception of history. Combined with the idea of the spirit of the age and simplistically applied to architectural history, this forms a dangerous cocktail of concepts when applied to architectural design that removes humanity from the frame. History helps to give us insights into the essential nature of humanity. Reflection upon the architecture of the recent past through a consideration of history, tradition and memory might more fruitfully guide action in the present. Such a critical history will help quicken and direct our activity.

Chapter 1: Vico and the 'New Science' of history

VITRUVIUS DETHRONED BY SCIENCE

The first history was written in ancient Greece by Herodotus in the fifth century BC. There are earlier accounts of events, but in naming his work *The Histories,* Herodotus pointed to its specifically new purpose and significance. Older societies such as the Sumerians and Egyptians, kept records but there is no evidence of their interest in history as such.[1] Herodotus set out to record singularly 'human achievements', which distinguished his work from earlier epic poetry such as Homer's *Iliad* or *Odyssey,* that focused on mythical heroes.[2]

Herodotus was born in about 484 BC, some 15 years before the birth of Socrates (c. 470–399 BC) and died about the time when the Parthenon was completed in 432 BC, so his mature years coincided with the time of Pericles (c. 495–429 BC) and Athenian classical greatness. F. M. Cornford described this as a time when ancient Greek thought shifted, in the title of his book, *From Religion to Philosophy* [1.1]. Herodotus' work marks a similar shift from mythology to history. But just as Socrates and his most famous follower Plato (c. 429–347 BC) mark the beginning of a rational world-view rather than its consummation, so *The Histories* announce only the inception of a new and ultimately modern way of looking at the past. For it was not until the eighteenth century that a modern philosophy of history, or historiography, emerged through a more rigorous investigation of sources and a critical weighing of historical facts and processes rather than the broad outline sketched by ancient historians. This marked one significant moment in the onset of modernity.

The earliest peoples conceived time as cyclical, quite different from our modern linear conception of time and progress. The monumental architecture of earliest societies symbolised the belief in an eternal order that Mircea Eliade called 'the myth of the eternal return': Sumerian ziggurats symbolised the sacred mountain around whose peak revolved the heavens: Egyptian pyramids made a place of eternal rest for the dead Pharaoh: Neolithic stone circles suggest a reciprocal

1.1   The Parthenon on the Acropolis, Athens

But simply establishing facts … does not make the historian. What makes the historian is understanding the significance of what he finds.

Hans-Georg Gadamer, *Truth and Method*

1.2 Ziggurat, from William Lethaby's *Architecture, Mysticism and Myth*

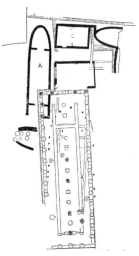

1.3 Temple of Apollo, Thermum, with older remains in outline

relationship between mankind's material culture and the eternal cycles of the sun and moon.[3] There is no reference to historical time in their development: rather they refer to an unchanging, timeless pattern of the cosmos [1.2]. Archaeological evidence indicates that the Greek temple form, in contrast, shows a historical development from the megaron house of early kings or chiefs to become a metaphorical house for a god or goddess, appropriately transformed from timber to stone, a material resistant to the decomposition of earthly life-forms [1.3]. This historical awareness, the use and transformation of a historical precedent, corresponds broadly with the new sensibility shown by Herodotus.

It was not until the rise of modern science in the seventeenth and eighteenth centuries, however, that the process of history became investigated. Modern historiography, in contrast to the work of Herodotus and his classical or medieval followers, has been described as resting 'on the discovery of man as a peculiarly historical being, subject to a development transcending the life of any individual, nation, or race'.[4] This new understanding of history, and by implication of humankind itself, was first defined by Vico, culminating in the *Scienza nuova*, whose work was a late flowering of the widespread advance in learning that accompanied the Renaissance.

Renaissance architects believed in a divinely ordered world that architecture could articulate. When a renaissance architect drew his 'lines and angles' in defining the plans and planes of a projected building, he believed that this emulated the way the Creator ordered the world. Harmonious proportions were the key to this and Leon Battista Alberti (1404–72) was the decisive figure in articulating this idea drawn from classical antiquity. The enormous importance of proportions for the history of architecture stemmed from a discovery reputedly made by Pythagoras (born c. 570 BC) of a link between harmony in music and numerical relationships. This had a profound impact on the renaissance belief in a closed, harmonious cosmos which found an echo in music and potentially in buildings through geometry and proportion.[5] But an equally vital part was played by the classical orders: 'the grammar of architecture … embodying all the ancient wisdom of mankind in building'.[6] The orders made proportions visible on the body of the building, as in the pilasters to Alberti's Pallazzo Rucellai (c. 1450–60) in Florence [1.4].

Behind Alberti stood the figure of the first century BC Roman architect Vitruvius. His importance cannot be overestimated, for his *De Architectura* was the only text on architecture surviving from classical antiquity. Humanists came to reaffirm the idea of 'natural law', which entailed stripping away the accidental to find the universal, unchanging order in nature. This lent support to Vitruvius' account of a timeless beauty predicated on symmetry and the proportional relationship of parts to a whole. The rise of science in the seventeenth and eighteenth centuries, however, came to challenge all such forms of ancient and received authority. In the words of Alexander Koyre, we moved *From the Closed World to the Infinite Universe*. Human beings on planet Earth became cast adrift in an infinite universe, such that the Vitruvian theory of architectural meaning became no longer tenable. So began the search for a new firm foundation for architecture. What this might be has preoccupied architects ever since. But scholars such as Vico investigating Roman law became increasingly aware that laws, like everything else, change with time and hence have a history.[7] Architecture's search for meaning became inextricably bound up with this new understanding of history and time.

1.4 Alberti, Palazzo Rucellai, Florence

The centre of architectural theory shifted from Italy to France in the seventeenth century, where the first serious challenge to Vitruvius emerged in the work of Claude Perrault (1613–88). Academies were being formed in this Age of Enlightenment to advance knowledge systematically, and Perrault was an active member of the Academy of Science founded in 1635. Elected to the newly formed Academy of Architecture in 1666, he was asked to prepare an authoritative edition of Vitruvius. The mandate of the new Academy was 'the reform of the classical tradition in light of the perceived abuses of the baroque period'.[8] Perrault's investigations, however, led him to deny any essential beauty embodied in proportional systems, hence undermining the bedrock of the Vitruvian tradition. 'Proportions are not certain and invariable' as those that produce 'harmony of sounds in music', he noted.[9] Perrault argued that there were neither laws of nature, nor 'logical reasoning' for precise proportioning of architectural elements. Beauty in architecture resided in richness of materials, fine workmanship, and symmetry, attributes obvious to all, as in beautiful music. This 'customary' beauty he contrasted with 'arbitrary beauty', which was 'more the result of a social consensus of perception' or 'what most educated people of taste enjoy'.[10]

The architect should be equipped with knowledge of many branches of study and varied kinds of learning, for it is by his judgement that all work done by the other arts is put to test. This knowledge is the child of practice and theory. … An architect ought to be an educated man so as to leave a more lasting remembrance in his treatises… A wide knowledge of history is requisite.

Vitruvius,
The Ten Books on Architecture

1.5 Claude Perrault,
*Ordonnance des cinq
espèce de Colonnes*

Perrault published the evidence for this in his *Ordonnance des cinq espèces de Colonnes* (1683), which he described as an appendix to his *Vitruvius* (1673). From accurate measurements of many Roman buildings he found no consistent systems of proportion, which undermined the Vitruvian claim for 'natural authority'.[11] From the range of measurements obtained, Perrault proposed instead fixing proportions empirically, 'probable' proportions 'derived from the arithmetical mean for each unit of the column and the entablature'[12] [1.5]. In making this survey, Perrault had exposed 'the fallacy that proportions are subject to influences outside of man's control'.[13] This chimed with the emerging view that everything might be measurable and hence controllable. In this recourse to precise measurement, analysis and calculation, we see how far Perrault and his compatriots had moved from a renaissance philosophy of nature, with its legacy of myth, to the Enlightenment's creation of a modern world dominated by science.[14] The new experimental method of science had produced remarkable insights into the workings of nature, which came to be seen, not as divinely created but, containing a 'formative principle which moves from within'.[15] The rise of the scientific world-view led inexorably to a split between a mathematical model of the world and the lived-world of everyday experience. Behind renaissance proportion and geometry, in contrast, lay a world of meaning shared by all involved in building: users, clients, architects and craftsmen.

1.6 Perrault, Le Vau, Le Brun:
The Louvre, Paris

The frontispiece to his *Ordonnance* illustrates both his argument and evidence by juxtaposing his design for the Louvre (1667–74) featuring a colonnade of coupled-up columns, an arrangement forbidden by Vitruvius, with an actual Roman triumphal arch that had just this arrangement [1.6 and 1.7]. (The design emerged from a committee comprised of Perrault, Le Vau, the *premier architected du Roi* and the painter Le Brun.)[16] This mixture of empiricism, reason and historical fact contradicting Vitruvius eventually had to prevail in an increasingly scientific age. The French had been shocked by Bernini's earlier Baroque proposal for rebuilding the Louvre where contemporary opinion saw his 'inspiration of the moment' at odds with Enlightenment reason and 'care for detail'.[17]

Perrault's rejection of Vitruvian precepts and his view that beauty resulted from 'chance, fancy and custom', caused a scandal amongst his fellow academicians.[18] The director of the Academy of Architecture, Francois Blondel (1618–88) angrily reaffirmed the theory that a model of beautiful or harmonious architecture had been established in classical antiquity and that this remained legitimate and binding.[19] This dispute initiated what became known as the 'Quarrel between the Ancients and the Moderns'. Followers of the 'Ancients' believed that their work came closer to the origins of the art, which gave Vitruvius authority, whereas the 'Moderns' considered that they benefited from reflection and reasoning, which gave them greater access to truth. These conflicting possibilities – origins or progress – dominated debate in the years that followed.

Ever since René Descartes (1596–1650) expounded his famous *'cogito ergo sum'* (I think therefore I am), in the mid-seventeenth century, only clear and distinct facts were accepted as guarantors of certain knowledge. This is more difficult for history than for a natural science such as physics.[20] Descartes 'dismissed history as mere opinion and arbitrary subjectivity'.[21] Vico was a Cartesian up until about the age of forty, when he came to see that the Cartesian method was not appropriate for understanding the humanities, from where emerged his *New Science*, the new science of history that reshaped the mental landscape of mankind and put history behind architects' search for new firm ground after the dethroning of Vitruvius.

VICO AND THE NEW SCIENCE OF HISTORY

Vico became the first to argue that mankind was essentially a historical being, and that his situation was largely shaped by historical circumstances. In so doing, the *New Science* called into question the fundamental precept of natural law, the prevailing belief in a set of unchanging principles with their source and legitimation in the order of the cosmos. In contrast to this essentially timeless proposition, Vico argued that we could only understand mankind by his own activity, by the things he made – including political and social

1.7 Perrault, *Ordonnance*, Frontispiece

I rightly conclude that my essence consists in this alone, that I am a thinking thing ... And although perhaps ... I have a body with which I am closely conjoined, I have, on the one hand, a clear and distinct idea of myself as a thinking, non-extended thing, and, on the other hand, a distinct idea of my body as an extended, non-thinking thing: it is therefore certain that I am truly distinct from my body and can exist without it.

René Descartes, *Discourse on Method*

systems – and that these could only be grasped by studying history. This implied that specific episodes or actions from the past could not properly be applied to the present. Although Vico doesn't discuss architecture, this would seem to render problematic the Renaissance use of the Vitruvian proportional system, for example.

The *New Science* shifted history from presenting personal feats – heroes, wars, treatises, alliances, and dynastic successions – to forms of social or economic organisation, customs, laws and institutions.[22] Vico's primary concern was to comprehend the constitution or construction of society. To do this he had to consider the origins of society and grasp patterns of development. 'Sciences must begin at the point where the subject matter begins', he wrote.[23] Only by comprehending the historical process could present conditions be understood. A focus on origins, founding principles, and processes was to become a major feature of Enlightenment thought.[24]

> Vico regards the historical process as a process whereby human beings build up systems of language, custom, law, government, etc. i.e. he thinks of history as the genesis and development of human societies and their institutions. Here we reach for the first time a completely modern idea of what the subject-matter of history is.
>
> R.G. Collingwood,
> *The Idea of History*

Vico admired the scientific method advocated by Francis Bacon (1561–1626) and Descartes, although he attacked their failure to appreciate the humanities. Notwithstanding this, his method aimed to emulate Descartes' system that established a secure foundation in wholly rational processes such as mathematics and geometry. 'In geometry we demonstrate because we create',[25] wrote Vico. His method lies in setting out axioms (114) against which he read evidence from ancient authors into his conceptual framework. He claimed that: 'My science proceeds like geometry which, by constructing and contemplating its basic elements, creates its own world of measurable quantities.'[26]

He raised two fundamental questions directed at 'natural philosophy' (as science was known in the seventeenth and eighteenth centuries). Firstly, he argued that mankind could never fully understand nature because God had created it. Only what man himself made could he truly understand. Because of this, he contrasted what he called the 'conditional knowledge' of natural science with the 'absolute knowledge' he believed history could establish. Secondly, he criticised the philosophy of natural law being applied to the earliest of men, because this philosophy had been the creation of minds from the sixteenth or seventeenth centuries. We could not, he explained, extend backwards our rational and developed understanding of society to explain the first human communities. He called this 'the conceit of the scholars'.[27] Ascribing unchanging universality to what Vico called the 'natural law of the philosophers' represented the problem, because the construction of social, economic and political structures was in fact temporal and relative, as his study of changing Roman law had demonstrated. At the end of the long gestation of the *New Science* Vico proclaimed his success:

> *the civil world is certainly the creation of humankind.* And consequently, the principles of the civil world can and must be discovered *within the modifications of the human mind.* If we reflect on this, we can only wonder why all the philosophers have so earnestly pursued a knowledge of the world of nature, which only God can know as its creator: while they neglected to study the world of nations, or civil world, which people can in fact know because they created it.[28]

The key to Vico's method lies in his sharply distinguishing humans from nature and his emphasis on the 'modifications of the human mind'. For while humans may or may not have an eternal essence, their ideas certainly changed and hence social and cultural forms, the products of minds, change through time. The possibility of understanding the origins of human societies before Greece and Rome had been widely dismissed, but this is what Vico set out to do. He attempted to reconstruct a history of mankind's earliest form of society by applying what he called a 'critical method', and what we would today call a comparative mythology, to the myths and fables recounted by classical authors. He found a set of three stages common to many different peoples' cultural development. These he called the ages of the gods, of heroes, and of men. Coexisting with these three stages was a common type of language: poetic, heroic, and vernacular.[29] His main source lay in the state of nature described by classical authors. But he felt obliged to begin with the biblical account of the origin of society since the Inquisition remained active in Naples. An outline of Vico's reconstruction of the development of the first societies and how they developed will help us understand the subsequent importance of origins and history.

He begins with the story of the flood in Genesis, where it describes the dispersal of Noah's descendants into the forests and falling to the level of beasts. After a long period during which the Earth dried out, thunder storms drove the terrified people to take shelter in caves. From these gatherings the first families arose, 'fearful' religions were formed, and from these settled conditions sprang farming, property

Vico's fantasia is indispensable to his conception of historical knowledge: it is unlike the knowledge that Julius Caesar is dead, or that Rome was not built in a day, or that thirteen is a prime number, or that a week has seven days... It is more like knowing what it is to be poor, to belong to a nation, to be a revolutionary, to be converted to a religion, to fall in love, to be seized by nameless terror, to be delighted by a work of art.

Isaiah Berlin,
Giambattista Vico and Cultural History

laws and morality. Out of these family-centred societies emerged leaders – kings, priests or wise men, such as Orpheus, whom he calls a 'poetic archetype' – who sacrificed to Jupiter-type gods in their despair.[30] Vico called this first primitive stage of society 'the age of the gods', from where emerged some universal customs, which he called his 'three first principles': religion, marriage and burial of the dead.[31]

Although Vico doesn't refer to Vitruvius amongst the classical authors he consulted, the essential characteristics of his description are similar to the Roman author's account of the origins of architecture. Vitruvius has the same elements of beast-like humans living in caves after being terrified by thunder and he also makes much of the advantage provided by natural outbreaks of fire in prompting social intercourse. In addition, he says that the unique vertical stance of men allowed them to 'make whatever they wished with their hands'.[32] With this ability some 'began to make roofs of leaves' and since men were observant, imitative and endowed with reason, the first built shelters were made, Vitruvius writes, by 'setting up forked posts, and putting withies between them' and finishing 'their walls with mud'.[33] Vico himself described an unfolding 'order of human institutions' that ran as 'first forests, then huts, next villages, later cities'.[34] Vitruvius' account of the origins of architecture in the primitive hut was to have a major impact on architectural theory in the years following Perrault's demolition of the belief in proportional relationships.

The state of nature was neither static nor timeless, Vico argued, but one of inequality and differentiation, which provoked change, the essential characteristic of his history. In the first 'age of the gods', some people would have remained outside the organised families, there would also have been inequality within and between families. This led to violence, resulting in some of those outside seeking refuge with the settled families. From this grew a new situation where father figures ruled not only over their own family but also the refugees, effectively forming a society of patricians and slaves or serfs. To protect themselves against uprisings from the lower orders, patricians formed alliances and allotted rights only to themselves. This second stage of social development Vico called 'the age of heroes'.

Conflict between patricians and plebeians inevitably arose in these 'heroic states', patricians wanting to preserve the status quo, the plebs pushing for change. Inexorably, rights had to be ceded to the underclass,

To Vitruvius, as to all his contemporaries, the notion of origins had cardinal speculative importance. His whole theory of architecture flowed from it.

Joseph Rykwert,
The First Moderns

resulting eventually in democratic states, which initiated the third stage of social evolution, what Vico called 'the age of men'. But the age of men also ran its course. The disciplined acceptance of social order gave way to a lesser regard for law and weakening of customs until societies broke down or were conquered. This brought about a reversion to barbarism followed by a new cycle of the three ages.

Vico had mostly in mind the fabled prehistory and history of Rome for these first three stages of social evolution. But he also drew upon Herodotus' account of the Egyptians' long recorded history, which they divided into three ages, the names of which Vico used for his system. This bore comparison with the Roman author Varro's similar three ages: (1) 'the *dark* age', (2) 'the *mythical* age', and (3) 'the *historical* age'.[35] The mythical account of the founding of Rome revealed certain facts that persisted into historical recorded time and supported his theory. For example, the presence of 'patrician fathers' and 'greater clans' lent support to the legend that 'from these Romulus assembled the fathers of the senate, and with the senate, the city of Rome.'[36] The fall of Rome led to what Vico called 'the second barbarism of the medieval period' from which emerged Christianity as the second age of religion.[37] The feudal institutions and courtly world of the later middle ages represented the second age of heroes, and the humanist and scientific studies that began in the fifteenth century and continued in his own time was the second age of men.

In formulating his three-fold sequence of the stages of social evolution, Vico may have had in mind the Greek's first mythical golden age that was succeeded by the ages of silver and bronze. But where the ancient classical schema indicated inevitable decline, Vico saw the collapse into barbarism as being followed by a new sequence of ascending social order. He called this 'the *ideal eternal history* through which the history of every nation passes in time'.[38] This dynamic cycle of rise and fall succeeded by further cycles Vico called the 'natural law of the peoples', which he contrasted with the timeless 'natural law of the philosophers'. He coined the phrase 'corsi e ricorsi' for this principal characteristic. The implication of 'return' in this should not be confused with the notion that history repeats itself exactly in the way that the Stoics had believed. Rather than any events or material facts repeating themselves, it was the historical process that recurs, the cycle of 'rise, development, acme, decline, and fall'.[39]

Here in Venice your profound book on the principles of a New Science concerning the Nature of Nations is circulating among men of distinction and winning unmeasured applause. The further they read into it the greater becomes their admiration and esteem for your intellect which composed it.

Carlo Lodoli, letter to Vico, January 15, 1728

From a close reading of Homer, Vico believed the Greek poet described a world just emerging from a primitive past to a noble world of heroes. 'Myths are the civil histories of the earliest peoples,' he said, 'who everywhere were poets by nature'.[40] This idea that poetic speech was the primary 'manner of thinking of entire peoples' ran counter to the prevailing view, but came later in the century to influence the Romantic Movement's opposition to the Enlightenment's concentration on reason alone.

Vico's work was not scientific in the modern sense where science came to be considered only such if modelled on the methodology of the physical sciences. Bacon, the 'father' of modern science, had pointed to a reciprocal relation 'between knowing more and knowing how to do more', which forged the link between science and technology.[41] At first this clearly promoted the idea of social progress taken up in the Enlightenment and would lead to emancipation from the 'tyranny of church and state'. But by ascribing progress in knowledge exclusively to the scientific method, as Bacon did, the link between science and technology came to predominate and eventually equated with material progress. In some senses, it is obvious that humankind has progressed, but when this is linked to the idea of history as an inevitable, predestined forward movement, human goals can become overlooked, and can lead to material advance being taken as a natural fact, i.e. technological invention and development. Reviewing the history of the Enlightenment, Max Horkheimer described this historical process leading to a 'means-to-an-end' society where we no longer establish truly human goals. He called it *The Eclipse of Reason*.

In contrast to this, Vico's idea of history aimed to understand the world humans lived in and constructed – social, political, cultural – as the product of our minds through time, with the implication that we create the kind of world we want, not one determined by a particular historical process, as emerged and expounded in the following century. In between times, history came to play a significant part in attempts to define a new firm basis for architecture following the overthrow of the Vitruvian tradition, in particular Vico's emphasis on origins and things made. More recently his idea of poetic origins came to support the resistance to the link between a linear conception of history and technological domination.

Vico is the true father of the modern concept of culture and of what one might call cultural pluralism, according to which each authentic culture has its own unique vision, its own scale of values, which, in the course of development, is superseded by other visions and values, but never wholly so: that is, earlier values do not become totally unintelligible to succeeding generations.

Isaiah Berlin,
Giambattista Vico and Cultural History

What we know contributes to what we make, and what is already made contributes substantially to what it is possible to know.

Dalibor Veseley,
Architecture in the Age of Divided Representation

Chapter 2: After Vitruvius:
The search for a new fundamental ground

The new perception of history coincided with the systematic extension of reason to all intellectual activity in the eighteenth century. The idea of history came to promote new ways of underpinning architecture, which might be pursued by reason, Neo-platonism (combined with gardening), or history itself. The three examples that follow illustrate each of these approaches.

TOWARDS A HISTORICAL ARCHITECTURE

With Vitruvius under attack and the philosophy of history in the air it is perhaps not surprising that the first history of architecture should appear at about the same time as Vico's *New Science*. This was the *Entwurff einer historischen Arkitektur* (Towards a historical Architecture) written by the Austrian baroque architect Johan Fischer von Erlach, first published in 1721 with a second edition following in 1725. The book's title alludes to the fact that Fischer's was no disinterested history but an exposition of his view that contemporary architecture had to be grounded on history.[1] In this we see the impact of the new consciousness of history that emerged around 1700. His book presented for the first time a comparative history of architecture that covered all periods from its origins up to his own time, and presented buildings from civilisations other than Greek or Roman.[2] The idea for such a work may have been inspired by Fischer meeting Sir Christopher Wren in London in 1704, for among Wren's papers left upon his death was a fragment of a proposed *Tracts on Architecture*, which began with an account of Solomon's Temple – as did Fischer's history – and continued with a description of the Tower of Babel and Egyptian pyramids, also illustrated by Fischer.[3] However, the conception of the work lies in Fischer's own earlier involvement with intellectual circles in Rome.

Fischer went to Rome when just sixteen years old, where he found a position with Philipp Schor, architect to the papal court. Through Schor he came into contact with the intellectual circle established by the exiled Queen Christina of Sweden and also the leading figure of late Italian Baroque, Carlo Fontana (1634–1714), who had inherited Bernini's studio. Rome had become a magnet for antiquarians and archaeologists, who featured in the queen's court, and it was from his involvement with this circle that Fischer acquired the grasp of the scientific methods for studying archaeological remains that was to play such an important role in producing his history.

Fischer came to know personally the polymath and speculative thinker Athanasius Kircher (1602–80), who was a central figure in Queen Christina's circle. French theory had become known and popular through the link forged in 1681 between the French Academy in Rome and the Academia de San Luca from which union Fischer would have become familiar with the 'quarrel' between the Ancients and the Moderns and aware of Perrault's rejection of Vitruvian proportional theory. In about 1684 he went with Schor to work in Naples where he would have moved in the intellectual circle from where Vico's *New Science* emerged. From this background mixture of archaeology, scientific investigation, up-to-the-minute architectural theory and new currents of thought about history, emerged Fischer's first history of architecture.

Fischer's history comprises four sections or 'books': the first begins with a reconstruction of the Temple of Solomon, considered then to mark the origins of architecture. Wherever possible he draws upon coins and medals that depict the buildings he covers. These are illustrated on the plates alongside the buildings, a novel way of showing historical sources. He refers to ancient authors – including the Bible – and modern descriptions by travellers or antiquarians for his reconstructions. Fischer's originality lies in setting out the development of European architecture from this first mythical great monument and in addition digressions on the architecture of Islam, contemporaneous Persia, and China. He goes on to show the Seven Wonders of the ancient world, including the Tower of Babel (where he makes use of Herodotus), the pyramids, the Mausoleum of Artemis, the Colossus of Rhodes, the Temple of Diana at Ephesus, and others.

His second book is devoted to Roman architecture where he depicts, amongst other famous monuments, a reconstruction of the Forum of Trajan, which shows evidence of the French influence. For Trajan's

The one unifying principle that runs through all of Kircher's work is an obsession with finding origins. He was fascinated alike by the Greek roots of Western music and by the subterranean sources of water and fire ... when he lived in Rome he researched the history of antique Latium ... most of all, he wanted to understand the beginnings of language and religion.

Joscelyn Godwin,
Athanasius Kircher: A Renaissance Man and a Quest for Lost Knowledge

Artists will see here that Nations differ no less in their Taste for Architecture than in Food and Rainment, and by comparing one with the other, they themselves may make a judicious choice.

Fischer von Erlach

column is set in the centre of a large square resembling a 'Place Royale', such as Jules-Hardouin Mansart's Place des Victoires (1685) and Place Vendome (1686) in Paris[4] [2.1]. The Roman Forum remained half-buried at this time such that their layouts were indecipherable. The third book illustrates mosques at Mecca and Isfahan, the Imperial Palace in Peking and the Great Pagoda at Nanking amongst other examples of oriental architecture. All of Fischer's reconstructed buildings are drawn pictorially, set in a landscape and in some kind of cultural context, depicted either as objects of interest to antiquarian travellers passing by and pointing, or with an imagined contemporary life going on around the buildings. Uniquely, he gave no account of the orders. All this was very new in books on architecture. More typically, the fourth book follows with several pages of drawings of his own designs.

In his introduction Fischer writes that his intention was more 'to raise new invention ... than to instruct the Learned'.[5] In doing this we can see how the idea of history became proposed as a new basis for architecture. Perhaps with Vico's contention that all things are subject to time and change, he projected his own work as the culmination of a long process of development which had begun with the Temple of Solomon, although the laconic captions to his plates leave the reader to decipher this.[6] The building where this idea of a 'historical architecture' announced in the title of his book is most clearly realised is the Karlskirche (1715–25) in Vienna[7] [2.2].

2.1 Trajan's column, from *Entwurff Einer Historichen Arkitektur*

2.2 Johan Fischer von Erlach, Karlskirche, Vienna, front view

The Karlskirche appears as an eclectic assemblage of motifs drawn from past epochs or moments of architecture. On the one hand Fischer was typically Baroque in synthesising elements of the design but, on the other, the building is unique in re-assembling recognisable elements from the history of architecture. The most striking feature of the building is the pair of columns that flank the entrance portico rising to embrace the dome. The columns are carved with spiralling relief sculpture, a clear reference to Trajan's column. Many reconstructions of the Temple of Jerusalem show a pair of columns either side of the entrance in the manner of the Karlskirche.[8] The particular pairing of columns also alludes to Hagia Sophia, which Fischer had drawn as the mosque that it had become surrounded by minarets, but signified here Constantinople as the 'second Rome'.

A pair of triumphal columns was also the heraldic emblem of the Holy Roman Emperor Charles VI, representing the mythical pillars of Hercules – Gibraltar and the Atlas mountains – that marked the westward extent of the empire. Relief sculpture on the columns represent scenes from the life of St. Charles Borromeo, canonised for fighting a plague in Milan and whose name was invoked when a plague struck Vienna in 1713.[9] A tradition of plague columns existed in Vienna, elaborate sculptures erected whenever a plague had been defeated, and Fischer had built one to commemorate the most recent [2.3]. The composition of the façade's principal elements, therefore, can be read as referring to the full span of history from the origins of monumental architecture to the most recent historical event. Other references include the portico – the Roman Temple of Concordia[10] – and the flanking towers that refer to François Mansart's Église de Minimes, which resembles Wren's St. Paul's which, of course, Fischer was familiar with as was Wren with the Paris church.

Behind the broad façade of the Karlskirche is a surprising slim and long plan. The Karlskirche is not simply an iconographical 'billboard', as in the post-modern 'decorated shed' theory of Robert Venturi, but also a richly symbolic plan that can also be read as a historical synthesis [2.4]. A typically baroque oval central space has transepts that form a cross, hinting at the renaissance idea of a centralised plan. A long choir housing the altar is terminated with a columnar screen after Palladio's St. Giorgio Maggiore (1564–80). The overall effect of the long and complex plan looks as if Fischer tried to evoke that of a Gothic cathedral.

2.3 Plague Column, the Graben, Vienna

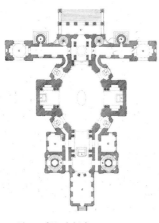

2.4 Plan of Karlskirke

In his biography, Hans Aurenhammer sums up the Karlskirke as a 'complex formal symbolic structure [which] is the result of its twofold functions – as a votive church and as a monument to the greatness of a dynasty'[11]. Fischer could have expressed this within the existing compositional conventions of the Baroque, but its shockingly original appearance shows that he reached beyond this to explore a new way of grounding architecture as a synthesis or collage of its own history. Although the Karlskirche is anything but a 'decorated shed', nevertheless Fischer's approach to re-grounding architecture through re-assembling historical elements was essentially iconographic, which became Venturi's position in the 1970s and beyond, as we will see.

ARCHITECTURE AND THE THEATRE OF NATURE

At about the same time as Fisher von Erlach published his history of architecture, a very different approach to re-establishing a firm foundation for architecture took place at Chiswick House in England. A re-use of recognisable historical forms once again played its part, although the aim and appearance were extremely unlike that expressed in Fischer's Karlskirche. He was clearly on the side of the 'Moderns' in conceiving the Karlskirche as a kind of overview of the past and building upon the best. The theoretical programme for Chiswick, in contrast, reaffirmed, but gave new expression to, the classical conception of a universal law in nature.

Chiswick House (1725–8) forms part of what is known as the 'Palladian Revival' [2.5]. Our modern understanding of architecture as a succession of styles was not formulated until later in the eighteenth century, although people at this time would have had some awareness of a progression from Greek, through Roman, Gothic, Renaissance and Baroque. However, England had a peculiar development compared with Italy or France. Curiously, Palladian Chiswick House followed the Baroque architecture of Wren, Nicholas Hawksmoor (1661–1736) and John Vanburgh (1664–1726), which had developed in the 100 years following the introduction of Renaissance architecture and Palladio to England by Inigo Jones (1573–1652). Art historical surveys present an orderly succession in time that implies an objective pattern, style following style in the 'stream of time'. But Palladian Chiswick reminds us that cultural forms do not fit the evolutionary hypothesis of biology but, as Vico said, are the product of men's minds. The idea of re-assembling historical elements that Fischer proposed is

2.5 Chiswick House, front view

2.6 Nicholas Hawksmoor,
St George, Bloomsbury

apparent in Hawksmoor's St. George, Bloomsbury (1716–31), although it is unlikely that he knew the Karlskirche. But Hawksmoor may have met Fischer when he visited Wren – Hawksmoor was Wren's assistant at the time – and did possess a copy of Fischer's book before he designed the extraordinary steeple for St. George, which is a stretched version of Tomb of Mausolus at Halicarnassus[12] [2.6].

At one level the reversion to Palladianism after Baroque was a political statement associated with the Whig party, which came to power at the Crisis of Succession caused by the death of Queen Anne in 1715. The Whigs associated corrupt government – the outgoing Tory regime – with distorted architecture, i.e. the Baroque of Wren, Hawksmoor and Gibb (1682–1745), all of whom were dismissed from their positions in the Office of Works. This notion had been formulated by Anthony Ashley Cooper, the third Earl of Shaftesbury (1671–1713), who compared Britain with Rome when she lost her liberty under the Caesars: 'not a tolerable Piece of Architecture could shew itself afterwards', he wrote.[13] However, Shaftesbury foresaw in Britain 'an Age when Liberty is once again in its Ascendant' and that this would lead to Whig Britain becoming 'the principal Seat of the Arts'.[14] His comparison between the decline of Rome under the Caesars and seventeenth century Britain, with a 'rebirth' of the arts under British constitutional government, has overtones of Vico's cyclical conception of history. This idea features in Shaftebury's *Letter Concerning the Art and Science of Design* written in 1712 from Naples, where he spent the last two years of his life, so he may have been familiar with the debates circulating in Vico's time.[15] The patron and gentleman architect of Chiswick House, Lord Burlington (1694–1753) was educated by private tutors, one of whom was Lord Somers, the ostensible recipient of Shaftesbury's '*Letter*'.[16]

Let us love our country, let us obey our senate, let us consult the interests of the gods … who by their council and labours have either increased the greatness or defended the safety, or preserved the existence of this great republic.

Cicero

A tableau in the garden of Chiswick House expresses this sentiment, for it shows Cicero in his well-known speech defending the Roman republic against two of the triumvirate who overthrew it, Pompey and Julius Caesar [2.7]. Behind sits the 'Temple of Romulus', a garden building based on a drawing so named by Palladio after the eponymous founder of the Roman republic. The Whig ideal of parliamentary democracy, or republican virtue, was to be expressed by the small Palladian villa in contrast to gigantic baroque palaces such as Wren's Hampton Court, which was associated with the Tories.

But there was a more philosophical aspect to all of this, which returns us to how conceptions of the past were competing at this time. Shaftesbury was the intellectual force behind this, for he articulated a new version of the natural law theory. 'Harmony, balance and proportion are the ultimate foundation alike of morality and beauty', he wrote, and these were provided by nature.[17] The underlying idea centred on the 'concept of simplicity and uniformity in nature.'[18] 'The ancients had sublimated the essence of nature in their art', consequently by imitating them, artists and architects would strive for an objective standard of beauty, one 'eternally valid and universally intelligible'.[19] Shaftesbury considered that this standard could only be found in sixteenth century Italy, where the Renaissance had reintroduced and refined classical architecture. Palladio's work was upheld as the epitome of this. This curious proposal for a re-run of the Renaissance, itself a rebirth of Antiquity, mixes Vico's idea of recurring cycles with natural law's eternal order. Shaftesbury was one of the Cambridge Platonists who opposed Descartes' separation of spirit from matter, proposing instead a 'vital principle' in nature.[20] The Philosophical Transactions of the Royal Society at this time promoted 'histories' – i.e. empirical studies – over a priori Cartesian 'systems'.[21]

Shaftesbury's advocacy of academies to promote 'correct' art was taken up enthusiastically by Burlington who, on returning from his first Grand Tour in 1715, established Handel and the Sculptor Guelfi at his London house. This became the Royal Academy of Music in 1719.[22] At this time Burlington showed little interest in architecture but the publication in 1715 of Colen Campbell's *Vitruvius Britannicus* and Giacomo Leoni's edition of *The Architecture of A. Palladio* opened

2.7 Chiswick House, view of garden from villa

Beauty will result from the form and correspondence of the whole, with respect to the several parts, of the parts with regard to each other, and of those again to the whole.
Palladio,
The Four Books of Architecture

2.8 Palladio (left), and
Inigo Jones (right)

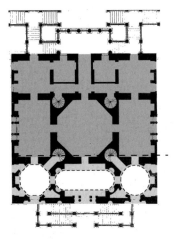

2.9 Chiswick House, plan

his eyes to the importance of architecture and the significance of Palladio in particular. A second Grand Tour in 1719 saw Burlington focus on Palladio's buildings and in Venice he acquired a copy of the 1601 edition of Palladio's *Quattro Libri*.[23] Upon his return to London he acquired a huge collection of Palladio's drawings. Armed with these precedents, guided by Shaftesbury's philosophy, assisted by his architect/draughtsman Henry Flitcroft (1697–1769), and the painter-turned-gardener William Kent (c. 1685–1748), Burlington set about designing Chiswick House and its garden.

The entrance front of Chiswick House announces its allegiance to Palladio and through him to the Ancients. It most resembles Palladio's Villa Badoer or Villa Foscari, although Burlington's main source was the Rocca Pisani by Palladio's pupil Scamozzi, drawings of which he possessed.[24] Statues of Palladio and Inigo Jones on either side of the monumental entrance stair reinforce the message [2.8]. But a distinctive feature not seen in Palladio's villas is the raised octagonal drum with its prominent 'Diocletian' window. This announces the specific purpose of the villa. Where Palladio's striking achievement was to represent the house as temple, the raised drum and 'Diocletian' window – so named from the Roman baths where it was found – proclaim Chiswick a place of pleasure, an academy and pantheon of supporters of liberty, a message reinforced by paintings in the central hall beneath the dome. The allusion to Roman baths and the broader cultural role they played is reiterated in the plan, for the sequence of rooms on the garden side – circular, rectangular, octagonal – copy those found in one corner of the Baths of Diocletian, a plan of which, drawn by Palladio, was in Burlington's possession [2.9]. Not unlike the Karlskirche, historical elements are re-assembled in new combinations to convey a specific message. But in the architectonic layout of the garden we see a different strategy where a first critique of the emerging scientific world-view is staged.

The idea of the villa inherited from Italy at this time was to make an idealised setting as a retreat from the city where contemplation of the arts, poetry, philosophy and politics could take place.[25] Underlying this lay the primary tenet of natural law philosophy, that of *natura naturans*, nature as a generative force. Shaftesbury linked beauty with virtue and introduced the idea of the virtuoso, who embraced good taste and fine judgement, which he argued, was more worthy than the scientist – a sideswipe at Wren, amongst others. There is a latent perfection in nature, he said, and that mankind's role was not to put 'nature to the rack to reveal her truths', as Bacon demanded, but to bring this potential to actual perfection. Shaftesbury bid men to:

> ... imitate the Divine maker and to form to themselves as well as they are able, a model of the superior beauties and endeavour to correct and amend common nature and to represent it as it was first created, which is the utmost mastery of human performance.[26]

Gardening played an important role in this project, which we can see worked out programmatically at Chiswick. Perhaps the time he spent in Naples led Shaftesbury to add an Aristotelian touch, to emphasise the art and skill in making a garden, rather than simply contemplation to draw out nature's perfection. At the notional centre of the garden sits the villa, representing the pinnacle of civilised virtue and the opposite end of the spectrum to the 'wilderness'. This idea can be traced at Chiswick by a series of arches. The villa's garden façade has three arched openings cut extremely precisely into the stucco inside each of which is a semi-circular headed window, the arch supported on stone Corinthian columns representing architecture as the epitome of civilised order [2.10].

However difficult or desperate it may appear in any Artist to endeavour to bring Perfection into his work; if he has not at least the Idea of PERFECTION to give his Aim, he will be found very defective and mean in his Performance.

Shaftesbury, *Characteristicks*

A path parallel to this façade leads to a gate designed by Jones, reclaimed from old Somerset House [2.11]. This has an arch formed from rusticated stone with a pair of Tuscan pilasters supporting an entablature and pediment. This evokes the earliest of the architectural orders emerging, as it were, from a background of stone closer to its 'natural' form. Turning left here, the visitor would come to the Orangery flanked by arched openings cut out of topiary. With its lawn in front, this appears as a theatrical scene as shown in

2.10 (Above) Chiswick House, garden elevations
2.11 (Left) Gate by Inigo Jones

2.12 Chiswick House, the Orangery © Devonshire Collection, Chatsworth. Reproduced by permission of Chatsworth Settlement

In Landskip, Inanimates are principal: 'Tis the Earth, the Water, the Stones and Rocks which live. All other Life becomes subordinate. Humanity, Sense, Manners, must in this place yield, and become inferior.

Shaftesbury, *Characteristicks*

the painting by Jacques Rigaud (c. 1681–1754) where orange trees are depicted 'on stage' as if having emerged through the topiary arches from wild nature behind, represented by unkempt trees [2.12]. With their spherical, golden form, the orange and its blossom smelling of paradise, oranges could be taken as a metaphor for mankind assisting nature to realise its latent perfection. Such a gradated sequence is implicit in Shaftesbury's theory as illustrated in the frontispiece to the 1714 edition of *Characteristicks*, where Shaftesbury is portrayed leaning on a volume of Plato against a backdrop extending from garden, across orchard/meadow to hills in the distance. He described setting out his own garden at Wimbourne into 'three different ranks' through a graded sequence of 'regulated nature'.[27] Other elements and scenes in the garden reiterate this belief in natural law, an eternal nature to be attended upon by the sensibility of the virtuoso.

The introduction of theatrical settings for statues, garden buildings and orange trees, combined with a narrative sequence, raised the level of awareness to the themes staged at Chiswick. Movement and participation, in conjunction with theatrical settings, played a significant part in a narrative sequence that imparts meaning. The twentieth century critic Walter Benjamin described the essential characteristic of architecture as that it forms a background to our lives and typically is not in the foreground of our attention as is the case when we read a book, watch a film, or a play. Where at Chiswick this theatre of nature was a critique of the rising dominance of science, a little later in France the Abbé Laugier set out a theory of architecture predicated on reason that aimed to be as rigorous as science itself. This led to a yet different historical analysis and another proposal for re-grounding architecture.

ARCHITECTURE IN THE LIGHT OF REASON

One of the most striking images in the history of architecture is the primitive hut depicted as the frontispiece to Laugier's *Essai sur l'Architecture* (Essay on Architecture) published in 1755 [2.13]. An allegory of his theory, it shows the muse of architecture sitting amongst the ruins of the classical tradition – a pedestal, piece of fluted column, and Ionic capital. She points to the primitive hut comprised of four trees joined by horizontal branches and some fallen at an angle to form a roof. Laugier was not an architect but described himself as a *philosophe* and was associated with the circle writing the *Encyclopédie,* the vehicle for disseminating Enlightenment research.[28] His subjection of the mythical primitive hut to the severe scrutiny of reason produced the most influential proposal for a new theoretical basis for architecture at this time. Like Perrault, he rejected the Vitruvian argument for an essential beauty and truth residing in proportional relationships and was particularly critical of the analogy with musical harmony.[29]

2.13 The primitive hut. Frontispiece to *Essai sur l'Architecture*

Nevertheless, he formulated his theory from Vitruvius' description of the origins of architecture in the primitive hut. 'The primitive hut is a rough sketch which Nature offers us', he wrote, 'and with architecture as with all other arts: its principles are founded in simple nature.'[30] Illustrations of the primitive hut had featured in architectural treatises before this, but only to show how far architecture had developed from its crude prototype.[31] For Laugier, in contrast, the primitive hut was presented as the essential axiom for constructing a new rational theory: 'I have my principle from which I cannot depart.'[32] In this he aspired to emulate Newton's explanation of how the principle of gravity controlled the movement of the planets in the infinite universe.

> Here it was no longer a matter of a particular natural phenomenon, it was not merely the reduction of a limited field of phenomena to rule an order: on the contrary, in Newton it was a question of establishing and clearly expressing a – rather *the* – cosmic law. This law seemed assured in Newton's theory of Gravitation.
>
> Ernst Cassirer,
> *The Philosophy of the Enlightenment*

Laugier's interpretation of the primitive hut only loosely resembles Vitruvius' account, whose descriptions are rather vague and scattered.[33] Laugier makes much of the pervasive belief that the Greek temple was derived from a timber prototype.[34] From his own reading of the primitive hut he found '... it easy to distinguish those parts which are essential components of an order of architecture from those parts which are only introduced through necessity or caprice'.[35] The essential components were columns, entablature and pediment. Walls, windows, doors, etc. were accepted as necessary and therefore admitted, although the column must be given sole responsibility for

> Vitruvius has in effect taught us only what was practised in his time ... Always avoiding the depths of theory, he takes us along the road of practice and more than once goes astray.
>
> Laugier

support. Features such as pedestal, pilaster or arch were considered capricious and hence had no place in a rationally conceived architecture. Laugier clearly had Baroque and Mannerism in his sight for he gives a long list of abuses, all of which could be found in buildings from the preceding period: broken pediments, columns on pedestals, swelling engaged columns, etc.

Laugier's essay had an enormous influence throughout Europe but particularly in France, where its radical and rationalising ideas gave the rising generation of architects a sense of participating in the intellectual ferment of the Enlightenment. This was the most provocative book since Perrault's *Ordonnance*. It was a time of remarkable change in ideas emanating from the Enlightenment and Laugier's essay came to play a decisive role in establishing Neoclassicism, an architectural style closer to the severe form of Greek temples than any seen during the Renaissance.

But Laugier's description of the origin of architecture in the primitive hut became challenged by the Italian Giovanni Battista Piranesi (1720–78). He ridiculed Laugier's argument for the evolution of architecture from a wooden prototype, which struck at the heart of his own belief in invention. His response came in a series of striking engravings of Roman remains – *Della Magnificenza ed Architettura de'Romani* (1761) – to demonstrate how the magnificence, richness and variety of Roman architecture could not have been derived from a timber hut. He proposed instead their derivation from Etruscan stone buildings.[36] Piranesi criticised what he saw as the excessive importance given to rationality – *rigoristi*, he dubbed the French approach. He opposed to the primitive hut, the primacy of invention and imagination, most dramatically shown in his engravings of imaginary prisons – the *Carceri invenzione.* These gave expression to the emerging idea of the Sublime. Piranesi may have been familiar with Vico's ideas, for in the *Scienza nuova* he wrote that 'poetry was born sublime precisely because it lacked rationality'.[37]

In this we see a new use of history. In place of the tendency amongst Enlightenment philosophers, such as Newton, to look for a single law to explain natural phenomena, which Laugier emulated for architecture, Piranesi pointed instead to the history of Roman architecture where nature was seen as a source of complexity and variety. The dispute between Laugier and Piranesi, reason or invention, informed the work of the generation succeeding Laugier in Enlightenment France, particularly the work of Claude-Nicholas Ledoux (1735–1808) and Etienne-Louis Boullée (1728–99), both described as 'revolutionary architects' because of the way their later projects did away completely with the classical orders.

Before this, some of Ledoux's town houses in Paris, such as the Hôtel d'Hallwyl (1766–7) and the Hôtel Guimard (1770–1), show the influence of Laugier by having an entrance niche for the rhetorical display of columns and lintel. The Hôtel Guimard also recalls Piranesi's view of the ruined temple of Venus and Rome from his *Vedute di Roma* (1759). The Hôtel de Thélusson, built in the late 1770s, shows a more direct influence from Piranesi. Seen through a Roman triumphal arch entrance, is a circular, columned pavilion attached to the front of the house, which transposes Piranesi's etching of the Temple of Vesta at Tivoli and is set in a sunken garden, as if an archaeological excavation.[38] Piranesi's inventive portrayal of Roman ruins and architectural fantasies showed Ledoux one way he could break from classical norms and produce a new and radical architecture. But Ledoux also insisted on reason as the fundamental basis of architecture, which chimed with the Enlightenment's rejection of tradition and called into question the use of the classical language. With the undermining of historically established meaning of geometry embodied in proportion and the orders, geometry became open to experimentation.

The forty '*barrières*' (toll gates) on the roads entering Paris that Ledoux designed and built from 1785 demonstrate his powers of invention generated from a manipulation of pure geometric forms [2.14]. But his most radical work was in the designs he produced for the imaginary

2.14 Claude-Nicholas Ledoux, Barrière de la Villette, Paris

2.15 Arc-et-Senan, detail

town of Chaux, an ideal settlement based upon the actual saltworks at Arc-et-Senan (begun in 1775). In this body of work he breaks free from all established conventions to design buildings that aim to transmit their purpose directly to the eye, an approach that became known as *'architecture parlante'* – speaking architecture. In this we see an allusion to the importance placed upon precise observation in Enlightenment science. Instead of the orders, Ledoux concentrated on simple geometrical solids and figures in the conviction that these represented the fundamental elements of nature. These basic elements that he adopted for his architecture represented reason in the works of mankind, and could be grasped by reason alone. Ledoux used the experimental possibilities in the utopian project for Chaux to explore new ways by which architectural form could convey meaning and which might allude directly to the building's purpose.

At Arc-et-Senan *architecture parlante* appears in the space beneath the entrance portico which is constructed as a natural cave. On either side barrels are carved as if pouring out water but which has turned to solid, as salt appears from the evaporation of water [2.15]. At the centre of the saltworks is the Director's House, similar in composition to some of the *barrières* [2.16]. It is striking for the curious portico with columns made up of juxtaposed cylindrical and rectangular blocks of stone, the latter perhaps an allusion to its quarried origin [2.17].

2.16 (right) Arc-et-Senan, the Director's House
2.17 (above) Arc-et-Senan, detail

Some of the buildings he designed for the ideal town of Chaux were extremely radical, showing no relationship to the history of architectural forms or conventional propriety, and with no vestige of the orders. Consequently they have become some of the most iconic images in architectural history, often read as representing the moment when modernity first shook off the past. Perhaps the most striking is the house for the Director of the River, which appears as a giant water pipe, set on a stepped podium, through which pours the river itself. A house for a cooper is expressed in the form of a series of hoops as would bind a barrel. Several are designed as simple cubes on a podium such as the Temple of Memory, the House of Union, and the *Pacifièré*, a place of peace or reconciliation [2.18]. Ledoux said that the 'form of a cube is the symbol of peace'.[39] The *Pacifièré* is ringed with bound axes framing tablets upon which noble thoughts were to be engraved. Ledoux omits all but the essential form, adding decoration, such as the axes, only where it directly explains the function of the proposed building. If the River Director's house most clearly expresses the function of the building, Ledoux's most radical design was for a perfectly spherical, white building, sometimes known as the House of the Rural Guards, the sphere chosen to represent the ideal in nature. It has been suggested that this project inspired the pure form of Le Corbusier's white, abstract villas, which played such an important role in establishing the Modern Movement.[40]

Where Ledoux combined reason with Piranesian invention, Boullée responded more to new theories of perception. His late unbuilt projects attempted to make explicit what he saw as a direct relationship between primary forms and the sensations they aroused. Disturbed by Perrault's contention that architecture was based on custom and arbitrary rules, and critical of over-emphasis on reason, Boullée developed '*la théorie des corps*', by which he believed the emotive effects of forms could be found. He sought first principles derived from nature. Reason alone could not reveal these, only the sensibility of the artist/architect, a view not dissimilar to Shaftesbury's virtuoso. Boullée connected clear ideas to regularity and argued that the most regular solids – cubes, cylinders, pyramids – should form the principal forms of architecture. The sphere was the most perfect form and taken to be the ideal, reflecting the sun, celestial movements and the cycle of nature [2.19].

He developed the notion of 'character', arguing that the aim of architecture was to produce images out of the corporeal form of building that, analogous with characteristic features of the human body, would evoke the purpose of the building while at the same time reflecting the primary ground of nature. His Cenotaph for Newton is the most striking and well-known example of his symbolic

2.18 *Pacifièré*

To him, the cube of the Pacifièré is the symbol of justice ... it was as simple as the law for which it stands.

Emil Kaufmann,
Three Revolutionary Architects

Boullée explicitly asserts that he has discovered the architecture of shadows, and hence the architecture of light. With this insight he taught how light and shadow are nothing but the other faces of chronological time.

Aldo Rossi,
A Scientific Autobiography

2.19 Antoine-Laurent-Thomas Vaudoyer, House for a Cosmopolitan

projects that explore this idea, its spherical form appropriate homage to this greatest of scientists, its immense size and dramatic lighting a Sublime metaphor for the immensity of the infinite universe recently discovered. The elementary forms of the earliest architecture, such as the pyramids were at the back of his mind, as they captured something of the essential, Platonic order of the world. Alberto Pérez-Gómez summarises Boullée's achievement as 'rejecting the value of the classical orders and its proportions *without* loss of meaning'.[41] The 'revolutionary' work of Ledoux and Boullée was little known until the mid-twentieth century, its recovery part of the new histories that sought an origin of ideas underlying the Modern Movement.

Where Ledoux and Boullée's visionary projects tried to show how architecture might re-establish meaning in response to the Enlightenment's elevation of reason over the traditional Vitruvian schema, Boullée's pupil Jean-Nicholas Durand postulated a purely rational theory in his *Précis des Leçons d'Architecture* (1822). He rejected the Vitruvian column and body analogy with its meaning embodied in proportional relationships and he disavowed Laugier's primitive hut as a model for architecture on the grounds that it was not a natural object.[42] In contrast, Durand asserted that there was no deeper meaning to architecture, that it was purely pragmatic, aiming no more than to evolve solutions to practical problems, and that buildings 'were to be convenient and economical'.[43] Countering Ledoux's and Boullée's ascribing metaphysical properties to the circle, for example, Durand proposed its use simply because its perimeter is the smallest to surround a given area of plan, hence the most economical. Durand was the first to treat architectural design as autonomous and cut off from its traditions. Ledoux and Boullée saw the passage of time as corrupting the essential forms of nature, which were to be recovered. Durand, in contrast, viewed history simply as the accumulation of knowledge and know-how, an idea that chimed with a linear conception of history emerging at this time.

Durand taught at the École Polytechnique, a relatively new institution associated with the independent emerging profession of engineering, where architectural education became influenced by its methods. Durand's book, which had enormous influence, aligned itself with purely rational principles of design, stressing the importance of the plan in design and the disposition of spaces arranged for economy and efficiency. The basis of what he called the 'mechanism' of composition

In Durand's theory, number and geometry finally discarded their symbolic connotations. From now on, proportional systems would have the character of technical instruments, and the geometry applied to design would act merely as a vehicle for ensuring its efficiency.

A. Perez-Gomez,
Architecture and the Crisis of Modern Science

Insofar as time is a fixed measure, it is derived from the revolutions of the sky. Time begins there.

Marie-Louise von Franz,
Time, Rhythm and Repose

was to be the grid. His *Précis* illustrates several examples of different kinds of buildings arranged on a square grid [2.20]. Architecture in Durand's schema becomes reduced to a graphic formula with walls, columns, doors and windows purely rationally distributed. Style became simply a conventional and decorative skin wrapped around a rationally organised and calculated box of space. In stark contrast to Boullée's interpretation of character, for Durand it was no more than the relation between the organisation of a building's plan and its form. His prescriptive methodology proved to be useful for the nineteenth century's new building types, such as prisons, barracks and hospitals. The grid began as the cross, concretising the movement of the sun (east – west), and the axis of the sky or day (north – south), but Durand's Cartesian grid neutralises these existential dimensions.[44] His grid became the template for twentieth century practice built around a rational distribution of space arranged in a steel or concrete frame. Durand's enthusiasm for the new discipline of the engineer and rational planning, followed by nineteenth century Positivism, led ultimately to architecture becoming cut off from history, the unfolding cultural circumstances to which it gives expression, and became increasingly driven by technological progress. From where we stand today, this marks a decisive moment in the march of modernity when architectural meaning shifted from primarily a concern with human ends to the means-to-an-end rationalisation of society that took place in the twentieth century. Dalibor Veseley describes this as leading from 'continuity of shared meaning' to our modern condition of 'broken fragments of understanding'.[45]

We have traced how the Vitruvian tradition of meaning embodied in geometry and proportion under challenge from Enlightenment science and history prompted a search for a new basis for architecture. Durand's organisational grid is a striking image and harbinger of things to come. In the early twentieth century the Modern Movement sought meaning in a mechanistic model of architecture with geometry purely an instrument of efficiency. But re-grounding architecture on rational criteria proved not to satisfy deeper human needs. Writing after World War II, the philosopher Gaston Bachelard's The Poetics of Space (1958) argued that 'inhabited space transcends geometrical space'. At the same time Durand was writing, a conception of history emerged that supported the idea of progress. But architects and philosophers raised questions against this which became a source for later re-appraisal, and it is to these we must now turn.

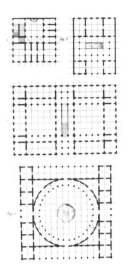

2.20 *Précis des Leçons d'Architecture.* Detail of plate showing the *mécanisme de la composition*

The absolute stasis of the grid, its lack of hierarchy, of centre, of inflection, emphasises not only its anti-referential character, but – more importantly – its hostility to narrative.

Rosalind Krauss,
The Originality of the Avant-Garde

The man-made world of things, the human artifice erected by homo faber, becomes a home for mortal men, whose stability will endure … only insomuch as it transcends both the sheer functionalism of things produced for consumption and the sheer utility of objects produced for use.

Hannah Arendt,
The Human Condition

Chapter 3: Aesthetics and questions of style

3.1 William Chambers,
The Pagoda, Kew Gardens

The second half of the eighteenth century was a time of intellectual and social ferment, a time oscillating between architectural innovation and recourse to history. As we have seen, in France there was the radical work of Ledoux and Boullée. In England the Palladian movement morphed into a refined academic tradition with the work of Robert Adam (1728–92) turning to Roman Pompeii for inspiration and William Chambers (1723–96) demonstrating his knowledge of Oriental styles in gardens, such as the Pagoda at Kew (1757–63), in contrast to his classically correct houses and civic buildings [3.1]. 'The changes which became manifest in the arts about the year 1750', wrote John Summerson in his *Architecture of the Eighteenth Century* (1986), 'have less to do with style than with the complete reorientation of European man to his historic past'.[1] Summerson is alluding to how the coexistence of specific historical references – Roman, Palladian, Chinese, and to be joined by Gothic – reflects a new consciousness of history that had come to replace a general deference to the classical tradition. New theories of association by Kames, Addison and Hartley that emphasised mental processes of the subject played a part in undermining the authority of the orders and led to a relativism where it became difficult if not impossible to assign ultimate authority to any one style.[2] Historical styles came to be associated with the values of the societies that produced them. But at the same time, the publication of books illustrating for the first time Greek temples gave support to Laugier. This led to 'porticoes and colonnades of the strictest classical purity … [on] churches and public buildings throughout Europe'.[3]

WINCKELMANN AND THE GREEK IDEAL

Classical Greece came to be seen more directly as the source of Western culture rather than as mediated through the Renaissance. Johann Joachim Winckelmann's (1717–68) pioneering work *On the Imitation of the Painting and Sculpture of the Greeks* (1755) proved decisive. He argued for nothing less than the direct imitation of Greek art and architecture [3.2]. Winckelmann's pamphlet of 1755 had a profound impact, not only in elevating Greek art to pre-eminence but also emphasising and redefining the role of imitation. 'There is but one way for the moderns to become great and perhaps unequalled,' he wrote, 'I mean by imitating the ancients'.[4]

Where Le Roy's and Stuart and Revett's *Ruins of the Most beautiful Monuments of Greece* (1758) was an archaeological, and first, presentation of Greek buildings, Winckelmann took an aesthetic approach. He had followed the lectures of Alexander Baumgarten (1714–62), who coined the term 'aesthetics', which Winckelmann applied to the study of Greek sculpture. Baumgarten aimed to show that taste could be as rigorously determined as any subject governed by reason. As pure contemplation of an object, aesthetics removes us from the world of time, hence Winckelmann's presentation of Greek art and architecture as a timeless ideal. The idea of the classic was born here at the same time as Neoclassicism. With this we see two parallel and contradictory procedures set in motion which shaped the years leading up to the Modern Movement. The relative value of styles led to the historicism and the style revivalism of the nineteenth century. Aesthetics, in contrast, promoted the idea of viewing an object unrelated to anything outside itself, an idea that led to the call for a 'pure' art, that eventually came to influence the austere form of Modern Movement architecture.

Winckelmann articulated a distinction between copying and imitation: copying was simply 'reduced to a single object', whereas imitation 'gathered information from single ones' and composed a new whole from the best of each, which led 'to general beauty, and its ideal images, and is the way the Greeks took'.[5] By observing many bodies, a classical Greek sculptor formed a 'just resemblance, and, at the same time, handsomer one', wrote Winckelmann with echoes of Shaftesbury, an idealised image of 'a more beauteous and perfect Nature'.[6] True to Enlightenment principles, he described this as 'a Nature ennobled by reason'.[7] As librarian for Count Bünau, the historian of the Holy Roman Empire, Winckelmann had access to a library of 40,000 volumes – possibly including Shaftesbury's books – and his early work was based on vast reading, for he had yet to set eyes on Greek sculpture.[8]

3.2 Karl Friedrich Schinkel, Royal Guard House, Berlin

Were a Man to form himself by one single Pattern or Original, however perfect: he wou'd himself be a mere Copy. But whilst he draws from various Models, he is original, natural, and unaffected.

Shaftesbury, *Characteristicks*

The ideas of beauty with most artists are formed from their first crude impressions, which are seldom weakened or destroyed by loftier beauties, especially when they cannot improve their minds by recurring to the beauties of the ancients.

Winckelmann, *The History of Ancient Art*

Winckelmann eventually went to Rome, where he came to hold a position with Cardinal Albani, who possessed one of the greatest art collections of the eighteenth century. From his first-hand study of Roman copies of Greek sculpture sprang Winckelmann's *The History of Ancient Art* (1764). This not only 'eclipsed all the antiquarian researches that preceded it' but also effectively founded the discipline of modern art history.[9] Combining detailed observation with refined aesthetic sensibility, Winckelmann detected a developmental sequence to Greek art. He proposed a four-phase developmental process: beginning, progress, state of rest, decline.[10] This was to become the staple model for art and architectural history. It also had a significant impact on architecture in the following century.

Winckelmann wrote only one essay on architecture, *Observations on the Architecture of the Ancients* (1760–2). He attacked Vitruvius for wanting 'to determine his dimensions ... according to the mystery of certain numbers'.[11] The discovery of an early Doric temple at Agrigentum had columns five times as high as the diameter, he noted, not the seven prescribed by Vitruvius. Winckelmann expressed disappointment upon seeing the Greek temples at Paestum, but he was able to locate these in his schema as works 'beginning' the development that led to the refined style of fifth century BC Athens.[12] He further criticised Vitruvius for proposing that architectural rules were derived from the primitive hut, arguing instead that formal criteria 'depended not on rules but on aesthetic experience'.[13] This can be read as a tacit critique of Italian Renaissance architecture for founding itself upon the faulty foundations of Vitruvius.[14] In place of Vitruvius and the Renaissance, Winckelmann advocated the 'noble simplicity' and 'absence of individuality' in classical Greek art.'[15]

Harries wonders whether the aesthetic approach led to architecture losing its way.[16] Aesthetics over-emphasises the role of sight at the expense of the experiential meanings that architectural form, space and details have to convey. In considering architecture from the spectator's point-of-view, an aesthetic approach all-too-easily degenerates to the truism that 'beauty is in the eye of the beholder'. Allied with the Romantic idea of the genius, aesthetics helped promote personal taste over ideas and meaning, the latter in contrast, facilitating a collective cultural discourse. Up until Winckelmann's time, art combined beauty and truth: aesthetics beauty and taste.

Winckelmann said that only by returning to the source of
Western civilisations by a process of properly pursued imitation,
might the Moderns 'become great and perhaps unequalled'.
History had difficulty in demonstrating 'clear and certain knowledge'
as compared with physics; similarly imitation was not as easy for
architects as it was for sculptors or painters. He gave no specific
guidance for imitation in architecture, but an architect might proceed
in an analogous way, perhaps by taking the proportions of several
temples and deducing an ideal. Although what this might be is
harder to imagine than an idealised human body. In practice more-
or-less literal copies of Greek temples appeared in European cities and
America. The Brandenburg Gate (1789–93) in Berlin by C.G. Langhans
(1732–1808) is perhaps the most dramatic and well-known example [3.3].

3.3 C.G. Langhans
    Brandenburg Gate, Berlin

Winckelmann's subtle distinction between imitation and copy may not
have always registered with architects. The 'real nature of Neo-classicism
in architecture', wrote Summerson, 'is in a combination of the ideal
of "noble simplicity" with that of rational application of the classical
elements.'[17] The literal copy of the Greek temple form became more

3.4 Robert Smirke,
    The British Museum, London

3.5 Jacques-Gabriel Soufflot
Église Ste-Geneviève, Paris

pronounced in the early part of the nineteenth century. In England William Wilkins (1718–1839) proposed a variation on the Propylaea to the Acropolis for Downing College, Cambridge in 1806. The Royal High School (1825–9), Edinburgh has a Doric temple projecting from flanking colonnades (Edinburgh indeed became known as the Athens of the North). One of the most familiar Neoclassical buildings is the British Museum (1823–7) by Robert Smirke (1780–1867), with its long, Ionic colonnades flanking the central entrance portico [3.4]. However, in France Laugier and reason continued to predominate. His insistence on the primary role of the column became integrated with the conventions of composition inherited by architects of his generation less radical than Ledoux or Boullée. They followed the example of Jacques-Gabriel Soufflot at Ste-Geneviève (1773–91), as for example, did Jacques Gondoin (1737–1818), in his design for the École de Chirurgie (1769–74), Paris [3.5].

GOTHIC: A SHORT LITERARY INTERLUDE

At the same time as Winckelmann's influence grew and the Greek ideal became established, there developed a parallel interest in Gothic, which came to be seen as an organic tradition native to northern countries. This first appeared in English literature. In Germany a philosophical movement played its part in helping the Middle Ages coming to stand beside classical antiquity as an ideal. In England it was the associations prompted by medieval buildings that became an increasingly popular motif, in contrast to the structural rationalism of Gothic structure in France. A stream of poetry emerged evoking what Kenneth Clark calls 'Gothicism', which linked melancholy sentiments with images of medieval buildings: 'Cloisters pale': 'awful arches': 'Column grey with moss': 'The Time-Shook arch'. Such ruined buildings were now only 'the Raven's bleak abode', or places where 'the poisonous adder breeds'.[18]

3.6 Gothic Pavilion, Painshill Park

Post-Reformation England was dotted with ruined abbeys but it was the presence of buildings in landscape gardens prompting associations that led to the erection of mock Gothic follies, often replacing classical pavilions [3.6]. William Gilpin (1724–1804) described how these associations ran deeper than mere gloom and superstition: 'A ruin is a sacred thing. Rooted for ages in the soil, assimilated to it: we consider it rather as a work of nature than of art.'[19] Ruins might be built to emulate literary scenes, but where new Greek buildings

represented a fresh dawn, ruins depicted the triumph of time. The garden at Stourhead (1744–56), for example, was laid out as an allegory of Aeneas' journey through the Underworld, a narrative garden walk embracing a number of classical pavilions but ending with a vista across a lake to a quintessential English village scene with its medieval church and a medieval market cross brought from Bristol [3.7].

Later in the eighteenth century Horace Walpole (1717–97) prompted the fashion for Gothic novels with his *Castle of Otranto: A Gothic Story* (1764), inspiring followers such as Matthew Lewis (1775–1818) with his immensely popular *Ambrosio, or the Monk* (1796).[20] Walpole was the decisive figure in this new sensibility, for not only did he write about Gothic but also 'gothicised' his villa at Strawberry Hill (1749). He made a first attempt to measure Gothic against classical architecture in aesthetic terms.[21] Acknowledging the 'simplicity and proportion of the Greek orders' he praises nevertheless the 'thousand graces and effects, magnificent yet genteel, vast yet light, venerable and picturesque of the Gothic style. It is difficult for the noblest Grecian temple to convey half so many impressions to the mind as a cathedral does of the best Gothic taste.'[22] Walpole made a series of additions to Strawberry Hill in an unapologetically asymmetrical manner and with features borrowed from a wide range of medieval sources [3.8]. He involved a number of his antiquarian friends in addition to architects such as Robert Adam and James Wyatt (1746–1813), as well as the master mason of Westminster Abbey, Thomas Gayfere. Despite the presence of a mason, Strawberry Hill was built for effect not substance, 'wood and plaster' Gothic as it has been described.

The lower part of the castle was hollowed into several intricate cloisters... An awful silence reigned throughout these subterranean regions, except now and then when some blasts of wind that shook the doors she had passed, and which, grating on the rusty hinges, were re-echoed through the long labyrinth of darkness.

Horace Walpole,
The Castle of Otranto

3.8 Walpole, Strawberry Hill

This new interest in indigenous architecture and English history was fuelled by a steady stream of antiquarian books, such as J. Bentham's *History and Antiquities of Ely* (1771) and John Carter's (1748–1817) *Views of Ancient Buildings in England* (1786–93) and *Ancient Architecture of England* (1795). New theories of experience that emphasised sensation over reason were partly shaped by the interest in Gothic architecture. This new challenge to the classical tradition has been described as a 'tendency to dethrone architecture, to replace the traditional Renaissance architect with historians'.[23]

Another source of the sublime is infinity… Infinity has a tendency to fill the mind with that sort of delightful horror, which is the most genuine effect, and truest test of the sublime… As the management of light is a matter of importance in architecture, it is worth enquiring how far this remark is applicable to building. I think then, that all edifices calculated to produce an idea of the sublime ought to be dark and gloomy.

Edmund Burke,
A Philosophical Enquiry into the Origins of Our Ideas of the Sublime and the Beautiful

In his *Inquiry into the Origins of our Ideas of the Sublime and the Beautiful* (1765), the philosopher Edmund Burke (1729–97) argued that there existed two primal passions which were prompted by the imagination: 'self-preservation' and 'self-propagation'. Burke categorised as Sublime those objects that threatened self-preservation and prompted sensations of fear, such as vastness, the infinite, terror and obscurity. We saw the idea of the Sublime presaged in Piranesi's engravings and fully expressed in Boullée's projects. Beauty, in contrast, sprang from objects that 'awakened sensations of sex, tenderness, or pleasure … the attributes of Beauty were Smallness, Smoothness, Gradual Variation and Delicacy of form and colour'.[24] For Burke, aesthetic experience was wholly direct and sensuous, thus he ruled out the beauty of proportion which required the intellect to grasp it.

The study of pictures can only produce any real advantage if we use it as a school in which we may learn to enlarge, correct and refine our view of Nature and by that route become good judges of scenery.

Uvedale Price,
Essay on the Picturesque

At the end of the century, limitations perceived in these two theoretical concepts led to the formulation of the idea of the Picturesque. According to Richard Payne Knight (1750–1824), the Picturesque belonged solely to the sense of vision: 'Could not some term be invented to describe this class of objects which, obviously not beautiful, was yet stimulating to eyes accustomed to painting?'[25] As the name suggests, it was prompted by qualities seen in paintings that conformed neither to the Sublime nor the Beautiful. In his *Essay on the Picturesque* (1794), Uvedale Price (1747–1829) summarised Picturesque qualities as 'roughness, sudden variation and irregularity'.[26]

These two new aesthetic categories indicate a turning away from the idea of beauty as defined by the classical tradition and as such they had far-reaching implications for the history of architecture. This elevation of new modes of vision, sensuous experience and imagination over reason reflected a growing mistrust of science in the latter part of the eighteenth century. This was taken up in more systematic philosophical work in Germany, which had greater long-term significance, if less immediate effect, on architecture.

* * *

In the late eighteenth century there arose a flowering of German metaphysical philosophy which set itself against some of the certainties espoused by Enlightenment thinkers. German idealists – as they became known – were against the tendency to abstract reason from the full richness of human life, as if reason alone could explain all man's actions. They felt that the mechanical or clockwork Newtonian Universe had removed God and to fill this gap they substituted metaphysics for faith. One of the most important philosophers, Johann Gottfried Herder (1744–1803), attacked the pursuit of 'logical clarity' in language and opposed the suggestion that the German language could be improved by the imitation of foreign languages. He implicitly opposed Winckelmann's claims for the superiority and imitation of Greek art, for Herder insisted on concentrating upon the origin, history and development of an indigenous folk culture.[27] Homer might have been the greatest poet but his use of language was culturally and 'historically conditioned' and, therefore, Herder argued 'his practice cannot be taken as a norm.'[28]

Herder proposed four stages to the development of a language by making an analogy with an individual's development: a 'childhood' phase dominated by passions and feeling: the poetic phase of 'youth': a third phase of 'manhood' when prose developed in concert with poetry: and a final phase of 'old age' when 'life and richness are sacrificed to pedantic accuracy'.[29] He later modified this by making an analogy between organic life and societies with a threefold cycle of growth, maturity and decline.[30] He associated this with three phases in the development of the European spirit: the Roman and Germanic societies that developed religion and political organisation: the Renaissance and Reformation: and his own era of scientific knowledge, the outcome of which he considered difficult to predict.

This is very suggestive of Vico's conception of social development and his emphasis on poetry as the well-spring of a culture. Herder had, in fact, been introduced to Vico's *New Science* by his mentor Johann Georg Hamann (1730–88). Herder travelled to Italy in 1789, reporting

For now as never before may man justly boast of his mastery over the natural world. However much remains undone, enough has been accomplished to make him to feel lord over the earth... But even so I regard the whole sense of a common material progress to be of little value: it is not further gain in this direction that I desire for the world: it causes me mortal agony that this, an unholy waste of its holy powers, should be regarded as mankind's entire task.

Johann Gottlieb Fichte, *Soliloquies*

that he learnt more for his philosophy of history in the first eight days of his stay in Naples than in three or four months in Rome. At Naples he found men 'quite different from those at Rome … and quite different writings'.[31] Like Vico, he also rejected the projection of laws and values from eighteenth century natural sciences upon earlier periods of human activity. He argued that earlier societies could only be understood by studying them in the round, but in particular as transmitted through mythology, poetry and song, and pointed to the importance of understanding origins and the historical development of societies.[32]

Herder attacks the idea that history should be interpreted as a movement of progress towards the modern State. He implies at least that the development of a modern State has little to do with reason, and that it was due rather to purely historical factors. The members of a tribe may very well have been happier than many inhabitants of a great modern State, in which 'hundreds must go hungry so that one can strut and wallow in luxury'.

Frederick Copplestone on Herder, *A History of Philosophy, vol. 6*

Herder shared the Enlightenment's commitment to reason in the development of humanity, but argued like Vico that it would be accompanied by setbacks. Against the universalising tendency of the Enlightenment, however, he stressed the need to respect cultural differences – poetry, food, clothes, manners, etc. – in order to understand the potential for humanity's development. Herder characterised this as the '*Volkgeist*', the spirit of a people, a concept that came to play an important part in the Romantic Movement and later. As Isaiah Berlin says in his commentary on Herder: 'Men are not self-created: they are born into a stream of tradition, above all their language, which shapes their thoughts and feelings, which they cannot shed or change, which forms their inner life.'[33]

German philosophers at this time were much concerned with reconciling the emerging scientific world-view with the traditions of human moral or religious consciousness. However, God was not to be so easily dethroned as Vitruvius. They posited a metaphysical concept whereby some kind of generative spirit was inherent in the world rather than an anthropomorphic Creator.[34] In trying to grasp its essential character, this allusive notion was given a number of names: 'Absolute reason'; 'productive reason'; 'ultimate productive principle'; and 'supra-individual principle'.[35] This was to become a crucial aspect of Hegel's conception of history which dominated the nineteenth century and lingers on.

German idealism had much in common with the emerging Romantic Movement. It is notoriously difficult to define Romanticism but there are certain common traits, such as turning against the Enlightenment's concentration on rationality and the privileged position given to analytical and scientific understanding. The conception of an inherent generative principle or spirit in the natural world could not be grasped by such means, Romantics argued, but only by intuition, feeling and the imagination. In opposition to the heroic status given to a man of science such as Newton, Romantics emphasised the creative imagination or genius of the artist. Friedrich Schlegel (1772–1829) said that 'there is no greater world than the world of art', and Novalis (1772–1801) asserted that the poet embodies the creative power of humanity, the human creative spirit being the highest expression of the generative principle in nature. In *Die Christenheit, oder Europ* (1799), Novalis praised the Middle Ages for being an age where an organic unity of faith and culture found expression in works of art.[36] Gothic represented the organic society proclaimed by Herder.

The Romantic Movement found its clearest philosophical expression in the work of Friedrich Wilhelm Joseph von Schelling (1775–1854), who transmitted these ideas to Coleridge and through him to England.[37] Enormous importance was placed on historical continuity. Coleridge's and Wordsworth's Preface to their *Lyrical Ballads* (1798) aimed to revitalise poetry by drawing upon the everyday speech and native traditions of people working close to nature, such as shepherds and ploughmen. Schelling's insistence on the primacy of imagination, transmitted through Coleridge, proved crucial to Ruskin's particular form of argument for Gothic, as we will see. Polemically pitched against the Enlightenment's characterisation of it as the 'dark ages', Romantics came to see the Middle Ages as more worthy than the Greek art championed by Winckelmann: faith and feeling over reason, traditional culture against an alien import. These contrasting positions on Classicism and Romanticism reverberated throughout the nineteenth century.

Vico's idea of distinct phases of cultures combined with Herder's notion of the *Volkgeist* to have an enormous impact on nineteenth century historicism, or Style Revivalism. The emergence of new approaches to understanding art and architecture – aesthetics, Gothic, Romanticism, the Sublime and the Picturesque – contemporaneous with the revolutionary projects of Ledoux and Boullée complicate the picture of a positivist thrust to culture in the mould of Durand. For most of the century historical styles were chosen to mask the reality of a fast-developing industrial society. The idealist philosopher's notion of a 'World Spirit', on the other hand, came to form the basis of Hegel's philosophy of history. Combined with the idea of progress,

All truth is a species of Revelation, and the function of Imagination is through symbols, to mediate truth to the Understanding: We cannot reason without imagination.

Samuel Taylor Coleridge

Imagination represents the afterlife either on high or in the depths... We dream of journeys through the universe, but is not the universe within us? We do not realize the profundities of our spirits. Inward is the direction of the mystic path. Within us or nowhere is eternity with its worlds of past and future. The external world is the world of shadows: it casts its shadows into the realm of light.

Novalis,
Pollen

Hence the romantic idea of Nature could be and was allied with a marked appreciation of the continuity of historical and cultural developments and the significance of past cultural periods for the unfolding of the potential of the human spirit.

Frederick Copplestone

this came to play a major part in the search for a style appropriate to an industrial age. But before we consider this, we can see how these new intellectual currents affected architecture at the end of the eighteenth century by looking at the work of John Soane (1753–1837).

SOANE AND THE ABBÉ LAUGIER

There are ten copies of Laugier's *Essay on Architecture* in the Soane Museum, all collected as part of his working library.[38] It is most likely that it was a teaching aid for the pupils he took on – there were five in 1790 who worked from 7am to 7pm in summer and 8am to 8pm in winter. Whatever role the book played, it was clearly of prime importance to Soane. Trained in the classical tradition, Soane came to be aware of the European debates but also the impact of Romanticism and the late eighteenth century theories of the Sublime, Beauty, and the Picturesque, all of which played a part in his work.

Soane's life is indicative of the social changes taking place at the end of the eighteenth century. The son of a bricklayer, his architectural training began when he was fifteen in the office of George Dance (1741–1825). He became a student at the Royal Academy in 1771 and won the Travelling Scholarship six years later. Travelling via Paris, where he met Jean-Rodolfe Perronet, founder of the *École des Ponts et Chaussées* and who had also contributed an article of engineering to the *Encyclopédie,* he arrived in Rome in May 1778.[39] He probably made contact there with French *Prix de Rome* students, where he may have learnt of Laugier's essay. Prompted by advice from Chambers, he certainly met Piranesi in the first months of his stay.[40] Piranesi gave the young Soane four of his engravings. In later life Soane collected eighteen volumes of Piranesi's prints, an indication of how highly he valued his work. So from an early age Soane became aware of the conflicting views on the origins of architecture: Laugier's rational reading of the timber primitive hut and Piranesi's imaginative rendering of Roman monuments derived from Etruscan stone predecessors. The argument to be advanced here is that Soane was aware of this conflict and that his work shows how it might be resolved.

Summerson (who was curator of the Soane Museum for many years) argues that Soane's style is characterised by a particular motif; a unique form of dome which he calls a 'pendentive dome' [3.9]. Unlike normal domes that have distinct separate pendentives to

There is no work as yet that firmly establishes the principles of architecture, explains its true spirit and proposes rules for guiding talent and defining taste ... it is not sufficient to know how to work: it is above all important to learn to think.

Laugier,
Essay on Architecture

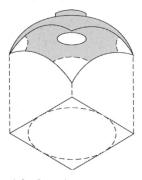

3.9 John Soane's 'pendentive' dome

make the transition from a square support to the circle of the dome, the 'pendentive dome' is simply one continuous surface rising from segmental arches. It has also been called a 'handkerchief dome'.[41] This can be read as making a primitive form of dome and Soane might be suggesting that this signature motif of his style – the pendentive dome rising from four columns – reconciled the idea of the primitive hut (Laugier) with a stone form of construction (Piranesi).

Soane's very personal and idiosyncratic style emerged in his design for the Bank of England's Bank Stock Office (1792), where the pendentive dome, capped by a circular lantern light, is supported on pilasters that are little more than incised vertical lines [3.10]. All most irregular, and his work became subjected to considerable criticism for departing from classical convention. The pilaster-strips can be read as 'symptoms of a "primitivism" to which Soane subscribed', argues Summerson.[42] Soane's allegiance to Laugier reappears in witty form at the gateway of Pitzhanger Manor (1800–3), the house he built for himself in Ealing. A solid form of the pendentive dome caps the gate posts which have a pilaster at each of the four corners made of flint – a solid 'primitive hut' made from the most 'primitive' form of stone [3.11]. Incised strip pilasters with residual capitals continue the primitive theme on the rear elevation of the house [3.12]. And the ceiling of the Drawing Room at Pitzhanger is given the form of the pendentive dome.

3.10 Bank of England, Bank Stock Office © The Governor and Company of the Bank of England

The architect, by close study and unwearied attention, should be learned in history, well informed of the primitive destination and origin of things, and on all occasions be able to trace every invention up to first principles and original causes.

John Soane,
Royal Academy Lectures

3.11 Pitzhanger Manor, gate post as 'primitve hut'

3.12 Garden elevation

None of these examples, it will be noticed, embraces the structural rationalisation sought by Laugier. In contrast, Soane was more interested in the associations they produced. Other aspects of Pitzhanger made clear his attachment to the new theories of perception

The night was now fast advancing. The Lamps were not yet lighted. The faint beams of the rising Moon scarcely could pierce through the gothic obscurity of the Church. Lorenzo found himself unable to quit the Spot. The void left in his bosom by Antonia's absence, and his sister's sacrifice, which Don Christoval had just recalled to his imagination, created that melancholy of mind which accorded but too well with the religious gloom surrounding him.

Matthew Lewis,
Ambrosio, or the Monk

and sensation gaining ground. In the basement Soane designed what he called 'The Monk's Dining Room', in a mock Gothic style. In the gardens he built the mock 'ruins of a Temple', half-buried remains of curious assembled forms. 'It is from the association of ideas [that ruins] excite in the mind that we feel interested', Soane wrote in his Royal Academy lectures.[43] He added that, 'if artificial ruins … are so cunningly contrived … they may be considered as histories open to the world'.[44] Amongst the visitors to Pitzhanger was Matthew 'Monk' Lewis, and Soane contributed to the 'Gothick' fun of his guests by inventing an elaborate fantasy whereby the ruins were of a building found in the garden and excavated.

The great Romantic painter J.M.W. Turner (1775–1851) became a close friend of Soane and frequent visitor to Pitzhanger. Soane shared the painter's obsession with light, finding in Gothic architecture a greater range of moods evoked by effects of light in addition to its association with the new categories of the Sublime and Picturesque. This expanded range of emotional effects Soane came to call the 'Poetry of Architecture'.[45] His buildings were frequently rendered in conditions of dramatic light. The Drawing Room and Library at Pitzhanger, for example, were depicted with curtains drawn back as if looking into a stage lit by a bright spotlight. The leading stage lighting designer of the time, Philippe de Loutherbourg (1740–1812), was another guest at Pitzhanger.

Soane's interest in Gothic resided in the moods that effects of light produced, rather than in associations prompted by the forms. The Dulwich Gallery (1811–12) offers a striking illustration of this. It was designed to house paintings left to Dulwich College by Soane's close friend Sir Peter Bourgeois, but included a mausoleum for the benefactor and accommodation for six poor women of the parish. A dramatic contrast of mood is effected by different lighting for the galleries and the mausoleum, the former bright and lucid lit by clear glass lanterns, the latter sombrely lit by yellow-glazed clerestory windows set into what appears from the outside to be a stone tomb.

The gallery is built of London stock bricks, reflecting the tight budget, and articulated by plain brick pilasters with a residual stone 'capital', another indication of Soane's allegiance to Laugier's primitivism [3.13] The mausoleum's top is in Portland stone with incised pilasters and capped by funerary urns, one of which sits on top of a solid form

of Soane's signature pendentive dome. Idiosyncratic stone surrounds frame doors to three sides of the mausoleum, but the doors have no handles or hinges: these doors indicate that there is no return from death, *architecture parlante* in detail [3.14]. He may have been aware of *architecture parlante* at an early age, for Dance's Newgate Prison (1768–85) used this idea by having rusticated masonry set inside arched openings, themselves rusticated, the combined effect suggesting an impenetrable wall. Soane was one of the first English architects to acquire a copy of Ledoux's *'L'architecture'* on its publication in 1804.[46]

Soane became professor of architecture at the Royal Academy in 1806, a position he took very seriously, filling eighteen notebooks from his reading in preparation for his first lecture.[47] He had an extensive library and, during the course of the lectures, showed himself to be aware not only of all important architectural writings but also the aims of the French *Encyclopédistes*.[48] Soane was also familiar with eighteenth century aesthetic theory from Burke to Winckelmann, and in preparing his lectures developed a keen interest in the Picturesque theories of Payne Knight and Price.[49] In addition to his idiosyncratic details, Soane was at his most inventive in the manipulation of space where qualities celebrated by the Picturesque such as 'sudden variation joined to irregularity' characterised some of his best-known work, especially his house at 13 Lincoln's Inn Fields (1812–24).[50]

Unlike the conventional arrangement of rooms linked formally by a visual axis, the plan for 13 Lincoln's Inn Fields consistently thwarts development of an axis but at the same time offers an oblique glimpse of a space beyond [3.15]. Soane established this experience from

3.13 (Left) Dulwich Gallery
3.14 (Above) The Mausoleum at Dulwich Gallery

Every building, whether great or small, simple or elegant, must, like the picture, speak intelligibly to the beholder. Each must have appositie character peculiar to itself, sufficient to point out the purposes and uses for which it was erected.

Soane,
Royal Academy Lectures

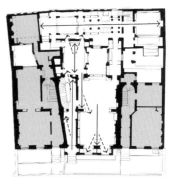

3.15 13 Lincoln's Inn Fields, ground floor plan

the outset, for an axis projected from the front entrance passes through a lobby where it hits the wall to the stairwell. But an opening beside the lobby gives an oblique glimpse to the stair rising against the oblique party wall. Ambivalence was preferred to resolution by Picturesque theory and this characteristic of the plan is pursued further in some critical details. For example, in the Breakfast Room a pendentive dome floats over the centre of the room but is disengaged from two sides such that it is impossible to see where wall and ceiling meet [3.16]. A lantern light above is one of the many varied sources of lighting that Soane deployed to add to the sense of mystery and/or ambiguity in spaces.[51] Forty-four convex mirrors attached to the pendentive dome emphasise the fragmentation of perception.

Soane also employs mirrors in the Library to create a particularly interesting spatial illusion. Mirrors high up above bookcases on the party wall create an impression of there being a space beyond [3.17]. Given that the house is easily recognised as a typical London terrace house divided by two party walls, it raises the question as to whether Soane is making a witty reference to Laugier here; the wall, which the French theorist allowed only by licence as a necessity, is here apparently removed. Hanging arches not unlike those in Henry IV's chapel at Westminster Abbey, in conjunction with the mirrors and the glazed bookcases, create more ambiguity as to where the boundary of the space exists, or if indeed there is one [3.18]. Soane's pendentive motif appears as bosses beneath the springing of the arches and a Gothic association is introduced by brackets in the form of miniature fan-vaulting.

3.16 13 Lincoln's Inn Fields
   The Breakfast Room
   By Courtesey of the Trustees of
   Sir John Soane's Museum
   Photo: Derry Moore
3.17 Library detail
   By Courtesey of the Trustees of
   Sir John Soane's Museum
   Photo: Derry Moore

There is an extreme contrast between the tiny Breakfast Room, its space compressed by the pendentive dome, and the triple-height 'Dome space' immediately beyond at the back of the house. It is crammed full of architectural fragments, statuary and funerary urns in the basement. Here Soane designed the Monk's Parlour equally full of fragments and casts of Gothic details and lit by yellow glass to provoke an appropriately melancholy mood. In the light-well adjacent to this room, called the Monk's Yard, Soane erected a memorial stone to Mrs Soane's beloved dog, Fanny, capped by a Corinthian capital resting on a pendentive dome. Beside this is another architectural tableau where the pendentive dome sits between a Corinthian capital and a Gothic pinnacle, material evidence, I believe, of how Soane considered that his architectural style could reconcile classical and Gothic in the same way as he set out to reconcile Laugier with Piranesi [3.19]. In a *Guide to the Museum* that he wrote in 1812 he considered aloud whether visitors in future years might imagine the house to have been a heathen temple, or a convent of nuns, or whether it was 'supposed to have been a residence of a magician'.[52]

Summerson has argued that Soane had a limited number of themes and that he invented 'no new themes … after 1806' and that one of his most obsessive 'themes is the "pendentive dome"'.[53] Yet despite this, his architecture is one of the most extraordinarily complex in the history of architecture. Soane's idiosyncratic interiors are indicative of the emergence of a modern sense of personality present in architectural design. His attempts to combine Laugier's theory with Piranesi's, reason with Romanticism, the Sublime and the Picturesque, illustrate the fragmenting character of European culture on the cusp of the eighteenth and nineteenth centuries. Acknowledging these new theoretical challenges to Classicism in his architecture, Soane can be taken as a paradigm of the argument advanced here. A critical use of history saw Soane re-configuring the classical tradition to accommodate these new theories and in the process create extraordinarily inventive buildings where classical elements were reinterpreted and re-combined with new ways of handling space that gave architecture an expanded vocabulary to express the changing times.

3.18 13 Lincoln's Inn Fields Library
By Courtesey of the Trustees
of Sir John Soane's Museum
3.19 Tableau in the Monk's Yard

Chapter 4: In what style should we build?

HEGEL'S PHILOSOPHY OF HISTORY AND HISTORICISM

George Wilhelm Friedrich Hegel (1770–1831) expounded a philosophy of history that exerted a profound influence on succeeding generations and has left its mark on how we operate in the world today. Born into the Age of Reason, Hegel soon found Christianity to be incompatible with reason. Like other idealist philosophers he sought a metaphysical explanation for the creative role religion conventionally ascribed to God. Drawing upon what his predecessors named the 'Absolute', Hegel coined the term 'World Spirit'.[1] For Hegel this was not a transcendental deity, rather it was the 'Totality', the whole of reality and an immanent process. 'The true is the whole', he said, and this could only be apprehended in history.[2] To grasp the spirit of their own time, people must understand its beginnings and its development, which he considered to be the key to understanding. Nature is a manifestation of the Absolute or World Spirit and a necessary precondition for the existence of the human spirit, which is where, Hegel says, the Absolute, or reality, attains consciousness of itself.[3] A more contemporary expression of this idea was given by the anthropologist Joseph Campbell; pointing to his face in a TV interview, he exclaimed, 'What are these but the eyes of the Earth?'[4]

For Hegel, however, humans were to be sharply distinguished from nature. Where natural phenomena endlessly repeat themselves, humans develop by a freedom of consciousness that enables them to reflect upon what Hegel calls 'the variations and deviations from the truth formerly established'.[5] Therefore reason in itself, or divorced from philosophical traditions, was not sufficient; 'the true is a process not a conclusion'.[6] Adapting the idea of *telos* from Aristotle, Hegel translated it from a biological concept to define 'human history in which we observe myriad processes attaining their fulfilment and goal.'[7] This is where history became of the utmost importance for Hegel's project. Hegel pronounced history a teleological process. That is, he said: 'It becomes concrete or actual only by its development and through its end.'[8] His conception of history as an unfolding process towards a higher end marks a decisive moment in modernity when the idea of a timeless ideal in nature as the basis for culture became replaced by a 'potential ideal', one in which 'historical events were *leading up to*'.[9] The goal became all-important and the process of history allowed its aim to be ascertained. Hegel's conception, however, was of the development of human self-consciousness, but this became distorted with the emergence of Darwins theory of evolution and, when combined with the Enlightenment's drive for progress, led to the belief in time as an arrow, a future-facing conception. A group called the Young Hegelians saw in his suggestion of mind's supremacy the instrument for radical changes in society, most famously Karl Marx. This continues to support all uncritical ideas of material progress, an idea that first found architectural expression in the Modern Movement. In his *The Open Society and its Enemies,* Karl Popper blamed the Hegelian idea of a 'predictive history' for the rise of Marxist and Fascist totalitarian regimes. More recently the teleological conception of history has been seen as supporting the tyranny of technological domination over the Earth and human affairs.

An important correlate of his history was Hegel's conception of the State and how it developed.[10] Like Vico, he pictured the family to be the first component of society, which developed by a dialectical process to require eventually a constitution and ultimately the State.[11] This is connected to the importance of history because, as Hegel explains: 'a constitution is no mere artificial product; it is the work of centuries, the idea and the consciousness of the rational in so far as it has been developed in a people'.[12]

The State for Hegel was not an 'essence' or timeless ideal but a movement towards perfection, the essential outline of which could be discerned. The Enlightenment's belief in the potential perfectibility of mankind was given concrete form in Hegel's conception of the State. The present State might be the best yet but would be improved in the future, an idea endorsing Prussia's rise to dominance at this time. Why his conception of history had such impact lay in the significance Hegel placed on the *Zeitgeist* – the spirit of the age – and how this intersected with Herder's *Volkgeist.* As Frederick Copplestone explains:

> the historian is concerned with nations rather than individuals. Hence the unit, so to speak, in the concrete development of the World Spirit, is the national spirit of a people (*der Volkgeist*). And by this Hegel

means in part a people's culture as manifested not only in its political constitution and traditions but also in its morality, art, religion and philosophy. It is a living totality, the spirit of the people as living in and through that people.[13]

The importance that Hegel gave to the *Zeitgeist* in conjunction with his teleological view of history had a defining influence on art and intellectual history. Hegelians came to see history as a pattern of 'dialectical' movement through successive stages such that each stage moved towards a kind of 'completion' in the next. Hence, the movement, as reflected in history, has a 'forward-looking' character.[14]

The combination of *Volkgeist* and *Zeitgeist* was to have an immediate impact on architectural thinking in nineteenth century historicism, giving it the peculiar character of simultaneously looking backwards to go forward. The *Volkgeist* presents itself at any one time as the *Zeitgeist,* which implies a particular nation or State at any one time. This led Hegel to criticise the culture of his own time. For example, the art and religious practice of ancient Greek people formed an integral part of their culture – a specific *Volkgeist* connected with a particular *Zeitgeist* – which made Winckelmann's Greek temples inherently alien to Germanic peoples. The organic development of an indigenous German culture had been broken by importing Greek (and before that, Renaissance) styles of architecture. This notion became reinforced with the rise of the Industrial Revolution, which became seen as breaking up organic societies that had developed over centuries. Given that the idea of the *Volkgeist* embraced everything in a particular culture, it was but a short step to see Gothic architecture as indigenous to peoples of northern Europe, whereas Classical architecture belonged to Mediterranean countries. This gave an impetus to the Gothic

4.1 Cologne Cathedral

Revival. In Germany the decision to complete Cologne cathedral in the wake of the Napoleonic occupation of the Rhineland proved to be a rallying point for those who equated Gothic architecture with national character [4.1].

A vociferous advocate of this was August Reichensperger, editor of the influential German periodical *Kölner Domblatt,* whose views were coloured by the writings of Augustus Welby Northmore Pugin (1812–52), one of the most influential writers on architecture in the nineteenth century.[15] Son of a French émigré, Pugin was influenced by both French rationalism and Schlegel. His first book, *Contrasts* (1836), presented in a novel pictorial form the case for adopting a particular historical style, which shows the influence of Hegel's *Zeitgeist*. The book is subtitled *A Parallel Between the Noble Edifices of the Fourteenth and Fifteenth Centuries, and Similar Buildings of the Present Day; Shewing the Present Decay of Taste.* This is exactly what it does. In the most dramatic example, a pair of illustrations depicts a town in 1440, dominated by church spires, and the same town in 1840 where the churches are in ruins or with broken spires, with the skyline now dominated by factory chimneys. In the foreground a panopticon planned prison replaces a Christian hospice [4.2]. Pugin associated a particular historical form of society with a specific style of architecture and attached a moral value to it. The typical fourteenth century Gothic of English parish churches 'answered both a useful and mystical purpose', he asserted, seeing it as 'the only correct expression of the faith, want and climate of our country'.[16] Mixing morality with Christianity and associating this with a particular style of architecture from a particular moment in history and described in such graphic manner proved to be immensely effective in promoting Gothic. Pugin stated that he was opposed to imitation or copying, arguing that fourteenth century Gothic was not so much a style as a principle.[17] With this sleight of hand he pointed the way to those who followed in the nineteenth century. Style Revivalism can be seen as masking the reality of an increasingly industrialised society and the fragmented cultural condition of advancing modernity.

Alan Colquhoun identifies three inter-related facets to the word historicism: 'the theory that all socio-cultural phenomena are historically determined and that all truths are relative; a concern for the institutions and traditions of the past; and the use of historical forms'.[18] Although all three definitions clearly bear upon nineteenth century Style Revivalism, it is the first that makes the other two possible. Growing with the rise of detailed historical studies, which demonstrated differences in cultural development, it became incontrovertible that cultures were relative to one another in space and time, an understanding exploited by Pugin. Writing at the end of a century dominated by Style Revival and attempts to break free, the historian Friedrich Meinecke (1862–1954) said that there were two

4.2 Augustus Pugin, *Contrasts*

I seek *antiquity* and not novelty. I strive to *revive and not invent* and when I have done my best and when compared with the puny and meagre abortions of the day, I have produced a sturdy effect.

Pugin

ways to avoid the implications of relativism: 'by setting up one period as a paradigm', as had Pugin and most nineteenth century architects. Or what he called the 'flight into the future'.[19]

Whilst the idea of a *Zeitgeist* obliged architects to consider what should be the appropriate style for their own time, Hegel's teleological, forward-looking idea of history implied they should have one eye on the future, as Meinecke deduced. This eventually led from a focus on retrieving and advancing a past to imagining a future. Hegel's idea of a teleological process was connected in his own mind to the idea of the unfolding of the World-Spirit, but this idea became easily transferred to technological progress and linked to material production. After Hegel the World-Spirit as self-actualising process became material progress. If we compare the fundamental characteristics of the earliest societies – living within what Eliade describes as 'the horizon of the eternal return' – with our own, we find totally opposing aims. The circumstance we find ourselves in today, resulting from human/technological impact on the planet, raises serious questions about our immediate future, if Hegel's teleological view of history applied to material progress is correct or slavishly followed.

IN WHAT STYLE SHOULD WE BUILD?

In the early years of the nineteenth century a search for a style more appropriate to the age did take place, although the arguments for choosing a particular historical style and advance from there persisted. An intense debate arose in Germany following the publication in 1828 of a short book by Heinrich Hübsch (1795–1836) titled *In What Style Should We Build?* Hübsch had studied under the severe Neoclassicist Friedrich Weinbrenner (1766–1826), went on to study in Rome and visited Greece, but came to the conclusion that imitating classical antiquity represented a false hope.[20] He argued for 'a new style alive to the demands of the present' and proposed what he called the *Rundbogenstil* (the round arch style).[21]

In the second half of the eighteenth century the meaning of the word 'style' had become part of a broad reappraisal of architectural terminology following the Vitruvian tradition's fall from favour. In the Renaissance 'style' was used in rhetoric as a synonym for *maniera* – a mode of handling words to give a particular expression.[22] Thus there was a 'lofty style' and a 'familiar style', the style of writing chosen as appropriate to the content of the work in hand. J-F Blondel (1705–74) developed the analogy for architecture in his *Cours d'architecture* (1771–7) where he stated that there could be a 'sublime, noble and elevated style' for building, or a 'naïve, simple and true character'.[23] By the early nineteenth century, this qualitative description of style had changed under the influence of historicism to become its modern descriptive form, i.e.: 'the styles as they have differed according to peoples and epochs'.[24]

This 'materialistic' approach to understanding architecture was diametrically opposed to Winckelmann's 'idealistic' theory. Disagreeing with the prevailing importance given to aesthetics, Hübsch proposed instead 'material, technical expertise, climate and present needs' as the basis of a style.[27] For example, Greek architecture had been true to hard material (marble) and large stones for its primary structure, he said. Roman architecture he described as a 'sham', but nevertheless, he praised the Romans for introducing the arch, which dealt logically with small stones or brick [4.3]. Hübsch concluded by stating 'that essentially there are only two original styles: one with straight, horizontal stone architraves; the other with curved vaults and arches'.[28] Where Winckelmann deduced 'higher ideas, inner forces, and spiritual concepts' from meticulous observation of the external form of Greek sculpture,[25] which led him to a timeless ideal of beauty, Hübsch countered with a materialistic argument that may have been partly inspired by the rationalist theory of Durand.[26]

4.3 Basilica of Constantine, Rome

Later in the book he reviewed the evolution of Christian architecture culminating in effusive praise for the Gothic of 'Cologne cathedral, among the most beautiful works of art, and comparable to a finely constructed poem in which not a single syllable strikes a discordant note'.[29] Despite this, he compared Gothic unfavourably to earlier Byzantine structures, lamenting that 'we nevertheless look in vain for the moving simplicity of the former', i.e., Byzantine or Early Christian architecture[30] [4.4]. Hübsch's own few buildings, such as the Church of St. Cyriacus, Bulach (1834–7) shows a distinct resemblance too the Early Christian style, but the strongly expressed brick semi-circular arches of the nave carries the stamp of his argument for advance. The Trinkhalle in Baden-Baden (1837–40), with its segmental arched colonnade is his best known building.

4.4 Early Christian church of Santa Fosca, Torcello

The emergence of academies and journals fuelled the increasingly urgent debate about an appropriate style. The editor of *Museums*, Franz Kugler, contrasted Hübsch with the leading Neoclassicist Leo von Klenze (1784–1864), but remained unconvinced that 'a work of art could ever evolve out of the material and extraneous conditions'.[31] Kugler believed that an authentic style could only be based on a nation's religious sentiment. On the other hand, Eduard Metzger, professor of the newly formed Munich Polytechnikum, declared that if 'a building has been declared constructionally correct, it is essentially perfect'.[32] In the first issue of another new architectural journal, *Zeitschrift für praktische Baukunst,* its editor declared bluntly: 'Form expresses construction.'[33]

Von Klenze ridiculed 'misguided German scribblers and dilettantes' for believing that they could invent a new style. Johann Heinrich Wolff agreed, arguing that modern needs could be accommodated by 'modifying and rearranging the architectural elements that naturally evolved in antiquity'.[34] Greek temple architecture represented the epitome of classical repose, he asserted, whereas all following styles produced 'an impression of restless mobility'. In contrast, Metzger saw the arch as being 'the last art form known to the world' with fourteenth century Gothic its epitome and hence any new form of architecture would develop from the pointed arch.

In all this we see the shadow of Hegel. Reviewing the past, architects and academics looked for a point of interruption in the evolution of styles, either seen as a peak, or where it had not been brought to its perfection, and advance to a new style from there. Not everyone was optimistic about developing a new style, however. Carl Gottlieb Wilhelm Bötticher (1806–89) was both pessimistic and aware of the Hegelian position: '[we] find ourselves alone in an immense void', he said, 'having lost all the historical ground that the past has provided for us and for the future as the only basis on which further development is possible.'[35]

Very soon I fell into the error of pure radical abstraction, by which I conceived a specific architectural work entirely from utilitarian purpose and construction. In these cases something dry and rigid emerged, something that lacked freedom and altogether excluded two essential elements: the historic and the poetic.

Karl Friedrich Schinkel

Karl Friedrich Schinkel (1781–1841) was the most influential German architect of this era and his architecture indicated how to alleviate this despair by a more considered use of the elements of architecture. Central to his conception of architecture were matters of construction: 'any masking of the construction is an error', he wrote.[36] Historians emphasising the functionalism of the early Modern

Movement erroneously claimed support from Schinkel, for he in fact qualified this by saying that 'mere need does not give rise to beauty ... Only someone who moves freely above material need will be capable of beauty.'[37] He was an accomplished painter and his paintings reveal a Romantic disposition. An early fascination with the expressive and spiritual qualities of Gothic became combined with his readiness to use brickwork for the church of Friedrich-Weider (1824–30) in Berlin. He also designed a brick church in the *Rundbogenstil* and used brick for the Berlin Bauakademie (1832–5) [4.5]. Most of his buildings, however, were classical, but he disagreed with Winckelmann on imitation, arguing rather that the Greek ideal represented only 'a reference point and point of departure.'[38] Slavish imitation was, he said, 'no way historical, but rather opposed to the historical. History has never copied earlier history ... The only truly historical act is one that introduces in some way an extra, a new element, into the world, from which a new history is produced.'[39]

4.5 Schinkel, Bauakademie, Berlin

Schinkel's Altes Museum (1822–30) illustrates how he approached this by taking elements, or units of form, from the classical tradition and re-assembled them into new wholes. For this first public museum in Berlin, he designed a long, open colonnade of 18 Ionic columns as the principal façade [4.6].

4.6 Altes Museum, Berlin

This original conception draws upon the idea of the Greek stoa, which represented the public openness of the agora as well as embodying an existential openness, in contrast to the more typical temple front of Neoclassical buildings. Walls at either end of the wide colonnade emphasised the frontal openness of the institution, which has at its centre a circular hall modelled on the Pantheon. Where the Roman's statues represented gods here they became god-like statues. Schinkel's Schloss Charlottenhof (1824–5) showed, in a different way from Soane, how the classical tradition and Romanticism could be reconciled [4.7]. Like Soane, whom he admired, Schinkel exemplifies the argument advanced here, that elements drawn from architectural history, critically appraised, can be re-assembled to constitute new meaningful wholes that establish a continuity with the past.

I believe it might be worthwhile to go back to architecture's historical experience; to return to those elements which define its specificity.

Giorgio Grassi

A few years later Bötticher – a pupil of Schinkel – gave expression to an increasingly aired view that a new style would only evolve from the use of new materials; 'such a material is iron'.[40] Germany lagged far behind

4.7 Charlottenhof, Potsdam

4.8 Notre Dame, Paris,
West entrance

England which led the field in the use of iron. An early use of iron in France shows the influence of the *Rundbogenstil* and the continuing grip of Gothic on the question of style at this time. In his essay 'The book and the building', Neil Levine shows how the Bibliothèque Ste-Geneviève (1838–50), Paris, by Henri Labrouste (1808–75) was a riposte to issues raised in Victor Hugo's novel *Notre-Dame de Paris*. In the eighth edition of this best-seller published in 1832, Hugo added a chapter called '*Ceci tuera celi*' (This will kill That); 'This' refers to the printing press with architecture as its victim. From 'the origin of things up to and including the fifteenth century', wrote Hugo, 'architecture was the great book of mankind, man's chief form of expression'.[41] Gothic cathedrals were 'accessible to every soul ... as easily understood as nature', he continued.[42] Gothic cathedrals epitomised this, their façades and fabric embroidered with the meaning of their sacred purpose [4.8]. 'The architect is like the stylus who writes at the dictate of the general idea of an epoch', explained Hugo, giving concrete expression to how Hegel's *Zeitgeist* operated. With a sideswipe at Renaissance architecture, Hugo saw Gutenberg's invention of the printing press as marking the transition from the 'reign of architecture' to the 'reign of printing'.[43] As Levine explains: 'Hugo's description of the "death of architecture" was grounded in a dialectical understanding of history. It ... paralleled Hegel's contemporary discussion of the successive primacy of each of the arts.'[44]

Labrouste rose to this challenge with his design for the Bibliothèque. He had been among the leaders of Romantic students urging reforms of teaching at the École des Beaux-Arts and had been invited by Hugo to criticise the sections on architecture in drafts of '*Notre-Dame*'.

Despite this, he was not drawn to Gothic. Instead he designed the library as utilitarian in appearance, dominated by a long row of large semi-circular arches – 'like a blind Roman aqueduct' – on the upper storey and small round-arched windows on the lower. The façade is not decorated with pediments, pilasters or porticoes but rather with panels on which are carved the names of authors whose books are housed in the library. Eight hundred and ten names are inscribed in chronological order in columns as if they might be typed on the page of a book [4.9]. Labrouste likened the façade to a 'monumental catalogue'.[45] Decoration is applied like printing; repetitive and mechanical. And black cast iron discs bearing the library's book stamp – an interlaced S and G – reinforce the idea of a printer's stamp.

The reading room on the upper storey is spanned by two rows of semi-circular iron arches, an early non-utilitarian building to use iron [4.10]. The arches are supported on cast iron columns resting upon tall base pillars of stone, as if Labrouste acknowledges the compatibility of old and new materials, the new resting on the old. The entrance vestibule also has an iron structure, but of shallow segmental arches. A spatial narrative is initiated here that is part of Labrouste's answer to Hugo's representational model of architecture. Busts of eminent philosophers, writers, scientists and artists line the walls whose upper parts are painted with trees. In conjunction with green iron lattice-work beams springing from a forest of columns, which suggests a grove of trees [4.11]. The whole arrangement evokes the grove of Plato's academy, an idea reinforced by a copy of Raphael's painting the 'School of Athens' on the wall of the stair to the reading room. Students passing through this sequence of spaces could enjoy the thought that they were following in the footsteps of famous thinkers. Just as the collection of books assembled in the lofty, light reading room rest upon that tradition of knowledge represented in the vestibule below, so their own achievements might build upon that of their illustrious forebears. Labrouste's intelligent, imaginative attempt to deal with the changing reality posed by new materials stands out like an isolated beacon amongst the widespread resort to Style Revivalism that dominated nineteenth century Europe.

4.9 Henri Labrouste, Bibliothèque Ste-Geneviève, Paris, Façade Detail

4.10 Reading room

4.11 Foyer

RUSKIN AND THE OXFORD MUSEUM

Perhaps the most interesting building in this period that broaches the question of history and style is the Oxford Museum (1854–60). John

Ruskin (1819–1900), who emerged as the major nineteenth century critic, was closely involved in the programme for the building, which raised profound questions about architecture in an industrial age. His writings on art and architecture at the time of the museum's conception reveal an awareness of not only Romanticism and its criticism of Enlightenment rationality but also the debate on history that we have seen reverberating throughout Europe.

Like Pugin (whom he despised) and others, Ruskin advocated Gothic architecture. But his argument for its use differed significantly and is best grasped by considering his notion of 'savageness', which he made the main point of *The Seven Lamps of Architecture* (1849). What Ruskin meant by 'savageness' is often taken to be simply 'imperfection in the execution of work or roughness in texture'.[46] But this superficial reading masks Ruskin's deeper meaning, which reveals the influence from Europe of thinking about history. He replaced the reprehensible overtones of 'savageness' – describing 'the charm in savageness which there is not in science' – with a suggestion of vitality.[47] In his book, *Modern Painters*, volume 2, he wrote of 'barbarism' and refers to Jules Michelet's book *The People* published in the same year, 1846.[48] Michelet (1798–1874) links 'barbarism' with 'the rise of the people' whom some compare to 'Barbarians! Yes! That is to say, full of sap, fresh, vigorous and forever springing up.'[49] Michelet expands the Romantic idea of the individual genius to a whole people, untrammelled by reason, who pierced directly to the heart of things by intuition and feeling:

> this gift which is rare in civilised countries, is, it is known, very common amongst simple nations, whether savage or barbarous. The simple sympathise with life and are endowed, as their reward, with the magnificent gift – that the slightest sign is sufficient for them to see … And here is their secret affinity with the man of genius.[50]

Some years before this, in 1827, Michelet had produced an abridged translation of Vico's *New Science*.[51] It has been said that 'the decisive event for Vico's reputation in the nineteenth century was Michelet's discovery of the *New Science* in 1824'.[52] Michelet enthusiastically adopted what he called Vico's 'great historical principle', transforming it from simply a mode of understanding to a criticism of Enlightenment rationality.[53] Michelet saw the vitality of a people, the *Volkgeist*, the spirit of the people, as the means to revitalise culture, as had Coleridge and Wordsworth. Unlike Herder, who found it hard to

The virtue of the Imagination is its reaching, by intuition and intensity of gaze (not by reasoning, but by its authoritative opening and revealing power), a more essential truth than is seen at the surface of things.

Ruskin,
Modern Painters, volume 2

predict what would follow his own scientific age, Michelet followed Vico in seeing a return to barbarism at the end of a seemingly high point in civilisation. But with Romantic blood in his veins, Michelet saw this as an immediate necessary good in order to revitalise culture.

For Ruskin, it was the medieval mason whose labours had made this possible. He characterised Gothic – or 'Gothicness' as he preferred – as a style recognisable by the mind of its makers, which crystallised in his notion of savageness. Making a distinction between building and architecture, he argued that architecture consisted of impressing upon built form 'certain characters venerable or beautiful, but otherwise unnecessary'.[54] Thus Ruskin equated ornament with mind and this constituted the emotional part of architecture. It was the memory of the mind of the people that Ruskin saw in Gothic and which he contrasted with the factory system and division of labour. 'It is, not truly, speaking the labour that is divided; but the men: – divided into mere segments of men – broken into small fragments and crumbs of life.'[55]

It was this way of working – the 'thinking hand' – that Ruskin wished to revive.[56] His notion of savageness overlapped with his belief that 'Gothicness' should show a love of nature, for Gothic's 'changefulness' bore witness to nature's cycle and vitality. The freedom given to the mythical medieval mason allowed him to demonstrate his faith in work by carving specimens of nature directly from his own observation and imagination, that other great work of God; Imagination opposed to Fancy, in Coleridge's formulation, or Mechanical Toil according to William Morris (1834–96).

The architects Deane and Woodward brought over from Ireland the masons James and John O'Shea and their nephew Edward Whellan who had previously executed work in the Ruskinian manner. Plant specimens were brought from the parks every morning for the masons to carve directly onto the window surrounds and column capitals [4.12]. The carved capitals in the glass-covered courtyard at the heart of the building are undoubtedly the finest ornament on a nineteenth century building [4.13]. This appeared to vindicate Ruskin's thesis, but the project ran into difficulties and much of the carving remains unfinished. What Ruskin called 'the Liberty of the Workman' or quite simply 'the Life of the Workman'[57] fell foul of the university authorities for some of the O'Sheas' witty animal carvings upset a college Master's sensibilities and they were dismissed.[58]

4.12 Deane and Woodward, Oxford Museum, unfinished carvings to window surround
4.13 Oxford Museum, column capital in museum space

4.14 Oxford Museum, main façade

4.15 Glass-covered courtyard
4.16 Detail of iron structure

The Oxford Museum was the only full-blown attempt to implement Ruskin's ideal. It was the first building dedicated to the study of science in Oxford, with the important aim of reconciling science with faith. The driving force was Henry Acland (1815–1900), a friend of Ruskin from their student days at Christ Church and who, as Lees Reader in Science, became closely involved in the programme for the building.[59] The university voted for 'a school of Natural Science' in 1849, a competition was held in 1854 and work began the following year. The building's form is similar to medieval secular buildings from the Low Countries, with a steep slate roof capping the yellow sandstone walls [4.14].

The glass-covered courtyard is a breathtakingly majestic space. Surrounded by a brick and stone cloister, iron columns rise up to support an iron pointed-arch roof structure covered with glass tiles, the space filled with dinosaur skeletons and glass cabinets displaying all aspects of natural life and form [4.15]. But iron represented the Industrial Revolution for Ruskin, which he raged against. So how did he reconcile himself to its use here? F.A. Skidmore, an iron master from Coventry employed to fabricate the structure, proposed making it out of wrought iron, and one can imagine Ruskin being appeased by this, the thousand hammer marks of the iron workers left on the metal as a record of their skill and labour.[60] Ruskin wrote an essay 'On Iron and Polity' at this time where he described the process of rusting as the 'life' inherent in iron, absorbing oxygen and returning to its original mineral condition.[61]

But, high drama ensued: The Minutes of the Oxford Museum Delegates for 23 February 1858 describe having 'learnt that the iron columns supporting the roof of the new museum have in several instances given way'[62] Skidmore was summonsed and described the difficulties in predicting how iron might perform, but offered to pay for replacement cast-iron columns. The remnants of the original wrought iron tubes were reused and rise like slender branches from which spring delicate leaves of native trees beaten from the iron [4.16].

Proposals to re-build the columns in stone were resisted by Acland as iron was central to his vision. *The Builder* reported him as performing an experiment to see how Gothic art would deal with 'railway materials – iron and glass'.[63] Ruskin saw iron as the material manifestation of the industrial process not only destroying the imagination of workmen but also despoiling town and country. As well as being appeased by the 'thinking hand' in work, he would have approved of the structure appearing ambiguously either as a forest of trees or a Gothic cathedral interior. The iron columns resting on stone – as did Labrouste's Bibliothèque Ste-Genevieve, which was illustrated in *The Builder* in 1853[64] – and embraced by the brick and stone cloister, can be read as reconciling science with faith, history with progress. A purely verbal description of the space – glass roof and lofty central space – would make it sound no different from atriums that characterise commercial or financial buildings at the heart of modernity. But at the Oxford Museum the essential meaning of the building is embodied in the material and details of the construction. Acland described it as transferring appropriate associations from the surroundings – native marbles form the columns and plants are carved on the capitals from the region where the marble originates – to the activity – the study of science. The carvings belong to both the material body of the building and the idea. On the one hand the Style Revivalism of the Oxford Museum denies the fragmenting condition of that age, but on the other it attempted to re-assemble a new meaningful whole. An overriding purpose in setting up the Museum was to point out an alternative to Bacon's maxim of putting 'Nature to the rack to reveal her truths'. The experience of the Oxford Museum is of a man-made world that is a metaphor for a view of the Earth as a living whole in which we are immersed and from which we draw meaning as well as minerals.

SEMPER ON STYLE AND WAYS OF MAKING

Gottfried Semper (1803–79) has been described as the first architect to grasp the condition of modernity, the first to consider architecture detached from its origins in historical styles.[65] He elaborated a theory of style that proposed a radically new way of considering the relationship between material, making and design, shifting the emphasis on to how a style was formed. Semper described his theory as 'practical aesthetics', which he contrasted with Winckelmann's preoccupation with perceptual experience, or 'spectator reactions'.[66] At one level he explained style as a product of material properties and techniques of making. This dimension of his theory, which Semper denied as being 'materialistic', occupied much of his major work *Der Stil* (1863), and became a significant influence on the early Modern Movement. More recent scholarship has highlighted his notion of *bekleidung* or 'dressing', a concept which might help explain why his buildings paradoxically are in a flamboyant Renaissance style.[67]

After a period studying and working in Paris, he was appointed to the chair of architecture at the Dresden Academy of Fine Art in 1834, a position that gave him the opportunity to build. His early designs were eclectic and show the influence of the *Rundbogenstil*.[68] With echoes of Herder, Semper argued for reconnecting to an early style – Pevsner described one unbuilt design as the 'Byzantino-Romanesque style'[69] – by comparing it with the Nibelungen Saga, the primal Germanic myth. 'The Rundbogen is closer to our time than the pointed arch', he said somewhat paradoxically.[70] The great success for Semper during this time was his design for the Dresden Hoftheater (1835–41). Arguing that the form of the theatre should reflect its interior workings, he took the novel step of making the semi-circular form of the auditorium the principal façade. Its colonnade of round-arched openings and engaged columns marked the beginning of Semper's life-long use of renaissance motifs, which he considered appropriate to the festive nature of theatre.[71] He described the style as being 'second youth', an allusion to the popular argument that a particular style was capable of further development. In 1849 he was forced to flee Dresden for London, having manned the barricades against the Saxon army suppressing a revolutionary uprising for political liberalisation.

Wolfgang Hermann has said that 'The Great Exhibition of 1851 was the decisive influence on Semper'[72] and it is generally considered a significant visual marker of the arrival of modernity. He was impressed by the iron and glass building – later known as the 'Crystal Palace' – but appalled by the poor design of the vast spectacle of machine-made products. Unlike Ruskin and Morris, however, Semper did not despair of the machine. Reflecting upon pre-industrial cultural artefacts on display led him to his fundamental theory of style, a theory aimed at contemporary problems of design. Commissioned to design the layouts for exhibits from Canada, Denmark, Sweden and Turkey, Semper visited almost daily.[73] He particularly admired artefacts made by Native Americans and Lapps, noting how they 'far surpass the refined works of the civilised nations in what one calls style.'[74]

Semper's Dresden lectures formed the basis of his book *The Four Elements of Architecture* (1851), where he introduced theories he developed later in *Der Stil*.[75] His keen interest in the emerging disciplines of ethnology and archaeology can be seen in the way he formulated the four 'elements'. The first was the hearth around which formed the social groups of family, tribe and nation. He associated a technical process with each element. In this case, ceramics and metalwork, crafts requiring fire. The second element was a mound, which raised the fire off the damp earth and prevented inundation from heavy rainfall or rising rivers – associated with materials that were piled up, such as masonry. The third element was the roof, which sheltered the flame – and was formed by carpentry. The fourth was the wall that defined an interior space at the same time as protecting the flame from the wind. Semper argued that the earliest wall would have been of woven material.[76] This became the basis of his theory of 'dressing', for he maintained that whilst piling up a mound or platform might be extended upwards to form a masonry wall, nevertheless, this would have been draped by a textile.

In *Der Stil* he re-designated his 'four elements' to emphasise that these were not specific materials but what he called 'material-functional' categories: 1), materials that were malleable and could be moulded and fired (ceramics); 2), pliable and tough materials that could be woven (textiles); 3), thin, tensile materials (carpentry); 4), dense materials resistant to compression (stone and masonry). Semper described these 'elements' as more like ideas or 'motives', a term best understood as being like a typical form evolving to satisfy a need. This idea contrasted with architects' obsession with using historical forms and details at this time. The craft processes associated with these elements will 'very often give the key and basis for the understanding of architectural forms and principles',[77] he argued, and were the precursors to all monumental architectures. The overwhelming increase in historical knowledge and its use in Style Revivalism – 'historical treatises in stone and chalk,' lamented Semper[78] – had stifled creative thinking on how to respond to an industrialised world of new materials and techniques. He also pointed to how capitalism, or 'speculation', had changed the traditional pattern of need by stimulating new desires salved only by novelties.

At the Great Exhibition Semper found a building that perfectly fitted his schema of the four elements. A full-size replica of a hut from the Caribbean island of Trinidad was erected on a 'terrace' of clay at the centre of which was the hearth. Semper described the superstructure: 'Here is the roof supported by columns of bamboo; its structural parts

Style means giving emphasis and artistic significance to the basic idea and to all intrinsic and extrinsic coefficients that modify the embodiment of the theme in a work of art.

Gottfried Semper

It is already evident that inventions are no longer, as they had been in earlier times, means for warding off want and for helping consumption; instead, want and consumption are the means to market the inventions. The order of things has been reversed.

Semper,
Science, Industry and Art

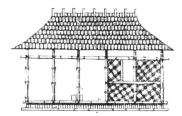

4.17 Caribbean hut, from *Der Stil*

4.18 *Situla* and *Hydria*,
after Semper, from *Der Stil*

We can quite rightly describe the old monuments as the fossilized receptacles of extinct social organisations, but these did not grow on the backs of society like shells on the back of snails ... nor did they spring forth from blind natural processes like coral reefs.

Semper

Let the material be true to itself ... Brick should appear as brick, wood as wood, iron as iron, each according to its own statical laws.

Semper

are tied together with rope of coconut fibre; it is covered with palm leaves; the terrace has a bamboo railing; the wall consists of mats'[79] [4.17].

The Four Elements had the subtitle, 'A Contribution to the Comparative Study of Architecture'. Using the then popular comparative method in *Der Stil,* he contrasts two types of water-carrying clay vessel, the Egyptian *situla* and the Greek *hydria*. The teardrop form of the *situla* may have been derived from a leather bag used earlier for carrying water, its form preserved as proving practical for scooping water from the Nile [4.18]. The very different form of the *hydria*, in contrast, had developed from collecting water from a spring and for carrying on the head. Its form had evolved from the common, tall thin *amphora* to become more rounded with a lower centre of gravity and third handle added to help with carrying on the head. The leather bag form of the *situla* is an example of what Semper termed *Stoffwechsel*. This literally means 'material transformation', the transformation of an artefact that occurs with a change of material and where a memory of an earlier material is preserved or recognisable. Neolithic clay pots were often decorated with a criss-cross pattern that is a symbolic reminder of woven baskets that preceded the invention of pottery.[80]

Semper has been described as an 'anthropologically oriented pragmatist',[81] and in his pioneering essay, Joseph Rykwert summarised *Der Stil* as investigating 'the elementary methods of making and fabrication … through a social and therefore a historic adaptation'.[82] A historical development in the production of traditional artefacts also implied a deeper rooted relationship between a society and its material culture. Semper's comparative approach aimed to emulate two of the greatest scientists of the era, Georges Cuvier in the field of botany, and Wilhelm von Humboldt in linguistics.[83] Rykwert explains how Semper developed Humboldt's view that languages represented 'the will of the people to represent itself' and, with echoes of Michelet's *The People*, Semper conceived material artefacts similarly as 'the products of the collective, of society, exactly in the same way as … language'.[84]

Semper gave no specific consideration to iron, the most obvious new material affecting building, a gap in his theory noted later by pioneer modernists. Many were convinced that a contemporary architecture had to deal with iron. Despite his praise for the Crystal Palace,

Semper was wedded to mass as an essential attribute of architecture. Because the fundamental property of iron was its relative strength, it must be made thin, he said, to be true to its material character. But to use iron in this way would be a contradiction, he argued, for a building needs mass and weight of material. Iron was acceptable for decoration, for 'delicate lacework, but not in girders carrying a great weight, as support for the building'.[85] He criticised Labrouste's Bibliothèque Ste-Genevieve for its iron structure.[86]

Semper's view of the history of architecture helps explain his attitude to iron. He felt that a significant moment came when the Romans developed the vault, which not only had structural advantages – using small stones or brick – over Greek trabeation, but also introduced the priority of space over tectonic form.[87] Semper saw this as opening up fresh areas for exploration culminating in the complex plans and spaces of Roman baths. Roman architecture, he said, represented 'the cosmopolitan future of architecture'.[88]

His reading of Roman architecture may also help explain Semper's use of the Renaissance style for his buildings, which seems at odds with the tectonic emphasis of *Der Stil*. In a way, the pilasters and entablatures that Romans added to their arched structures can be seen as a form of 'dressing'. This had been taken up in the Renaissance, the style he re-appropriated for the Darmstadt Hoftheater.

Architecture … must not have anything to do with this quasi-invisible material [iron] when it is a question of mass effects.

Semper

4.19 Museum of Natural History, Vienna

In his later years Semper had the opportunity to design major buildings: a Museum for Natural History (1872–81) and the Art History museum (1889–91) – the pair conceived as a Roman Forum in relation to the Hofburg Palace – and the Hofburg Theatre (1872–6), all in Vienna and each in his richly decorated version of the Renaissance style [4.19 and 4.20]. During this same period his Dresden Hoftheater

4.20 (Left) Hofburg Theatre, Vienna
4.21 (Above) Hoftheater, Dresden

burnt down and Semper was commissioned to rebuild it [4.21]. In doing so, the details reveal the consolidation of his theories.

Semper introduced an iconographic programme that centred upon Dionysus leading his bride Ariadne to her apotheosis. Apollo, usually epitomising civilisation's highest achievement, was here relegated to a minor position. This decorative scheme served as an allegory of the origins of art springing from a vital source yet to be recovered, renewed, or perfected by civilisation. Semper aimed this at 'the higher law of humanity ... to the causal connections of history, but understood in mythical terms and directed to the national consciousness of a people'.[89] The iconographic programme therefore reinforced Vico's well-assimilated idea of the rise and fall of civilisations combined with cycles of renewal. Semper's elevation of Dionysus over Apollo was a theme that was to have an enormous influence on Richard Wagner (1813–83) and Nietzsche in the following years. Nietzsche was to develop this theme, which Semper had drawn from his ethnological and archaeological research, and turned it into a vehement attack on nineteenth century culture, an attack that was to resonate into the twentieth century and beyond, as we will see.

Semper introduced an entirely fresh perspective on history. He did not identify history with architectural styles, their root in forms of construction and the values associated with the society in which the style had developed. Instead, Semper's theory of style proposed that architectural 'elements' were derived ultimately from the materials and traditional ways of making domestic artefacts. Following from this, he considered that architects had little alternative but to adapt traditional types of built form because of the historical orientation of the age. 'No century can be erased from world history', Semper asserted. Contemporary architecture, he continued, 'must therefore give some indication ... of the connections between the present and all past centuries'.[90] Architects should neither slavishly copy historical examples nor try to invent new forms, he said, 'but rather try and express new ideas with the old types'. With a sentiment that could be aimed at the novel forms of 'iconic architecture' peculiar to our own time, he continued: 'Architecture has over the centuries created its own store of forms from which it borrows the types for new creations; by using these types, architecture remains legible and comprehensible to everyone.'[91]

Chapter 5: Nietzsche and the 'history beyond history'

Nietzsche's essay *The Use and Abuse of History* was one of his first forays into cultural criticism. In it he targets the stultifying embrace of history upon culture in the nineteenth century. It could be argued that the opposite is true of our own time; that the forces of modernisation and globalisation shape culture in ways that primarily further the ends of progress and profit. Future-focused aims, rather than specifically human ends, which, as Tosh says, necessarily embrace time past. Nietzsche was the first to explore the root of these concerns in cultural criticism. Although there is virtually nothing on architecture in Nietzsche's published writings, he did make comments in his notebooks, and his views were clearly coloured by historical Style Revivalism. He read Semper's *Der Stil* but was less sanguine on the role of industrialisation. Like Ruskin, but with a completely different prognosis, Nietzsche expressed 'anguish at the fragmentation of men's lives' under industrial production.[1]

The essay was published in 1874 under the title *Von Nutzen und Nachteil der Historie für das Leben*. (It is often translated more literally as 'Of the Use and Disadvantage of History for Life').[2] The second of four essays published as *Untimely Meditations* (1873–6), it is a particularly useful work to understand Nietzsche because it was the last written in conventional essay form. The aphoristic style of his later work is easily misread, a form of writing that requires the reader to complete his thoughts, as Nietzsche himself observed.[3] It also contains in preliminary form the key concepts of his later philosophy.[4]

The *Untimely Meditations* present a critique of a complacent culture, a society made up of 'cultural philistines', wrote Nietzsche, a public 'warding off a real artistically vigorous cultural style'.[5] He wrote in hope that 'the whole noisy sham-culture of our age could be silenced for ever'.[6] He is upheld as the first critic of modernity because he saw the roots of this cultural crisis in the Enlightenment with its zealous commitment to science and progress: 'Is not the nineteenth century … merely a stronger brutalized eighteenth century', he wrote, 'that is to say a *decadence* century.'[7] Nietzsche coined the phrase 'herd-man' to characterize the emergence of a mass culture fed by a mass media.

In *The Use and Abuse of History* he identifies three kinds of history: the 'monumental', 'antiquarian', and 'critical'. Monumental history he condemns because its adherents do not want to see a new greatness emerge, claiming that greatness already exists. 'Monumental history is the masquerade costume in which their hatred of the great and the powerful of their own age is disguised as satiated admiration for the great and the powerful of past ages.'[8] Antiquarian history he condemns for its insatiable thirst for antiquity, its excessive reverence for 'ancient custom', 'religious belief', and 'political privilege'. Antiquarian history 'knows only how to preserve life, not how to engender it'.[9] Antiquarian history revered the past such that it stifled creativity.

In contrast to these two disadvantages of history, he says we should 'employ critical history for the sake of life'.[10] 'Every man and every nation requires … a certain knowledge of the past', he wrote, 'but always and only for the ends of life'.[11] He goes on to explain that history can be of use but, 'If he is to live, man must possess and from time to time employ the strength to break up and dissolve a part of the past.'[12] The essay is scathing about history as then practised but, by qualifying it with 'life' or 'to live', he insisted upon its usefulness. How he imagined a living culture might be revived involved both a particular reading of history and a specific moment in history. This underlay all his writings and will be the focus of my investigation because, after all, the aim of architecture must be to support life.

It is notoriously difficult to grasp exactly what Nietzsche is arguing for, much easier to see the monumental and antiquarian history he is railing against in nineteenth century Style Revivalism. Nineteenth century historicists tended to parcel up the past into discrete and contained pieces. Historical styles became the emblems of ideas associated with the societies that produced them, as we have seen in the way Pugin associated Gothic with Christian values. It was from this vantage point that what he called an 'antiquarian' relationship to the past felt the full force of his criticism, for Nietzsche described his compatriots as 'walking encyclopaedias'.[13]

In contrast, Nietzsche's critical history would allow us to gain a past, he said, 'from which we *might* spring, as against that from which

I am here attempting to look afresh at something of which our time is rightly proud – its cultivation of history … I believe, indeed, that we are all suffering from a consuming fever of history.

Nietzsche,
Untimely Meditations

If, behind the historical drive, there is no drive to build, if destroying and clearing away does not enable a future alive with hope to build its house on liberated ground … the creative drive is weakened and discouraged.

Nietzsche,
The Use and Abuse of History

we do spring.' This implied examining the past to discover the vital sources that brought artistic forms into being and how this process might be emulated rather than seeing a historical period as a closed and circumscribed entity whose form could be resurrected. Nietzsche peeled away the layers of an ossified culture to look for the seed of a new and vital one. Nietzsche's thinking has been called a form of 'unmasking' that helped shift nineteenth century preoccupation with historical decorated form to modernism's interest in space.

The crucial issue for Nietzsche was the suppression of creative action by the excess of history that dominated the nineteenth century. History is only 'fruitful for the future', he said, when it is 'directed by a higher force and does not itself dominate and direct.'[14] The historicism of his time was coming to determine everything. It was the antithesis of art, and 'only if history can endure to be transformed into a work of art will it perhaps be able to preserve instincts or even evoke them', he said. 'Such a historiography would be altogether contrary to the analytical and inartistic tendencies of our times.'[15]

Here we see the importance of art and artists to Nietzsche's prescriptions for change. He called for 'the production of the great man', an early formulation of his controversial notion of the *Übermensch* (translated as 'superman' or 'over-man', although without the connotation of domination). He had in mind artists such as Michelangelo, or Richard Wagner, the subject of his fourth *Untimely Meditations*. But Nietzsche was against unbridled originality: 'Most original thoughts are foolishness', he wrote.[16] Rather, a critical history could be used to break free of positivistic historiography and Hegelian historicism to recreate something like the cultural condition of archaic Greece. Nietzsche had explored this in his first published book, *The Birth of Tragedy out of the Spirit of Music* (1872). He argued there that Greek tragedy – no higher art form existed, thought Nietzsche – arose from a 'coupling' of the Apollonian and Dionysian principles. Apollo he identified with sculpture and 'dreams', Dionysius with intoxication and music, Apollo with individuation and Dionysus with ecstatic immersion in nature. In calling for a history directed to 'the ends of life', Nietzsche insisted that priority must be given to the Dionysian principle, where 'artistic energies … burst forth from nature herself.'[17] In this early work he hopes for '*the gradual awakening of the Dionysian spirit* in our modern world', and sees hopeful signs in German music 'from Bach to Beethoven, from Beethoven to Wagner'.[18]

With a hundred such men – raised in this unmodern way, that is to say become mature and accustomed to the heroic – the whole noisy sham-culture of our age could be silenced forever.

Nietzsche,
Untimely Meditations

Man is a rope tied between beast and *Übermensch* – a rope over an abyss … What is great about man is that he is a bridge and not an end: what can be loved in man is that he is an *overture* and a *going under*.

Nietzsche,
Thus spoke Zarathustra

* * *

'A historical phenomenon, known clearly and completely and resolved into a phenomenon of knowledge, is, for him who has perceived it, dead',[19] wrote Nietzsche. The immense historical knowledge proudly accumulated by the Germans weighed down the capacity for action and stunted original thinking. History, in the modern sense of a profession embracing teaching and research, was most advanced in Germany at this time. The leading figure was Leopold von Ranke (1795–1886), whose Berlin seminars played an important part in disseminating the practice of critically evaluating documents and sources.[20] In opposition to Hegel's vision of history, Ranke coined the maxim *'wie es eigenlich gewesen'* (how it really happened).[21] His insistence on documentary sources – in contrast to Winckelmann's emphasis on aesthetics – and belief that an objective representation of the past could be reconstructed from the facts was bound up with positivism and became the bedrock of the profession. In *What Happened to History*, Willie Thompson argues that this 'historiographical revolution', which began with Ranke, 'was one aspect of the experience of modernity starting to overtake Europe'.[22]

History was very much in the ascendant during the 1870s when Nietzsche wrote *The Use and Abuse of History*, with faculties of history being founded at Oxford and Cambridge, and Henry Adams (who had been trained in Germany) introducing seminars after the style of Ranke at Harvard in 1871. As a philologist, Nietzsche had been trained in the approach to sources taught by Ranke, but had become frustrated by its narrowly fact-based application. Hence his shift towards philosophy. With its stifling piling up of facts, positivist history was the principal target of Nietzsche's monumental history, but Hegel also came under fire. He detected the notion of progress latent within Hegelian-inspired historicism, and criticised the teleological conception of history, both for its implied determinism and Hegel's belief that 'modern man' is the 'summit and target of the world-process'[23] and (with echoes of Shaftesbury) that 'we are nature perfected'.[24] He opposed this complacency, which ran counter to his own belief in the need for 'great men' to turn against the tide of history so conceived. However, critical history remained fundamental to his own thinking and his work has been characterised as a 'historical approach' to philosophy.[25] At the start of his next book, *Human, All Too Human* (1879), he wrote: 'A lack of the historical sense is the congenital defect of all philosophers.'[26]

Lack of historical sense is the family failing of all philosophers … But everything has become; there are *no eternal facts,* just as there are no absolute truths.

Nietzsche,
Human, All Too Human

Such was the progress made, not only in technology but also in social reform, that history and the emerging social sciences had become convinced that 'the method of science [was] applicable to other fields'.[27] But gradually the difference between science and history became clear: science aimed to be prescriptive, whereas history is descriptive; science deals with observable present facts, whereas history has to retrieve an elusive past bound up with more complex human goals.

The first to grasp that the methods of natural science were inappropriate for history was the philosopher Wilhelm Dilthey (1833–1911). He had been appointed professor of philosophy at Basel two years before Nietzsche's arrival there in 1869 as professor of philology. Dilthey described his work as 'a philosophy of life', a view that must have influenced his younger colleague.[28] Dilthey developed the concept of 'understanding' as more appropriate to history than the scientific method. Understanding was the process of grasping meaning, which he argued permeated the human world. It would take us away from the task here to explore this forerunner of modern hermeneutics, sufficient to say that Dilthey's importance lies in insisting that every experience of being human is meaningful, that there is 'pattern and meaning' everywhere, and that 'meaning in human life is linked to its temporal structure'.[29] Understanding implied an 'inside view of human nature which we all possess' and, with echoes of Vico, provided 'insight into the workings of the human mind', the only way history made sense.[30]

Comprehension of the meaning and significance of the historical world is often derived, as by Hegel or Comte, from ascertaining a general direction in the movement of universal history. This telescopes the interaction of many elements into one indeterminate vision. In fact we find that the historical movement takes place in the individual context of interactions.

Wilhelm Dilthey,
Pattern and Meaning in History

Understanding and interpretation is the method used throughout the human studies and all functions unite in it. It contains all the truths of the human studies. Everywhere understanding opens up a world.

Dilthey,
Pattern and Meaning in History

* * *

Nietzsche took a keen interest in architecture and was dismayed at what he called 'the fairground garishness of the modern world',[31] an opinion that many today share at the rash of outlandish forms. Nietzsche contrasted Style Revivalism with the 'unity of artistic style ... of a people' which he believed had once existed in Europe but had now gone, perhaps for good.[32] Despite this he argued for 'contemplation of the past in its monuments' because 'the greatness of the past' showed that it 'was at least *possible* then and will therefore surely be possible again'.[33] He hoped it could be feasible to 'set a new world alongside the old' given the proper use of history. But in darker moments he despaired that such a possibility had become practically extinct since Schinkel showed how the past could be broken apart and re-assembled to form a new whole.[34]

In this struggle of the organic vital force against both the material and will power, nature unfurls her most glorious creations; it is manifested in a beautiful elastic curve of a palm, whose majestic corona vigorously straightens up while bending to the law of gravity ... This struggle is found to be still more active in organisms with volition, as in the Artemis or Apollo created by ancient art. Here the freedom of will and movement is in an equilibrium with the conditions of mass and life – the greatest diversity in a unified working together of forces that is possible for man to conceive.

Gottfried Semper,
Style in the Technical and Tectonic Arts

Nietzsche's view on how culture might be resuscitated gained impetus from his association with Wagner, whom he met in 1869 and whose opera *Tristran and Isolde* he upheld as a creative use of history and myth in *Untimely Meditations*.[35] Nietzsche might have been introduced to Semper's ideas by Wagner. Semper had sent Wagner (an old friend) his recently published lecture 'On Architectural Styles', where he outlined the iconographic programme for the rebuilt Hoftheater in Dresden, the elevation of Dionysus over Apollo.[36] Nietzsche took notes from Semper's *Der Stil* in the autumn of the same year, 1869, as he prepared his first public lecture at Basel. Nietzsche's lecture on 'The Greek Music Drama' became the basis for his first book, *The Birth of Tragedy,* in which he wrote that the Dionysian Greek wanted 'truth and nature in their most forceful form'.[37]

Although Nietzsche referred explicitly to architecture in only a handful of published aphorisms, scholars have unearthed statements from his notebooks that shed light on his thinking and which also elaborated how he viewed the Dionysian/Apollonian dialectic as the possible basis for regenerating culture.

> The architect represents neither a Dionysian nor an Apollonian state – what impels him to act is the great act of will ... the architect has always lived beneath the mental sway of power. In a building, pride, the defeat of gravity, the will to power must manifest themselves. Architecture is a kind of eloquence of power conveyed through forms: now persuasive, even cajoling, now starkly commanding, the supreme feeling of power and assurance is conveyed by that which possesses the *Grand Style*.[38]

The word 'Dionysian' means: an urge to unity, a reaching out beyond personality ... the great pantheistic sharing of joy and sorrow that sanctifies and calls good even the most terrible and questionable qualities of life.

Nietzsche,
The Will to Power

The Dionysian rites of ancient Greece were an attempt to be 'one with life', the barrier of individuation broken down and mankind plunged back into the primordial unity. Apollo, on the other hand, was 'the symbol of light, of measure, of restraint' – i.e. of individuation.[39] 'True culture', said Nietzsche, 'is a unity of the forces of life', the Dionysian element, with the love of form and beauty, which is characteristic of the Apollonian attitude. His exceptional ability as a philologist enabled Nietzsche to develop a thesis that the conjunction of Dionysus and Apollo was responsible for the emergence of Greek tragedy, an art form that epitomised his idea of both a living and higher culture. This could only take place in his own time, Nietzsche believed, if priority were to be given to the Dionysian side, if men were to immerse the creative spirit in the raw drive for life rather than reusing received historically circumscribed cultural forms, the ossified forms of archaeological history. He considered the will to power to be the only drive that remained alive in mankind, and that only the *Übermensch* could reactivate something like the Dionysian immersion in nature that would form the essential basis of a revived culture. Music and participation were essential to this, which explains his support for Wagner's grandiose operas at this time. In all his later work Nietzsche tried to find different ways of reaffirming this idea and how something like a new living culture might be restored.

Nietzsche found guidance as to what this 'Grand Style' of architecture might be from Jakob Burckhardt's *Civilisation of the Italian Renaissance* (1860). Burckhardt was an older colleague at Basel, much admired by Nietzsche and, like him, a follower of Schopenhauer.[40] Burckhardt had studied under Ranke but was considered a 'deviant' pupil for straying into the broad field of cultural history. His scornful dismissal of the Hegelian idea of history as 'our old friend progress in disguise' won Nietzsche's approval. Burckhardt said that there existed nothing more sublime than the Pallazo Pitti, attributed uncertainly to Brunelleschi. Nietzsche himself saw it as embodying his aspirations for architecture. 'No musician has ever built like the architect who built the Pallazo Pitti', he said.[41] It was probably the building's vast dimensions that lent it a suggestion of the Sublime, its extensive rustication evoking nature in its rawest form, and the absence of the classical orders that would locate it in a specific historical period that appealed to Nietzsche.[42]

Uniquely for his time, he interpreted the architectural experience as 'empty form' which, like music, could be a reflection of psychic states. He immersed himself in the spaces of the past, he wrote, in order to 'walk within them as if within myself'.[43] Nietzsche differed from many of his contemporaries in that his focus came increasingly to be on the individual – the *Übermensch* – rather than Herder's or Michelet's idea of a 'people'. 'The *Übermensch* … must organise the chaos within him by thinking back to his real needs', he wrote. 'Thus he will discover the Greek idea of culture … the idea of culture as a new and improved physis.'[44] (*Physis* was the Greek term for how natural forms emerge, rise and take shape in and out of themselves, to which *poiēsis* as an equivalent human form of production is related.) Of Style Revival buildings, he reflected that we 'godless people want to think our own thoughts in them' and rather than 'intercourse with another world … We want to have ourselves translated into stones.'[45]

[M]usic is a return to nature, while being at the same time the purification and transformation of nature; for the pressing need for that return to nature arose in the souls of men filled with love, and in their art there sounds nature transformed in love. Let us take this to be one of Wagner's answers to what music signifies in our time.

Nietzsche,
Untimely Meditations

In his essay 'Architecture as Empty Form', Tillman Buddenseig suggests that Nietzsche's advocacy of 'emptying forms' could be read as a precursor of the abstract forms of modernism. He goes so far as to say that Le Corbusier's 'Plan Voisin' for the redevelopment of the Latin quarter of Paris was a 'good example' of this. But, with its expression of exclusively rational planning and total obliteration of the historical form of the city, rather than setting 'a new world alongside the old', this would have made no place where Nietzsche could 'think his own thoughts' in any meaningfully human sense. It was a triumph of objectivity leaving no place for the subjective emotional response demanded by Nietzsche in *The Use and Abuse of History*.[46] It would have been more 'life-denying' than 'life-enhancing', to use Nietzsche's terminology. This is a typical example of how Nietzsche has been misread, predicated on the erroneous view that his call for a revaluation of all values meant a total rejection of history. Buddenseig lists seven 'pioneers' influenced by Nietzsche, a proposition that will be examined in the next chapter. Pioneer modernists did tend to read Nietzsche's clarion call for a revaluation of all values in this way. But more recent studies of Nietzsche, have seen that the more nuanced opinions on the proper relationship between 'life' and history expressed in his early work remained, if masked by high rhetoric.

From the outset, Nietzsche's writings brought him notoriety. *The Birth of Tragedy* received a savage review questioning his fitness to be a professor of philology. Increasingly frequent illness led him to be retired early on a modest pension from Basel. For the rest of his sane life, Nietzsche applied his philosophical turn of mind to a critique of nineteenth century culture, hoping to redirect it.

History was essential, wrote Nietzsche, but the past had to be overcome and this could only be achieved by thinking 'supra-historically'. Three of his most important critical concepts – the 'will-to-power', the 'eternal recurrence', and the '*Übermensch*' – were crucial to this enterprise. His later form of thinking turned to origins, to a time when human cultural activity aimed to weave itself into nature's intrinsic processes of cyclical regeneration, such as in the Dionysian rites, a time outside of historical time, to which these three concepts are related. One of his last published writings before insanity gripped him was *Thus Spoke Zarathustra* (1883–5) where he cast his thoughts in the form of utterances from this earliest of mythical prophets. These critical concepts are given little explanation in his published

There is, indeed, rejoicing now that 'science is beginning to dominate life': that condition may, possibly, be attained; but life thus dominated is not of much value because it is far less *living* and guarantees far less life for the future than did a former life dominated not by knowledge but by instinct and powerful illusions.

Nietzsche,
Untimely Meditations

writings but his notebooks are filled with attempts to define them. Working through these in his *Nietzsche as Philosopher*, Arthur C. Danto finds Nietzsche describing the will-to-power as a 'plurality of powers bound together through a common nourishment process we call "life"'.[47] It is a fundamental drive which embraces all living creatures and life forms. The will-to-power became one of Nietzsche's most controversial ideas, taken in conjunction with the *Übermensch* to have lent support to Nazi ideology (although his ideas in fact do not). His violent rhetoric played a big part in his ideas being misunderstood in this way. The will-to-power, as Danto explains, 'is not something we have, but something we are'.[48] We and everything else, according to Nietzsche, because our passion, desires, and instinctual drives are the only givens, and are shared with all life-forms.

I consider life itself [to be] the instinct for growth, for continuance, for the accumulation of forces, for power; where the will to power is lacking there is decline.

Nietzsche,
The Antichrist

The combination of the will-to-power and the *Übermensch* returns us to Nietzsche's enduring fascination with archaic Greece. For the 'superman' is not an abstract ideal, but as Stanley Rosen says in *The Mask of the Enlightenment*, Nietzsche's Zarathustra calls for 'the fulfilment of human existence at its best.'[49] This entailed recapturing a history back beyond history, as it were, a call for a Dionysian 'superman'. Exactly how he sees the *Übermensch* is never made clear, but, speaking as Zarathustra, he contrasts the superman with what he calls 'the last man', humankind happy to be like everyone else. At other times he used the term 'herd man' to describe the emergence of the masses whose drives were increasingly shaped by the mass media. In contrast to the 'herd man', Zarathustra proclaimed: 'I teach you the *Übermensch*. The *Übermensch* is the meaning of the earth.'[50]

It is generally accepted that it is impossible to give a definitive account of Nietzsche's philosophy. Rosen ascribes this to his use of what he calls a 'double rhetoric'. By this he means that Nietzsche's texts set out simultaneously to accelerate the destruction of a decaying European civilisation at the same time as encouraging what Rosen calls 'warrior-artists' of great creative strength to revitalise it.[51] Nietzsche's own views on how cultural forms such as architecture should develop seem to reflect the legacy of the Romantic Movement that played a significant part in his youth, although unlike most Romantics he denies any possibility of transcendence. Benjamin thought so, citing Nietzsche along with Tolstoy and Strindberg as supporting his own 'deep attachment to the Romantic tradition'.[52] At school Nietzsche read Goethe and Schiller, for example, and wrote essays on Byron and Hölderlin. His doctorate thesis was titled 'On the Concept of the Organic since Kant'.[53] The world is will – argued Schopenhauer, a major influence on Nietzsche and subject of the third *Untimely Meditations* – and will is the inner driving force of life. He filled notebooks whilst on his countless walks in the landscapes where his wandering, solitary life took him in the years between Basel and madness in Turin.[54] Like Herder and other philosophers, Nietzsche could not accept an intuitive grasp of 'life' in nature. Rather it could only be grasped through what I have called a history before history, a reaffirmation of the Dionysian approach to life in nature as practised in archaic Greece.

Like his comments on the will-to-power, those on the eternal recurrence are given little explanation. Where he does expand upon this, it is curiously literal, as if 'a whole cycle of absolutely identical sequences results' and is 'infinitely repeated'.[55] But it is interesting to reflect that Nietzsche first hit upon this idea when on a mountain top '6,000 feet beyond men and time,' he noted.[56] This quasi-mystical experience of one-ness with the primal life-force is consistent with his characterisation of the eternal recurrence: 'But the knot of causes, in which I am tangled returns again … I belong myself to the causes of eternal recurrence.'[57]

Nietzsche's Zarathustra descends from a mountain top where he has spent ten solitary years. Before he descends, he speaks to the sun. Adopting the voice of Zarathustra and speaking thus from this particular location, Nietzsche implicitly offers the reader three different perspectives: the wise man; a person deeply involved with nature; and a non-European perspective. Philosophers call this 'perspectivism', but more recently cultural studies have labelled it 'relativism'. Because of this, Nietzsche has been claimed as the 'father of postmodernism'. But more philosophical commentators dispute this. Danto acknowledges the relativity of values produced by different peoples in different cultures but reminds us that Nietzsche/Zarathustra said 'the *one* goal is lacking; I teach you the *Übermensch*.'[58] Rosen argues that seeing things from a number of viewpoints 'does not entail a vitiating relativism' as promoted by post-modernists and as some of Nietzsche's twentieth century disciples have assumed.[59] Keeping in mind these early indications of modernity and impending post-modernity, it might be best to draw to a conclusion with Danto's philosophical summary.

Forgetting is as essential to action of any kind, just as not only light but darkness too is essential for the life of everything organic.

Nietzsche,
Untimely Meditations

What counts is what we eternally do, the joy in overcoming, whatever our task may be, and the meaning we give to our lives ... It is we who give value together with significance. This we must accept if there is to be meaning to our lives (for we could not change it if we wished to): we must affirm ourselves in our fate ... Heeding this, men might stop feeling *ressentiment*. In existentialist terms, it is a plea for authenticity.'[60]

Nietzsche's life's work is encapsulated in *Thus Spoke Zarathustra,* his call to overthrow a decadent European culture, a 'tradition founded on a mixture of Platonism and Christianity', the separation of the spirtual realm from the earth. This had been given new impetus by the 'doctrine of progress that marks the advent of the last man.'[61] 'Humanity should be the goal ... not progress', wrote Nietzsche.[62] He repeatedly criticizes the 'objectivity' of science and the creeping of positivism into history and the humanities. In this way, mankind had 'destroyed his instincts', he said in *The Use and Abuse of History.* Nietzsche's critical history, his history beyond history, was a call for what Rosen describes as 'a re-appropriation of the spirit of the archaic Greeks.'[63] Rosen argues that Nietzsche 'represents the crucial stage in the denial of the given'. By this he means the rise to domination of science and technology over everyday human lived experience and all aspects of life. In the early twentieth century, for example, we have seen Buckminster Fuller write an *Operating Manual for Spaceship Earth* (1968), a conception wholly at odds with the more recent and appropriate world-view of James Lovelock's *Gaia* (1979), the idea of the earth as a self-correcting living organism. Nietzsche's radicalism is often taken to mean that anything goes in culture. But his insistence on 'life', authenticity and meaning suggest specific themes to be embraced by culture, particularly in architecture with its special obligation to shape the environment of humankind.

Nietzsche is seen by Heidegger as a transitional figure marking the end of Western metaphysics, and the transition to an uncertain time as to how we think through modernity. Nietzsche cast scorn on the belief in a transcendental realm. His recourse to the eternal return was partly aimed at this and to hammer away at the ossified past-ness of the past, the 'It-was' that determined the present. To break free of the legacy of a transcendental tradition lead Nietzsche to the Dionysian, which became Heidegger's inspiration to investigate the pre-Socratic thinkers.

Nietzsche ... probably thought that his inverted Platonism could lead him back to pre-Platonic models of thought.

Hannah Arendt,
Between Past and Future

Stone is more stone than before. In general, we no longer understand architecture – certainly not as we understand music ... Originally, every part of a Greek or a Christian building had a significance in relation to a higher order of things; the sense of an original, inexhaustible significance hung over the edifice like a veil of enchantment ... What is the beauty of a building now? The same as the beautiful face of a vacuous woman: a masquerade.

Nietzsche,
Human, All Too Human

Have I been understood?
Dionysus against the Crucified.

Nietzsche,
Ecce Homo

Chapter 6: Approaches to modernism

PIONEER HISTORIANS

The history of the Modern Movement was given a particular bias by its first historians, who selected images and statements that demonstrated an outcome they actively desired. This is the subject explored by Panayotis Tournikiotis in *The Historiography of Modern Architecture* (1999). More recent detailed studies of the 'pioneer' architects involved, however, reveal that they had a more complex relationship to history than the picture of total rejection painted by Nikolaus Pevsner (1902–83), for example, in his *Pioneers of the Modern Movement* (1936). Nevertheless, Tournikiotis retains the idea of pioneer in explaining how modernism took shape.

There is a good deal of ambiguity in the meaning of the word pioneer. Pevsner defined it to suggest trail-blazers who had a fairly clear idea of the form of what would become a homogeneous Modern Movement. A more reasonable way of thinking about late nineteenth and early twentieth century pioneers is of architects rejecting historicism but with no clear aim or formal expression in mind. Their design work would inevitably be informed by the mode of practice in which they had been trained. As they sat at their drawing boards, their designs were bound to be informed by the habits and hand of practice. For an art historian such as Pevsner it was all too easy to overlook the ingrained nature of practice.

In histories written between the late 1920s and 1960s Tournikiotis traces what he describes as the 'genesis, triumph and decline of the Modern Movement'.[1] Three phases correspond to this, which he labels 'operative', 'revision' and 'critical'. In addition to Pevsner, Emil Kaufmann (1891–1951), Siegfried Giedion (1888–1968) and Henry-Russell Hitchcock (1903–87) are called 'operative' because of their 'repudiation of the past', which they claimed was 'predominant in the Modern Movement'.[2] Their writings show a common methodology in supporting the Modern Movement, argues Tournikiotis; namely that pioneer architects rejected historicism, noted a rift between

architectural practice and engineered structures, and made a
transition to a new architecture that reflected new technologies. This
also represented the spirit of the age, but is seen by 'pioneer historians'
to be good.[3] Hegel's future-forward conception of history was becoming
realised. Although they might select different pioneer architects, this
group of historians each looked for what Tournikiotis calls common
'morphological components' – plain surfaces, simple geometric forms,
white or strong colours, etc.[4]

Writing between 1930 and 1932, when, he says, the 'architecture
of reason and functionalism was in full swing', Pevsner begins
his account with Morris' attacks on 'sham craftsmanship'.[5] Three
kinds of architects form his chain of pioneers. A 'historical' set
loosely associated with the Arts and Crafts who produced designs
with relatively plain surfaces, architects who admired engineering,
followed finally by architects who most clearly broke with the past.
Pevsner identified three roots to Modernism: Morris, Art Nouveau,
and engineering. Art Nouveau formed an important link, he says,
because architects such as Victor Horta (1861–1947) using iron
decoration 'could take the innovation of engineers in their stride'.[6]
He concludes by arguing that while 'Morris laid the foundation of the
modern style; with Gropius its character was ultimately determined.'[7]

All four 'pioneer historians' followed Pevsner in highlighting engineers'
contributions to the Modern Movement, but Kaufmann and
Hitchcock also emphasised its white, abstract form. As the title of his
book *Von Ledoux bis Le Corbusier* (1933) suggests, Kaufmann argued
that the 'revolutionary' phase of French Neoclassicism influenced its
character: 'Anticipating the twentieth century, Boullée and Ledoux
restored the elementary forms to their rightful place in architecture.'[8]
Ledoux's revolutionary projects in particular provided a precedent for
the free-standing forms favoured by the Modern Movement.[9] After
publishing the first English-language book on *Modern Architecture*
(1929), Hitchcock organised, with Philip Johnson (1906–2005), the
seminal exhibition entitled 'The International Style' in 1932, which,
along with the accompanying book, did more than anything to
establish the canonical, white abstract form of the Modern Movement.

Pevsner, Kaufmann and Giedion all had their ideas shaped by studying
in the German tradition of art history developed by Heinrich Wölfflin
(1864–1945) and Alois Riegl (1858–1905). Psychological research in the

last decades of the nineteenth century shifted the focus away from associations with historical styles onto the impact of the architectural experience itself. This played a significant part in bringing to the fore notions of 'space' and 'abstract form', notions crucial to the exemplars selected by these historians. A decisive moment in this new focus on space came in 1893 when August Schmarsow (1853–1956) described architectural development as 'the history of the sense-of-space *(Raumgefuhl)* ... [and] is a basic constituent in the history of *worldviews.*'[10] In his *Space, Time and Architecture* (1941), Giedion (who had studied under Wölfflin) traced the lineage of the Modern Movement to a combination of Cubism's research into space and architects' interest in engineering.[11] He saw this new rendering of space – 'a hitherto unknown interpenetration of inner and outer space' – as the artistic achievement of the *Zeitgeist.*

At about the same time, Adolph Göller (1846–1902) argued that, for purposes of analysis, and stripping away the representational content, or historical detail, then architecture could be defined as 'the art of pure form'.[12] Robert Vischer (1847–1933) wrote that early dream interpretation theory led him to the notion of '*Einfuhlung*' (literally 'in-feeling', but usually translated as 'empathy'), which had a profound impact on architectural theory at the turn of the century.[13] 'Physical forms possess a character only because we ourselves possess a body', wrote Wölfflin, the first to broach this idea of a direct relationship between body and building. Indicating the influence of Nietzsche, he added that ornament was 'an expression of excessive force-of-form'.[14] This idea lent support to the removal of ornament, allowing form itself to be sufficient at this time, but came later to inform a phenomenological notion in late twentieth century theory.

Armed with these newly articulated concepts of space and form, reinforced by a psychological interpretation of architecture superseding a historical perspective, and surrounded by evidence of progress in technology and engineering, architects could advance beyond historicism to the abstract forms of the Modern Movement. Whilst this made for a compelling narrative shared and spread by what Tournikiotis called these 'operative' historians, the architects involved often in fact had a more nuanced attitude towards the past. Once the Modern Movement had become established, a younger generation of historians raised questions about their historiography. These revisionist and critical historians will be discussed in Chapter 10.

When we look upon the history of art no longer as mere history of artistic ability, but as a history of artistic will, it gains a significance in the general history of mankind ...For changes in will ... cannot be purely arbitrary or fortuitous. On the contrary, they must have a consistent relation to those spiritual and mental changes which are clearly reflected in the historical development of myth, of religions, of philosophical systems, of world conceptions.

Wilhelm Worringer,
Abstraction and Empathy

The sceptical argument is well known: time has no being since the future is not yet, the past is no longer, and the present does not remain. And yet we do speak of time as having being. We say that things to come will be, that things past were, and that things present are passing away.

Paul Ricoeur,
Time and Narrative

In his essay 'Modern Architecture and Historicity', Colquhoun points out that from the late eighteenth century onwards architectural thought oscillated between asserting that 'all styles are possible' and 'all styles are forbidden'.[15] Under the sway of Hegelian teleology the modernist view became that 'architecture possessed meaning as a reflection or symptom of a particular stage of historical development'.[16] Consequently 'meaning in architecture did not depend on the memory of its own past. The spirit of the age demanded that architecture be absolutely new.'[17] Colquhoun notes that architecture shared traits with avant-garde art, but points out that architecture's 'autonomous existence was intimately bound up with its own technology'. The conflation of 'instrumentalism and modernist formalism … made possible the idealisation of technology and its role in the production of a utopian society'.[18]

> Coming to terms with technology is possible only by coming to terms with the conditions of our earthbound cultural existence.
>
> Dalibor Vesely

Colquhoun's reflections take account of the rationalism that the Modern Movement came to embrace, to which the pioneers undeniably contributed. However, they did not all or always aim for an 'absolutely new' architecture, nor did they exclusively pursue abstraction and rationalism. The ambiguity between history and progress in the writings and buildings of the pioneers makes it valuable as a source of reappraisal, not only in itself but for how architecture might respond to our understanding since the fall of the Modern Movement followed in turn by post-modernism.

> Architecture inherits the consequence of general technological advance, occasionally encouraging, rarely determining. In fact we may say that despite the rhetoric, material and construction methods have charted a relatively slow path of change compared with other technologies.
>
> David Chipperfield,
> *Tradition and Invention*

WAGNER, LOOS AND THE SECCESSION

Otto Wagner's *Modern Architecture* (1896) has been described as 'the first modern writing to make a definitive break with the past'.[19] He rejected the prevailing historicist view that an architect must design 'through the choice of a so-called style'.[20] A contemporary review linked the book's focus on practicality to 'realism', a concept that emerged in cultural criticism referring to the paintings of Courbet and Millet and the novels of Flaubert and Zola.[21] The reviewer also detected influence from 'the rationalist teaching of … Cordemoy and … Laugier.'[22] Wagner himself, however, wrote of 'furthering our inherited traditions'.[23]

One of the five chapters of *Modern Architecture* is titled 'composition', anathema to functionalists. The importance he gives this indicates the wide gulf between his conception of architecture and the advocates of 'form follows function'. Pevsner insinuated that Wagner endorsed Adolf Loos' statement that from 'engineers we receive our culture'.[24] But he did not. To the claim that 'utility will discipline art', Wagner retorted: 'The error in this view lies in the assumption that utility can displace idealism completely and in the further inference that man can live without art.'[25] He added that the 'engineer who does not consider the nascent art-form but only the structural calculation and the expense will therefore speak a language unsympathetic to man.'[26]

Perhaps the most surprising aspect of Wagner's *Modern Architecture* and his innovative late buildings is that these were not the works of a radical young man but of someone past fifty and at the height of his profession. Acknowledged as the leading architect in Vienna, he was commissioned to design the city's new rail system in 1894 and later that year appointed professor of architecture at the Vienna Academy of Fine Arts. *Modern Architecture* grew out of his inaugural address.

Semper is mentioned on the second page and lay behind Wagner's call for architects to respond to practical needs: 'Semper first directed our attention to this truth.'[27] But need is not to be defined too narrowly and should embrace, he said, 'Styles of living, fashion, etiquette, climate, place, material'. To this end Wagner advised that, after a short period of study in Italy, 'the young artist might then visit the great cities ... and there he might train himself completely by observing and perceiving the needs of modern man.'[28] Given the historicism that prevailed, it is understandable that Wagner pressed the claim for need, utility and practicality. However, these basic requirements were not to be considered the generator of architecture as an art form. Rather, 'utility and realism precede in order to prepare the deeds that art and idealism have to perform'.[29] He criticised Semper's 'dressing' theory, which distracted from the idea of style emanating from methods of making. Rather than his 'symbolism of construction', he should have named 'construction itself as the primitive cell of architecture'.[30] Wagner argued that buildings should not be masked with Renaissance decoration, as Semper had, but rather 'composition must clearly reveal the material of construction and technology used'.[31]

Wagner's debt to Semper is well-illustrated in his Karlsplatz station building (1898–9), which clearly refers to the *Carib hut* illustrated in *Der Stil* . Where the hut had woven panels infilling a bamboo frame, Wagner has marble panels in an expressed iron frame that sits on a

Modern art must offer us modern forms that are created by us and that represent our abilities and actions.

Otto Wagner,
Modern Architecture

All modern creations must correspond to the new materials and demands of the present if they are to suit modern man.

Otto Wagner,
Modern Architecture

6.1 (Left) Otto Wagner,
Karlsplatz Station, Vienna
6.2 (Above) Detail

granite plinth. The tripartite articulation of the panels alludes to the classical column, where heavily tooled granite implies its base [6.1 & 6.2]. This residual classicism is modified by a contemporary note, for gilded flowers inlaid into the top of the marble panel suggest both a classical column capital or frieze and also Wagner's support for the Secession movement then taking hold of fashionable Vienna.

'The beginning of every architectural creation is composition', wrote Wagner.[32] But an acknowledgement of how far architecture had travelled since the certainties of the classical tradition comes in his remark that 'there is no recipe for architectural composition'.[33] Nevertheless, he insists that a plan must be axial and symmetrical. This ensures 'some measure of self-containment, completeness, balance … Gravity and dignity, the constant companions of architecture, also demand symmetry.'[34] These axioms of classical composition are present in his most successful building, the Post Office Savings Bank (1903–6, first phase), a building which can also claim to have the first modern interior, as all the materials of the banking hall are man-made. The symmetrical principal façade is arranged in the typical tripartite manner of a classical column; a granite rusticated plinth with smooth marble above and topped by an aluminium cornice. Bolt heads in the cornice evoke the metopes of a Doric temple. Acroteria of winged Nikes holding wreathes, marked the corners. (Perhaps a homage to Semper – who saw wreaths as the primary art-form – for a line of six more wreaths cap this façade) [6.3]. Despite the stone appearing to be traditional load-bearing construction, it is in fact cladding. Wagner acknowledges this by prominently displaying aluminium bolts that attach the stone to the brick wall behind [6.4].

6.3 (Top right) Post Office Savings
     Bank, Vienna, Main Façade
6.4 (Above) Entrance canopy
     and cladding detail
6.5 Lobby
6.6 Banking Hall

An aluminium entrance canopy leads to a relatively dark, low-ceilinged lobby dominated by a broad, stately granite stair [6.5]. This contrasts with the banking hall beyond, brightly lit with a glass ceiling and glass floor. Where the material of the banking hall is entirely modern, the space itself is given the profile of an early Christian church derived in turn from the Roman basilica form with vaulted 'nave' and side aisles [6.6]. Iron columns are sheathed to head height with polished and riveted aluminium plates, and cast aluminium hot air outlets mark out the boundary of the hall like classical herms. In *Modern Architecture* Wagner writes of what could be his approach here: 'Each new style gradually emerged from the earlier one when new methods of construction, new materials, new human tasks and viewpoints demand a change or reconstitution of existing forms.'[35] He added that the 'architect may dip into the full repository of traditional forms, but he must never copy a selected form; he must adapt it to us'.[36]

Referring to the 'uniformity of our apartment homes', he said that architectural treatments derived from 'the architecture of palaces are completely inappropriate'.[37] Nevertheless, when designing the adjoining apartment buildings Linke Wienzele 38 and Majolica House (1898–9), for example, he imposes an order that has a compositional relationship to a renaissance palazzo[38] [6.7]. He extends the iron framework of the ground-floor shops up to form a canopied balcony for the first-floor apartments, which suggests a piano nobile and provides a mezzanine break to the four floors of rationally positioned windows above.

A network of lines decorates the majolica-tiled façade on the eponymous Majolica House, which suggests weaving – Semper again – from which spring red flowers, increasing in density at the top like a frieze, as does the decoration on Linke Wienzele 38.

6.7 Linke Wienzele 38 and Majolica House, Vienna

The rampant historicism of the Vienna Ringstrasse development led Wagner to say that 'the language [which the architect] has directed to the public ... is completely unintelligible'.[39] If architecture 'is not rooted in life, in the needs of contemporary men, then it will be lacking in the immediate, the animating, the refreshing, and ... it will cease to be an art.'[40] But as his buildings demonstrate, the here-and-now, technology and function, were not sufficient in themselves; Wagner's art of architecture drew upon and transformed history and tradition.

* * *

The Vienna of this time has been called 'the crucible of modernity' when Viennese intellectuals were calling for an art and architecture that would reflect modern life. In the last decade of the nineteenth century, when Wagner published *Modern Architecture*, Sigmund Freud (1856–1939) was working on *The Interpretation of Dreams*, the Viennese Secession was founded in 1897, Karl Kraus (1874–1936) published the literary magazine *Die Farkel* (The Truth), Adolf Loos (1870–1933) wrote many critical articles, and Arnold Schoenberg (1874–1951) challenged classical musical conventions by his emphasis on dissonance.[41]

> Oh no, I'm not a bellyacher. My hatred of Vienna is not love gone astray. It's just that I've discovered a completely new way of finding it unbearable.
>
> Karl Kraus

The Secession was formed when a group of artists and architects walked out of the established association of artists, a move Wagner supported and joined in 1899. The Secession magazine was called *Ver Sacrum* (Sacred Spring) which showed its allegiance to Art Nouveau – fresh, vital spring growth – but also announced its interest in early Greek mythology where springs were sacred places. The leader was Gustav Klimt (1862–1912) and the two most prominent architect members were Josef Maria Olbrich (1867–1908) and Josef Hoffman (1870–1956), both of whom had been apprenticed to Wagner.[42] Olbrich's temple-like Secession building draws upon these themes [6.8 & 6.9].

> In art the important thing is not that one takes eggs and fat, but that one has a fire and a pan.
>
> Karl Kraus

> I have a shattering bit of news for the esthetes: Old Vienna was new once.
>
> Karl Kraus

6.8 (Above) Josef Maria Olbrich,
Secession Gallery, Vienna

6.9 (Right) Entrance detail

In contrast to more typical *Art Nouveau*, Klimt's paintings have been compared to Freud's work in bringing to the surface sub-conscious desires. Klimt had been early introduced to the idea of a vital, originating force underlying culture when commissioned to decorate the grand staircase of Semper's Burgtheater, for his task included representing the festival of Dionysus as the origin of drama. A later painting entitled 'Music' of 1898, for example, has no pictorial depth, its surface filled with enigmatic figures. Music is represented as 'a tragic muse, with the power of transforming buried instincts and mysterious cosmic power into harmony'.[43] This is a theme from Nietzsche's *The Birth of Tragedy*, and Klimt significantly shows Dionysian figures rising above Apollonian. Klimt's aim was to lay 'bare the instinctual life that has been sublimated or repressed in the classical tradition'.[44]

Freud was pushing back the interpretation of dreams from the personal unconscious to a 'mythic layer', which he equated with 'the universal archetypal experience of primitive man.'[45] Freud's discovery of the 'primitive' in everyman, and bringing to light 'repressed instinctual impulses' came to be of immense importance to our understanding of humanity, and played a large part in twentieth century art but not in modern architecture where a machine metaphor came to dominate.[46] This recourse to mythology can be read as a new, more vital way to overcome historicism. Alternatively, it has been interpreted as stripping away the mask from the burgeoning rationalism of the age to reveal the creative impulses deep in the human psyche, an idea no doubt prompted by Nietzsche. Only in the latter part of the twentieth century did these deeper concerns of human meaning return to make an impact on architecture. Klimt's paintings became increasingly dominated by their rich surface decorative treatment, a kind of gilded mask behind which half-hidden meanings emerge. This parallels the way Wagner's later buildings – The Post Office Savings Bank, the church of St. Leopold, Am Steinhof (1905–7) – have a strong emphasis on the surface, perhaps also reflecting Semper's theory of 'dressing' and his own belief that art's role lie in covering utility [6.10 and 6.11].

* * *

The false facadism that concealed the commercial reality of the Ringstrasse was attacked in an essay by Loos for *Ver Sacrum* in 1898.[47] But Loos soon turned against the Secessionist's 'modern' style of decoration that obscured the utilitarian nature of things. He wrote a savage satire on the Secessionist obsession with total design, ridiculing Hoffmann for designing a client's clothes to match specific rooms.[48] In contrast to a Secessionist interior, Loos described his own childhood house where objects told a family story, and how his own was not a 'stylish' house but its rooms were full of memories.[49]

Pevsner's 'operative' history fixed on comments Loos made linking beauty to utility and his praise of engineers while illustrating the white, abstract garden elevation of his Steiner House (1910). He described this as having 'achieved the style of 1930 completely and without any limitations'.[50] Loos did not approve publication of photographs of his buildings, so Pevsner may not have been familiar with the extraordinary contrast between the austere façade and the comfortable interior. 'The house should be discrete on the outside', said Loos, 'its entire richness should be disclosed on the inside.'[51] This is why Loos designed houses with a plain, white exterior; the façade was a mark of discretion not a pioneering call to a wider abstraction, as claimed by Pevsner. A typical Loos interior, including his own apartment in Vienna (1903), features a living room focused on a fireplace built of exposed brickwork and covered with a copper hood, both materials transformed by fire, a congruence Semper would approve, if not Pevsner. Many of his interiors have an inglenook and exposed timber beams on the ceiling, too large and too far apart for logical structural support.[52] Furniture would be chosen by the client, not designed by the architect. Loos favoured English design connected with the Arts and Crafts movement, and particularly admired the English gentleman's unostentatious suits, which he contrasted with

6.10 Wagner, St. Leopold, Am Steinhof, Vienna, main façade

6.11 Interior with 'decorated' gilded suspended ceiling

The work of art wants to draw people out of their state of comfort. The house has to serve comfort.

Adolf Loos

Secessionist dandies.[53] Comfortable and well-dressed, this was the correct attire for the modern man in the modern city, not showing off his personality in public.[54] The same applied, in his view, to the house, for buildings should fit modern man like an unpretentious modern suit. He knew the book *Das Englische Haus* (1904–5) in which Herman Muthesius (1861–1927) identified Arts and Crafts disciples of Morris as initiating reforms in design and architecture that focused on reviving craft traditions, the practical rather than the historical. Loos was as much interested in cultural continuity as in making a break with the past.

In comparing unostentatious clothes with undecorated façades Loos drew upon Semper. In an early essay, *Glass and Clay* (1898), he discussed Semper's theory of the origin of form in the practical shapes given to material artefacts, and illustrated the Egyptian *situla* and the Greek *hydria*. He would have come across Semper's ideas while studying at the Dresden *Bauakademie*, following which he visited the United States from 1893 to 1896 where his enthusiasm for a modern, practical culture took root. Loos equated the 'evolution of culture … with the removal of ornament'.[55] His essay *Ornament and Crime* (1905) pointed to how unnecessary, uneconomic and unappealing were ornamented things to modern ways of living and which were 'no longer the expression' of twentieth century culture.[56] Cultural forms had been developed slowly by anonymous craftsmen making 'the objects of our daily use', he said, 'time created them for us'.[57] 'The craftsman creates the form subconsciously. The form is received via tradition.'[58] He contrasted this authentic culture with nineteenth century architecture and what he described as architects' 'fetish for ornament'.[59]

Here we see a clear distinction made between the use of tradition and the abuse of history. The forms of everyday objects and vernacular buildings had been created organically and refined by traditions slowly over time. Architecture, in contrast, had been subject to relatively rapid change in the nineteenth century as fashion followed fashion satisfying immediate desires rather than deep-seated needs. Loos considered that architecture had 'departed from tradition' at the beginning of the nineteenth century and that it was this point, he said, 'from which I want to continue'.[60]

Loos' initial response to architectural design was to eliminate superfluous decoration. This was evident in one of his earliest

All that Adolf Loos and I did – he literally, I linguistically – was to show that there is a difference between an urn and a chamberpot, and in that difference there is leeway for culture. But the others, the 'positive ones', are divided into those who use the urn as a chamberpot and those who use the chamberpot as an urn.

Karl Kraus

The real difference between me and the others is as follows; I maintain that use determines the forms of civilised life, the shape of objects, the others that new forms can have an influence on the forms of civilised life (the way of sitting, of living, of eating, etc.)

Loos

projects, the Café Museum of 1899. Situated near Olbrich's House of the Secession, Loos avoided anything that might be called 'art', the only decoration was mirrors and brass supports for electric lamps. The use of Thonet chairs were a mark of his belief in typical forms, industrialised productions for everyday use.[61] Ten years after it opened Loos wrote with relish that it had been dubbed 'Café Nihilimus'. Where it appeared still fresh, Secession decoration was a faded fashion. It would be mistaken, however, to see Loos as nihilistic and rejecting all of the architectural past. Kenneth Frampton argues that Loos combined 'the informal comfort of the Anglo-Saxon interior with the asperities of classical form'.[62] Loos evoked the essential character of Classicism through a tight control over form and careful modulation of the elements of building rather than adding classical details. This marks the emergence of the idea of the classic, a label attached to many strands of design in the twentieth century, such as the classic car and the Chanel 'little black dress'. 'The architect does not merely create for his time', wrote Loos, but also 'posterity … For this one needs a firm, unchanging standard; … this is classical antiquity.'[63]

6.12 Loos, Michaelerhaus, Vienna, main façade,

The bourgeois Viennese did not have the right to use the aristocratic ornament of classical architecture, argued Loos. Nevertheless, he did consider it legitimate for 'modern man' to use 'ornaments of past … cultures at his discretion'.[64] His sole building with applied ornament is the Michaelerhaus (1909–11), which has a colonnade of marble Doric columns, classical elements he considered appropriate here as it faces the entrance to the Imperial Palace [6.12]. Despite this concession to decorum, the design for this apartment building provoked outrage because of its unadorned white walls pierced with serried ranks of windows. The planning authorities took out an injunction to stop work, but support from Wagner combined with Loos' ironic proposal to add flower boxes to the windows proved sufficient to advance the project. 'The present is built on the past', Loos asserted, 'just as the past was built on the times that went before it.'[65]

No one man or even an institution created our wardrobes, our cigarette cases, our jewellery. Time created them for us … They change from year to year, from day to day, from hour to hour. Because our lives, our attitudes, our habits change from hour to hour. That is how our culture changes. But those people from the Werkbund confuse cause and effect … And thus, to the delight of all those who love culture, the activity of the Werkbund is futile.

Loos,
Cultural Degeneration

Loos' most original contribution to architecture came in his later houses where he developed the concept of *raumplan* ('plan of volumes' or 'spatial plan'). 'For this is the great revolution in architecture', wrote Loos, 'solving the plan by means of space.'[66] The consummation of this ambition Loos achieved in the Müller House (1929–30) in Prague [6.13]. Behind a plain, white façade he arranged a complex set of interrelated volumes tailored to the comfort of their respective purpose.

6.13 Müller House, Prague, front façade

6.14 Section. A; Living Room. B; Dining Room beyond. C; 'Ladies Room'. D; Library

His great skill was to accommodate a disparate range of volumes within the tightly controlled cubic form of the building itself, Loos' classicising predilection winning over the picturesque arrangement of English Arts and Crafts houses, which he otherwise admired. The plan of volumes is arranged to unfold a narrative sequence of visually linked spaces from public to private, from grandest space to the most intimate [6.14]. From the tall living room, steps rise to the dining room with its lower ceiling and balcony overlooking the larger volume. A short flight of stairs ascends here to the study and the library, leading finally to what is called the 'ladies room', an intimate alcove with an internal window looking over the living room and out to the city. Loos reinforces the sense of a comfortable volume of space by an appropriate selection of materials: Cipollino marble for the living room; a highly polished wooden ceiling for the dining room; leather sofas and mahogany joinery dominate the library; and the 'ladies room' has lighter wood panelling and seating covered with embroidered material. In the Müller House Loos draws together his primary influences: asperity of classical form, façade as mask, or mark of discretion, and Semper on materiality, into an extraordinarily original work through his concept of 'raumplan'.

STRUCTURAL RATIONALISM: BERLAGE, PERRET AND BEHRENS

The last decades of the nineteenth century saw iron begin to shape the development of modern architecture. Art Nouveau architects such as Horta and Hector Guimard (1867–1942) used iron to create ornament that drew directly upon nature 'to subvert the inertia of stone'[67] inherent to historical forms of architecture. Iron was associated with the notion of 'realism' that increasingly affected architects' thinking as more and more utilitarian iron structures were built. The Paris Exposition of 1889 provided a striking image of modern life presided over by the Eiffel Tower. Wagner praised the Eiffel Tower in the preface to a monograph devoted to his designs, but criticised it for 'too much realism'.[68] Because their work engaged with emerging new technologies, Hendrik Berlage (1856–1934), Peter Behrens (1868–1940) and Auguste Perret (1874–1954) were accorded pioneer status. However, each of the three had a more complex relationship with history and tradition than that painted by 'pioneer historians'.

* * *

Berlage's Amsterdam Stock Exchange building shows clearly the journey from historicism to a form of modern architecture. This was partly due to an unusual length of time from his initial competition design of 1884 – a typical late-nineteenth century eclectic mixture of renaissance motifs – to his final revised design of 1895. An essay he wrote during this period, called 'Architecture and Impressionism' (1894) reveals his attachment to the notion of 'realism' in the work of painters and writers mentioned earlier. Berlage argued for 'a simpler architectural concept', one which emphasised massing, simplified lines, modest detailing, and greater consideration of the material condition of building.[69]

His ideas about architecture were influenced mainly by Semper and the Gothic Revival, structural rationalist Eugène Viollet-le-Duc (1814–79). Berlage trained at the Eidgenössiche Technische Hochschule in Zurich under disciples of Semper following his departure for Vienna. On returning to Amsterdam in 1881 Berlage became associated with P.J.H. Cuijpers (1827–91), a disciple of Viollet-le-Duc and interested in honest use of materials. Cuijpers best-known building is the Rijkmuseum (1877–85), under construction when Berlage joined him, a building influenced by the Oxford Museum [6.15]. These two buildings had a major effect on the evolution of the Amsterdam Stock Exchange design. Berlage, however, 'only applied theories of Viollet-le-Duc without being fascinated by the middle ages'.[70]

6.15 P.J.H. Cuijpers, Rijksmuseum, Amsterdam

The *parti* of the Stock Exchange is similar to that of the Oxford Museum, a sky-lit main hall surrounded by a brick arcade. Unlike the Oxford Museum, however, any semblance of historical reference had been stripped away in the final design. The walls are load-bearing brickwork with shallow arches springing from straightforward granite imposts on plain brick piers. Consistent with the principles of structural rationalism, and curiously like the ideas of the obscure early Italian rationalist Carlo Lodoli (1690–1761), this uses a stronger material, stone, at points where compressive structural forces are greatest [6.16]. Modest patterns made with different coloured bricks and a crenelated capping are the only decorative additions to the wall.

6.16 Hendrik Berlage, Stock Exchange, Amsterdam

Unlike the gothicised iron structure at the Oxford Museum, here only a plethora of rivets 'decorate' the structure, not unlike the procedure advanced by Wagner at the Post Office Savings Bank, although much less rhetorical. In an essay written shortly after construction, Berlage

6.17 Stock Exchange, Amsterdam corner tower and entrance

wrote that architects should 'exploit … the various constructional difficulties as decorative motifs'[71] [6.17].

Berlage held very strong socialist views, censuring capitalism for its part in a decline in artistic standards and for placing individual interests over social ones. A lecture he delivered in the United States in 1911 opened with a reference to Ruskin and ended with a quote from Morris. With echoes of Morris, Berlage wrote of 'a naked wall in all its smooth and simple beauty'.[72] English Arts and Crafts architects believed that a revival of craftsmanship represented a necessary prelude to a revival of architecture itself. Berlage's use of load-bearing brickwork was inspired by Dutch traditional buildings of the Middle Ages as well as Morris who urged architects to transcend Style Revivalism by emulating traditional vernacular buildings.[73] The rationalised brick idiom of the Amsterdam Stock Exchange responded both to local traditions of building and accommodated Berlage's socialist views, for the bricklayers could demonstrate skill in their work.

However, he was aware of the movement towards *Sachlichkeit* that came to have a profound effect on the character of the Modern Movement. Usually translated as 'objectivity', it can also be taken to mean the most practical solution to a problem, a rendering Berlage preferred. For Berlage it had two particular nuances that differentiate his view of modern architecture from that presented by 'pioneer historians', one architectural – 'architecture is the spatial enclosure' – and one social – 'The *sachliche*, rational, and therefore clear construction can become the basis of the new art', and, he wrote, 'at the same moment the new universal spirit – the social equality of all men – will be revealed.'[74]

> The art of the master builder lies in this; the creation of space, not sketching façades.
>
> Hendrik Berlage

It is this nexus of ideas embodied in the Stock Exchange that gives Berlage's work its particular stamp and marks out the difference between his vision of a modern architecture and the Modern Movement as narrated by Pevsner *et al*. He believed in the development of simplified traditional forms to respond to new and more rational building techniques, but used brickwork to give mass to a building and acknowledge labour. 'It is, in fact, not easy to rid oneself of traditional forms', he wrote. 'And it appears to be a human characteristic not to look for new forms appropriate to the new demands of modern inventions, but to start by trying the old, established forms.'[75] Giedion criticised Berlage for being 'very sparing in his use of glass and iron'. In this we see the stark difference between the exaggerated emphasis given to engineering and 'space-time' openness by historians of the Modern Movement and the more humane Dutch modernism of the 1920s and 1930s inspired by Berlage's emphasis on brickwork. Buildings such as by W.M. Dudok and Michel de Klerk, although they were equally influenced by Frank Lloyd Wright and the Expressionist movement [6.18].

6.18 Michel de Klerk, Workers Housing, Spaarndammerbuurt district, Amsterdam

* * *

Perret's place in the roll-call of pioneers stems from his architecture being the first to express the use of a reinforced concrete frame. An active involvement in his father's construction business combined with enthusiasm for the broad tradition of French structural rationalism shaped his architectural outlook. Pevsner claims that Perret's buildings used concrete 'without adapting it to the spirit of past styles'.[76] More recent studies have shown Perret to have been highly critical of avant-garde modernism and, contrary to Pevsner's assertion, it was precisely the 'spirit' of classicism that Perret pursued.

'Viollet-le-Duc was my real master', Perret is reported to have said.[77] By this he acknowledged that structure and construction play a determining role in architecture, but rejected the historicism of Viollet's Gothic Revival. He preferred instead the interpretation of classical architecture as rational structure made by his teacher Julien Guadet (1834–1908): 'the sense, broad and severe, in which I understand the word "Classic"'.[78] Perret abhorred novelty – 'fashion, transitory conditions' – for its own sake, insisting instead upon the correspondence between what he called 'permanent conditions' and the classical spirit.[79] The creative tension between modern concrete construction and cultural continuity gives Perret's best work its distinctive stamp. In her biography of Perret, Karla Britton says: 'Although his work maintains an independence from the avant-garde, it is not independent of modernity with which it establishes a significant cultural dialogue.'[80]

Architecture can only equip itself with new forms if it seeks them in the rigorous application of a new structure.

Viollet-le-Duc

One of Perret's earliest projects, the eight-storey apartment building 25 bis rue Franklin (1903–4), best fits Pevsner's pattern for pioneers.

6.19 Auguste Perret,
25 bis rue Franklin

Architecture is the art of organising
space. It is through construction
that it expresses itself.

Auguste Perret

Construction is the maternal
language of the architect.
The architect is a poet who thinks
and speaks in construction.

Auguste Perret

Its canonical pioneer status stems from it being the first building to express its reinforced concrete frame [6.19]. The frame is emphasised by Perret's decision effectively to reverse the typical Parisian apartment plan. For instead of a light-well at the rear of the site, the centre of the plan is recessed at the front, which makes a complex perimeter to the street and requires a large number of concrete columns visible on the façade. These are clad in plain ceramic tiles and brick infill panels are clad with tiles decorated with a chestnut leaf motif.

The frame structure allows the plan to have a relatively open appearance, which led Giedion to identify Perret as being a pioneer of the Modern Movement's interest in the *plan libre* (free plan).[81] In reality the plans are quite traditional, symmetrically organised with rooms *enfilade*. Perret considered that the composition of space should be subordinate to construction: 'Architecture is the art of organising space, it is with construction that space is expressed.'[82] This traditional view of space led to a spat with Le Corbusier a few years later.

Looking for an architect working in a new direction, the young Charles-Edouard Jeanneret (1887–1965), later Le Corbusier, sought out Perret in 1908 and worked with him for fourteen months.[83] For Perret, being modern did not require a new conceptualisation of space nor the invention of form, two areas, of course, that came to mark Le Corbusier's achievement. With his conception of the *plan libre* went the strip window and it was this in particular that Perret criticised. He intimated that Le Corbusier's invention of new forms came at the expense of the window's role in lighting a room: 'owing … to an excessive taste for the bizarre in his design, he tortures the openings by stretching them to an exaggerated degree.'[84] An incensed Le Corbusier replied by pointing out that it was precisely to give more light to a space that engendered the strip window.[85]

The Théâtre des Champs-Elysées (1910–13) illustrates more clearly how Perret's architecture developed to combine the classical spirit with reinforced concrete. Henri Van de Velde (1863–1957) had been commissioned to design the theatre and engaged the Perret Brothers (as the firm became known on the death of Auguste's father) as structural consultants. Perret quickly pointed out that the proposed interior arrangements did not fit the demands of a structural frame. He persuaded the clients to make changes, prompting Van de Velde to resign, leaving Perret with the commission.[86]

Perret's façade acknowledges the structural concrete frame but uses travertine-clad pilasters and an emphatic cornice to shape a temple-like appearance [6.20]. A relief panel has Apollo as its central figure, evidence of Perret's more conservative stance on classicism than his Viennese contemporaries. Perret was affiliated with a group of French artists who shared his more conservative approach to modernism by way of a refined classicism that involved 'the distillation of a simplified vocabulary and attention to cultural continuity'.[87] These included the poet Paul Valéry, the painter Maurice Denis and the writer André Gide.

The exposed beams, coffered ceiling and unadorned concrete columns of the foyer make a conspicuous expression of the concrete structural framework [6.21]. The complex demands of the theatre proved decisive in convincing Perret that the classical spirit was capable of dealing with new building types thanks to a rigorous use of the tectonic character of the structural frame. Reynar Banham criticized Perret for using a frame and ignoring concrete's 'plastic potential' in his *Theory and Design in the First Machine Age*.[88] But Perret insisted that, because concrete was moulded in wooden formwork, the linear nature of wood machined from trees should characterise its use.

6.20 Théâtre des Champs-Elysée, Paris, main façade
6.21 Foyer

Perret's interpretation of the history of architecture, which emphasised the relationship between material, structure and architectural form, helps explain his attachment to trabeation. He accepted Laugier's thesis that the primitive hut marked the origins of architecture before its translation into stone Greek temples. The successive epochs of historical styles were determined first by wood, then stone, and followed more recently by iron, which had been succeeded in turn, he believed, by concrete.[89] Since the Renaissance 'architects have been speaking a dead language', he argued, by concentrating on decoration rather than construction until iron structures arose.[90] Because iron needs constant maintenance, Perret considered reinforced concrete to be both superior and more modern. The Parthenon (trabeation), Hagia Sophia (round arch), and Chartres cathedral (pointed arch) epitomised for him how the history of architecture had unfolded in response to materials and available techniques. He saw the use of a concrete frame cast in wood formwork as linking his approach to modernism with the origins of architecture and classical antiquity.

Perret's reading of architectural history was much influenced by the architectural historian Auguste Choisy (1841–1909). Trained

What will soon appear the most old, is that which at first appears the most modern.

André Gide

Novelty, the will for newness: the new is one of those exciting poisons which ends up being more necessary than any nourishment; thus once they are masters of us, one must always augment the dose and make it mortal unto death. It is strange to attach oneself to the perishable part of things, which is exactly their quality of being new.

Paul Valéry

as an engineer, Choisy achieved fame following the publication of his *Histoire de l'architecture* in 1899. This book, very different from Guadet's, expounded a theory of architecture drawn from an original interpretation of historical examples where he preferred the phrase 'art of building' to architecture; two earlier books were *L'Art de batir chez romains* (1837) and *L'Art de batir chez les byzantins* (1883). Although, like his French predecessors Cordemoy and Laugier, he admired both Greek and Gothic architecture, Choisy followed Hübsch in being drawn to Roman architecture for its invention of the vault. The vault was for him the essence of Roman architecture, for structure and decoration were 'distinct and quite separate'.[91] From the Renaissance onwards he considered that buildings had become little more than articulated surfaces. Choisy concentrated instead on structure and how it organised space, as Robin Middleton explains:

> In *L'Art de batir chez romains* he said – on the very first page – that the structure of buildings had never been properly studied, 'they have stopped at the surface of buildings without studying the skeleton'. This he felt was the essence of architecture. And the way in which he approached and analysed it was direct and consistent.[92]

Choisy developed a radically new form of representation, the upward, or 'worm's eye' view isometric as a way of showing in a single representation the structural system, the organisation of a building, the volumes enclosed and the massing. Ornamental details were played down as being extraneous to the essence of architecture. This form of representation was conceived as a way to think rationally about architecture in a different way from the focus on ornament and the orders of earlier treatises.

Perret himself advanced the additional argument of economy for using a frame. He described architecture as 'the utilisation of material subordinated to the laws of economy'.[93] A very restricted budget led to the Perret Brothers being commissioned for the church of Notre Dame du Raincy (1922–3) on the outskirts of Paris. Other architects had been consulted but historicist forms constructed from traditional methods of building proved too expensive. The church was built to commemorate those who died in the nearby World War 1 Battle of the Ourcq.[94] Concrete and glazed workshops predominated in this working-class district, so Perret's concrete would have been the new but everyday material familiar to the church's congregation [6.22].

6.22 Notre Dame du Raincy

The plan is the traditional basilica type of nave with side aisles. Circular concrete columns and the shallow vaulted ceiling are left with the marks of the formwork exposed. Transverse vaults over the side aisles echo Brunelleschi's early Renaissance churches when the basilica form was revived [6.23]. The abiding impression, however, is of a Gothic cathedral or perhaps the Sainte-Chapelle in Paris, spaces transfigured by light. The tall, slender columns, fluted with shuttering board marks, evoke Gothic ribbed columns. The outer row is disengaged from the wall – as proposed in Le Corbusier's 'Dom-ino' system – which here allows a coloured glass-block wall complete sovereignty, the wall's mass eliminated in the service of light. Otto von Simson has explained how the Gothic cathedral developed by making light itself the material substance of the wall, an audacious attempt to evoke the idea of the Heavenly City.[95] 'Measure and light', he says, were the ideas that transformed the Romanesque style into the Gothic cathedral. At Notre Dame du Raincy, Perret draws upon this history and translates into a modern form the essence of this idea of sacred space; not a glass wall to let light through, but the wall itself seemingly made of light.

6.23 Notre Dame du Raincy, interior looking east

In contrast to novel form-making and abstraction, Perret sought to construct an architecture that articulated an appropriate relation between tradition and innovation. Notre Dame du Raincy epitomises this with its space redolent of the long traditions of the church yet built in the most modern materials. Britton makes a distinction between 'career' and 'vocation' to revise Perret's position in the Modern Movement. 'Career' suggests a progressive development (when used as a noun, but running out of control as a verb). This fits less well with Perret than 'vocation', which implies a dedication to a singular end.[96] Perret's goal, writes Britton, 'was not merely to be an innovator, but also a translator of tradition ... Translation did not involve mere repetition: what was important to him was an amplification of tradition.'[97] In Perret's own words, 'a building must last, it must create a past that itself prolongs life.'[98]

* * *

> The architect is the constructor who fulfils the transitory through the permanent.
>
> **Auguste Perret**

> By modernity, I mean the ephemeral, the fugitive, the contingent, the half of art whose other half is the eternal and immutable.
>
> **Charles Baudelaire**

> Technique is found at the point where technology unites with poetic sensibility to yield true architecture.
>
> **Auguste Perret**

Behrens' AEG Turbine Factory has been hailed as 'the first piece of modern architecture'.[99] All the 'pioneer historians' concur, although one senses unease in their estimates. The building's formality and monumentality reveal Behrens' attachment to history, for it is hardly the 'frank industrial architecture' acclaimed by Hitchcock.[100] Pioneer historians glossed over Behrens' more ambiguous position as they advanced the cause of a purely functional modernism. In Jurgen Joedicke's *A History of Modern Architecture,* for example, Behrens was criticised for failing to live up to the ideals of structural rationalism. Joedicke praised the 'way points of intersection between structural members are given architectural prominence', but criticised the fact that 'creating form out of structure is not consistently followed out'. 'Behrens dramatizes form', he concludes, and 'the building loses its straight forward, practical, character and becomes a monument.'[101] Written in 1958, Joedicke's comments illustrate the way historians over-simplified the historical record, ignoring the tensions pioneer architects felt between invention and inherited design traditions in favour of a future-forward narrative. A closer look at the AEG Turbine Factory in the light of Behrens' thinking about architecture illuminates this distortion particularly clearly.

The Allgemeine Electricitats Gesellschaft (AEG) was founded in 1883 and within seven years had grown into a vast industrial combine. With limited access to raw materials, it became clear that Germany could only prosper with high-quality industrial production. (This laid the foundations of Germany's modern economic success, of course.) It was from this background and with the aim of improving the design of its products that Behrens was appointed 'artistic consultant' to AEG in 1907. On joining AEG he came face-to-face with the unavoidable facts of fast-developing industrial power.

Behrens' early career as a Jugendstil artist – the German version of Art Nouveau – and his deeply held convictions on art shaped his approach to design in industry. Before joining AEG, Behrens had been one of seven artists invited to form the Darmstadt Artists' Colony with its aim of re-vitalising the visual arts. Directed by Behrens, the opening ceremony in May 1901 was called *Das Zeichen* (The Sign), the title of the last section of Nietzsche's *Thus Spake Zarathustra.* In the late nineteenth century many artists read Nietzsche, and Behrens was no exception. Soon after the opening he designed an unexecuted theatre, intending to express the Nietzschean view that 'mime and dance

Just as nature is not *Kultur,* so the purely human fulfilment of functional and material needs cannot create *Kuktur.*

Peter Behrens

were the origins of the theatre and must become again its basis'.[102] Nietzsche's concept of 'will-to-power' was the source of Riegl's art critical term of *Kunstwollen* (translated either as will-to-art, or will-to-form), which enabled Behrens to adapt ideas developed at Darmstadt to the demands made of industrial design at AEG. A short period as director of the Kunstgerwerkeschule in Dusseldorf from 1903 brought him into contact with followers of Berlage, which coloured his ideas on how art and design could be applied to industrial production.[103]

On joining AEG, nevertheless, Behrens continued to hold to Nietzsche's view that positivistic science, which dominated nineteenth century Germany, ran counter to prospects for cultural development. In a lecture of 1909, when the Turbine Factory was under construction, he opposed, he said, 'the tendency of our modern architects to seek to devise all artistic forms from function and technology'.[104] Behrens was effectively the first industrial designer in the modern sense, designing electric lamps, kettles, and table fans in addition to the AEG company logo, an early example of creating a branded identity. His design for the Turbine Factory added to this, for it was to become the face that AEG turned to the world, with Behren's new logo emblazoned on its front façade [6.24].

Behrens began his design in 1908, construction commenced early in 1909, and the building was fully operational at the beginning of 1910. The AEG board issued a detailed specification prescribing a steel frame and full-glazed wall, so an engineer, Karl Bernhard, was appointed to work with him. Bernhard designed a three-hinged arch structure of latticework truss with a tie rod across the 26-metre span and capable of supporting a travelling crane to lift the enormous weight of assembled turbines [6.25]. But for Behrens the factory was not to be a utilitarian structure like nineteenth century railway station buildings. He said that 'iron and glass have a dematerializing effect on form', which his architectural concept aimed to conquer by drawing 'the construction together into an emphatic mass of iron'.[105] Setting the glass side wall back and inclined inwards, coupled with iron sheathing to the exposed columns helped achieve this [6.26]. The glazed side wall sits on heavily textured concrete panels which rest in turn on a long concrete plinth, like a Greek temple stylobate, that binds the structure together.

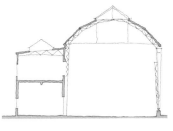

6.24 Peter Behrens,
    AEG Turbine Hall, Berlin
6.25 Section

6.26 Detail of steel column base

It is in the treatment of the front gable elevation, however, where Behrens' architectural concept triumphs over the dematerialising effect of glass and iron. Massive, battered concrete pylons at each corner are capped by a pediment-like gable whose profile echoes that of the steel roof trusses. Horizontal bands of steel embedded in the concrete pylons evoke rustication. The pylons were 'intended to close and connect', enhancing the corporeality that he insisted was essential to architectural form.[106] The gable overhanging the pylons, combined with a deep, over-sailing fascia running the full length of the side elevation, binds the building into a single massive form.

Bernhard criticised the façade on the grounds that the temple-like gable implied a trabeated construction hence contradicting the three-hinged arch structure, a criticism Joedicke made later. But this functional argument ran counter to Behrens' artistic convictions. He accepted the new technology as a historical fact, accommodating it rather than celebrating it, and certainly not as the ideal of culture.[107] 'Behrens attempted to raise the factory building to the level of high art', writes Mallgrave, 'with his insistence on monumental forms.'[108] He aspired to celebrate the power of the machine, the turbine assembled in the building, rather than producing machine-like architecture. The monumental, temple-like composition of the Turbine Hall shows Behrens bringing the factory into architecture rather than vice versa, as the narrative of pioneer historians would have us believe. As Frampton says, the Turbine Factory 'was a reification of industry as the one vital rhythm of modern life'.[109]

Gropius, Mies van der Rohe (1886–1969) and Le Corbusier all worked for Behrens during this time. Unlike the younger men, Behrens held to a belief that a re-formulated classical architecture could work with modern conditions. He believed that positivistic science was about to be replaced by 'a culture in which the will of the artist and the people' would prevail.[110] We detect here the persistent influence of Nietzsche, for Behrens explicitly claimed the higher role for the artist over the engineer in producing a modern culture; all great achievements have been produced, not by 'conscientious professional work', he wrote, 'but [are] the outcome of the energy of great and strong personalities'.[111] For Behrens a modern culture could only emerge from a Nietzschean 'higher man' exercising his will-to-form. Not as purely personal expression, but rather by exercising his will-to-form in recasting architecture's history against the functional thrust of an industrialised society. From this position, as Stanford Anderson says, Behrens could be 'critical of modernity and to claim that the artist had the will to reform the modern condition'.[112]

His later buildings for AEG show how far Behrens distanced himself from his younger pupils and others who came to adopt a *Sachlichheit* approach, as did his 'Festhalle' for the Cologne Deutscher Werkbund exhibition of 1914, with its stripped Renaissance form, wholly at odds with the rising clamour for 'Standardisation'. After World War I his work departed yet further from mainstream modernism. His Dombauhütte für Gewerbeschen (1922) in Munich is an extraordinary building of triangular gables of brickwork laid in diagonal patterns. The name *Dombauhutte* refers to the lodge where medieval craftsmen worked on a cathedral, a notion taken up at the Bauhaus. His Administration building for the Farbwerke Hoechst (1920–4) in Frankfurt is dominated by a Berlage-like tower in brickwork. Its reception hall, a five-storey top-lit atrium in expressionist brickwork, is as far removed from the *Sachlichkeit*, abstract language of the Modern Movement as can be imagined.

THE DEUTSCHE WERKBUND

Founded in October 1907, the Deutscher Werkbund became the most significant body in making the break from historicism. Behrens was a founder member, but it was Herman Muthesius (1861–1927) who shaped its character. The aim of the Werkbund was to improve the quality of German design, which it pursued by extending and adapting Arts and Crafts principles to industrial design. With this in mind the initial membership brought together twelve artists – included Behrens, Hoffman and Olbrich – and twelve craft firms.

Muthesius represents a new kind of figure in the debates about history and modernism, for he had studied art history and philosophy at the University of Berlin before studying architecture. In 1896 he was sent as cultural and technical attaché to the German Embassy in London with a brief to report on English art, architecture and technical achievements. His encounter with English design culture was to prove a pivotal step towards modernism. His investigations focused on the

Far more important than the material aspect is the spiritual; higher than purpose, material, and technique stands form. Purpose, material, and technique might be beyond criticism, yet without form we should still be living in a crude and brutal world.

Hermann Muthesius,
Aims of the Werkbund

Arts and Crafts movement, reports of which he sent back to Germany. It was the comfort, common sense and practicality of English middle-class domestic culture that appealed to Muthesius, as it did to Loos.

Muthesius identified as its leaders the young architects who had worked for Richard Norman Shaw (1831–1912) and were also followers of Morris – whom he called 'the father of this new artistic movement'.[113] Their 'thesis was sound workmanship, reasonableness, and sincerity; and its motive was a genuine, popular enthusiasm, for art, which had been particularly kindled by the widely read books of Ruskin.'[114] Ruskin had compared fine 'house-building' to ship building 'designed with the masculine reference to utility'.[115] However, where Ruskin valued ornament as the mark of a man's mind, Arts and Crafts architects studied traditional building crafts as a preliminary to reviving architecture itself, shifting the emphasis from 'style-architecture', to the more modest realism of vernacular building traditions. Muthesius' adopted Choisy's term 'art of building' in an early account of English developments entitled *Stilarchitektur und Baukunst* (1901) which, as the title implies, was a critique of Style Revival architecture. He may have been prompted to substitute the 'art of building' for 'architecture' by William Lethaby (1857–1931), for in 1895–96 – just when Muthesius arrived in London – Lethaby had generated a great deal of controversy by proposing to replace the word 'architecture' with a term such as 'reasonable building' or 'rational building'[116] [6.27]. How to translate Arts and Crafts principles from craft products to industrial production became the Werkbund's quest.

Returning to Germany in 1903, Muthesius took up a post with the Ministry of Commerce and Trade, where he implemented reforms to design education. He was joined by Behrens in leading the *Verband des deutschen Kunstgewebes* (Association of German Applied Arts), a forerunner of the Werkbund.[117] He criticised the search for a new style before a fundamental review of industrial design and production had been carried out. Manufacturers producing 'machine made surrogates' of Jugendstil exacerbated the situation and what was required was to focus attention upon 'the everyday to which the crafts and the building-art must be directed'.[118] A precondition for design reform, he said, lies 'in the conceptual bonding of arts and crafts to subdue "art" in the recovery of a suitable craft production.'[119]

Muthesius' ultimate aim was to produce high-quality industrial

I am full of hope that from the very necessary and unpretentious buildings will spring the new and true architecture, at any rate, [this is] more likely than from experimenting with the methods of some popular style.

William Morris

6.27 William Lethaby, All Saints, Brockhampton

products that would secure the country's place in the emerging world markets. A modern authentic culture, he was convinced, had to accept the machine. The scientific achievements of nineteenth century industry had led to demand from an expanding middle-class market for 'straightforward' domestic architecture and fittings of the kind developed for the English house as well as 'the electric lamp and the bicycle'. These captured 'the spirit of our time more closely that any new furniture or wallpaper of the Jugendstil or Secession style'.[120] According to Muthesius: 'the machine does not exist in order to produce art. This is a privilege of the human hand ... the human hand can use tools ... The machine is, however, only an improved tool.'[121] Anticipating the Bauhaus, he believed that if a craftsman-like sensitivity could engender 'forms that the machine can produce, then these, as soon as they logically evolve from the conditions of the machine will also be those that we will without hesitation call artistic'.[122] In this way 'not fakes of handwork' but rather typical machine forms, 'such as bicycles, would evolve'. Muthesius' call for a concentration on 'typical forms' sparked the seminal debate at the first great Deutsche Werkbund exhibition of 1914 held in Cologne.

Shortly before delivering the key-note address, Muthesius distributed a set of ten theses that he hoped would be adopted as an agreed programme in the approach to design. His proposal proved contentious, however, and, before the scheduled meeting van de Velde produced a set of ten 'anti-theses'. The dispute centred on Muthesius' call for the Werkbund to strive 'toward the development of types (*Typisierung*)'. Earlier historians translated *Typisierung* as 'Standardisation', the connotations of which so enflamed van de Velde: 'So long as there are still artists in the Werkbund ... they will protest against every suggestion for the establishment of a canon and for standardisation.'[123] Muthesius argued that 'a beneficial concentration' on types represented 'the most urgent task of the age', which was to create 'the preconditions for the export of its industrial arts'.[124] Van de Velde responded by asserting that 'the artist is a burning idealist, a free spontaneous creator. Of his own free will he will never subordinate himself to a discipline that imposes upon him a type, a canon.'[125]

On the surface this appears to be simply a disagreement about the priority given to either an artist's individual freedom to design or to work within the constraints imposed by the logic of industrial

The way in which the English achieved this goal, namely, by re-adapting vernacular and rural building motifs, promises the richest harvest.

Hermann Muthesius, *Stilarchitektur und Baukunst*

The well-being and the hope for the future lies in this: in the conceptual bonding of arts and crafts to subdue 'art' in the recovery of suitable craft production.

Hermann Muthesius, *Stilarchitektur und Baukunst*

Architecture, and with it the whole of the Werkbund's activities, is pressing towards standardization, and only through standardization can it recover that universal significance which was characteristic of it in times of harmonious culture.

Muthesius, *Werkbund Thesis No. 1*

production. But there was 'history' between the two men that helps explain deeper, underlying motivations. For in his *Stilarchitektur and Baukunst,* Muthesius had criticised van de Velde's leading role in promoting the Jugendstil. Of all the people involved in the Werkbund, no-one was more infatuated by Nietzsche than van de Velde. He read Nietzsche's works extensively and designed special editions of his works for collectors.[126] He also designed the Nietzsche-Archive (1902–3) in Weimar, in addition to a project for a memorial to commemorate the seventieth anniversary of the philosopher's birth in this same year, 1914. In a similar way to Behrens, van de Velde held fast to the Nietzschean idea of the 'higher man' who would lead culture out of its moribund condition and spoke of 'the will to truth that exalted Nietzsche'.[127] This would manifest itself through the will-to-form, which for van de Velde was represented by the mastery of line understood as a life-force, the inspiration behind Jugendstil and expressed in van de Velde's design for the theatre at the Werkbund Exhibition.[128] Fixing typical forms for design would instead mark a premature closing of creative exploration and cultural development. Muthesius, in contrast, was increasingly moving towards standardisation and 'creating the preconditions for the export of its industrial arts.'[129]

Central to the debates on art and industrialisation at this time were the words *Sachlich* and *Sachlichkeit.* In its adjectival form, *Sachlich* meant simply 'practical ... factual, matter-of-fact.'[130] *Sachlichkeit*, in contrast, implied a more rational focus on 'materials and processes'.[131] At the time of writing *Stilarchitektur and Baukunst,* Muthesius used the former to indicate a realist art and architecture of the kind Berlage would approve.[132] But the thrust of his Werkbund theses shows him moving towards greater objectivity in design. This is what set van de Velde against Muthesius. After World War I, a pure objectivity and increased rationalism took hold of architecture under the guise of *Neues Sachlichkeit.* But at this stage, and amongst participants in the 1914 exhibition, there existed much less consensus on this being the direction for architecture to take.

Van de Velde received much support for his 'anti-theses', including from Gropius, who apparently tried to organise a walkout in protest at Muthesius' programme. The mixed feelings about how best to proceed at this stage can be gauged from Pevsner's celebration of Gropius' and Meyer's Model Factory at the exhibition as the building that properly represented the style of a *Sachlichkeit* architecture for the twentieth century. Their design for a Model Factory represented, he said, 'the creative energy of this world in which we live and work and which we want to master, a world of science and technology, of speed and danger … that is glorified in Gropius' architecture, and as long as this is the world and these are its ambitions and problems, the style of Gropius and the other pioneers will be valid.'[133] Then, as now, not everyone was so convinced, although in the years immediately following an anti-historical view did prevail.

The Werkbund debate brought into clear focus the process of aligning architecture with rationalising criteria that had began with Durand a century earlier, and has played a significant part in the way architecture developed over the subsequent hundred years or so. In summing up his discussion of *Sachlich* and *Sachlichkeit,* Anderson contrasts what he calls 'realist architecture' with 'the calculation of mechanical needs' of *Neues Sachlichkeit* objectivity. 'Within a realist architecture there is an impetus to understand and use our received condition as much as to criticize and change it.'[134] As we have seen, many of the pioneer architects in fact adopted such an approach, from Otto Wagner's call to 'adapt' traditional forms through to Perret's Nietzschean aim of 'creating a past that itself prolongs life'.

It is at the Werkbund where we first see Muthesius moving from the 'realism' of the builder's art to standardisation as the precursor of an industrialised architecture. This became the dominant and long-lived narrative of the Modern Movement, a narrative established by 'pioneer' or 'operative historians' who selected images and phrases that served their own predilections. But, as we have seen, the work of the pioneers Wagner, Loos, Berlage, Perret and Behrens, in fact belied such a straightforward, future-forward narrative. In the clamour for the rationalisation of architecture to reflect an increasingly industrialised age and leave historicism behind, humankinds' experiential and psychological needs for shelter and orientation were all-too easily overlooked. A brief review of the 'isms', the radical architectural movements that burst upon the first years of the twentieth century, movements that vociferously rejected history, will help show why eventually history and the humanities regained a place in thinking about architecture.

The disease of reason is that reason was born from man's urge to dominate nature, and the 'recovery' depends on insight into the nature of the original disease. The true critique of reason will necessarily uncover the deepest layers of civilization and explore its history … Thus the derangement of reason goes far beyond the obvious malformations that characterize it at the present time. Reason can realize its reasonableness only through reflection on the disease of the world as produced and reproduced by man.

Max Horkheimer,
Eclipse of Reason

Chapter 7: Modernism against history

CIAM AND THE INTERNATIONAL STYLE

After World War I, new groupings of architects enthusiastically adopted Muthesius' call for rationalisation. A gathering of leading European architects in 1928 culminated with the founding of the *Congrès Internationaux d'Architecture Moderne* (CIAM).[1] The tenor of the 'La Sarraz Declaration', the manifesto signed by 24 major European architects, suggests that German influence remained strongest. The main points called for links between architecture and the 'general economic system' by means of 'rationalisation and standardisation.'[2]

Rationalisation became more emphasised at CIAM 2 the following year. The main topic of the congress, proposed by Giedion – the secretary – was to be '*Existenzminimum*'[3], how to design to the most efficient, minimal dwelling standards: *Die Wohnung für das Existenzminimum.*[4] Frankfurt was the chosen venue because under the leadership of Ernst May (1886–1970), rationally planned housing projects were being built there.[5] May had appointed Walter Schwagenscheidt to investigate scientifically the optimum orientation of dwellings for solar gain, which proved to be 22.5° from north – south[6] [7.1].

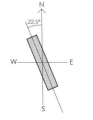

7.1 Walter Schwagenscheidt, orientation of dwellings

The clamour for rationalised production continued at the 1930 Congress, in Brussels (CIAM 3). The theme was 'Rational methods of Site Planning.' (*Rationelle Bebauungs-weissen*). Reversing his opposition to standardisation from the Cologne Werkbund, Gropius led the attack against traditional patterns of dwellings. 'Parallel rows of apartment blocks have the great advantage … that all apartments can have equally favourable orientation with respect to the sun, that the ventilation of blocks is not obstructed by transverse blocks, and that the stifled corner blocks are eliminated.'[7] Gropius produced a diagrammatic site section aiming to prove the advantage of high rise in such an arrangement [7.2]. Known as the *Zeilenbau* system, this arrangement became proclaimed as the optimum rational site plan combining economy, sunlight, ventilation, and even providing, it was contended, the advantages of garden city planning.[8]

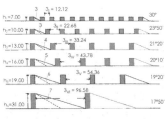

7.2 Walter Gropius, diagrammatic site section

These first CIAM meetings were dominated by the doctrine of *Neue Sachlichkeit*, the adjective shifting the term decisively to 'objectivity'. Gropius argued that a layout of parallel blocks 'is thus considerably functionalised'.[9] Mark Swenarton sees this emphasis on 'functionalised' as springing from contemporary American techniques of industrial production and management as espoused by Henry Ford and F.W. Taylor. 'Taylor's method ... involved the abolition of traditional, or, as he saw them, irrational working practices and their replacement by new, "rational" procedures based on scientific analysis and calculated for maximum efficiency.'[10] Ford, whose book *My Life and Work* (1922) had become a best seller when translated into German in 1923, stood for pre-production research and assembly line production.

May also employed Grete Schütte-Lihotzky to design the 'Frankfurter Küche', a radically minimal and prefabricated kitchen.[11] May emphasised the need for 'scientific analysis'[12] over architect's traditional concerns with the particularities of a brief or site. Circulation became prioritised by an analogy drawn from physiology to suggest a scientific method.[13] It 'was this belief in abstraction and science inherited from the Fordisation programme that, above all', Swenarton argues, 'distinguished the thinking of CIAM'.[14]

The La Sarraz declaration stated that: 'It is only from the present that our architectural work should be derived.'[15] This was an attack on established teaching of architecture: 'BY PUTTING ARCHITECTURE BACK ON ITS REAL PLANE, THE ECONOMIC AND SOCIAL PLANE; therefore architecture should be freed of the sterile influence of the Academies and of antiquated formulas.'[16] Architecture would no longer refer to history for any of its precepts, but align its concepts with those of industrial building production: 'rationalisation and standardisation'.[17]

In taking up Muthesius' call to engage building design with industrial production, the architects of CIAM pursued the Werkbund's aim to its logical conclusion. This signature of the Modern Movement first found coherent architectural expression at the Werkbund's *Wiessenhofsiedlung* held in Stuttgart in 1927 [7.3]. Hitchcock argued that this proved crucial in the new style 'winning acclaim'.[18] However, the exhibition 'The International Style; Architecture since 1922', which he organised with Johnson at the Museum of Modern Art (MoMA), New York in 1931, in conjunction with the accompanying book, arguably had a greater impact on establishing the style of the

We are approaching a state of technical proficiency when it will become possible to rationalize buildings and mass-produce them in factories by resolving their structure into a number of component parts. Like boxes of toy-bricks, these will be assembled in various formal compositions in a dry state.

Walter Gropius,
The New Architecture and the Bauhaus

The man-made world of things, the human artifice erected by homo faber, becomes a home for mortal men, whose stability will endure ... only insomuch as it transcends both the sheer functionalism of things produced for consumption and the sheer utility of objects produced for use.

Hannah Arendt,
The Human Condition

7.3 Le Corbusier,
Wiessenhofsiedlung, Stuttgart

7.4 J.J.P. Oud,
Wiessenhofsiedlung, Stuttgart

Modern Movement. Reflecting later, Hitchcock stressed that a primary aim of the book 'was devoted to defending the idea of style', an important tactic in the attack on nineteenth century eclecticism.[19] Their emphasis on style as a set of aesthetic qualities linked the industrial-technical developments with new directions in modern art. They argued that it was 'particularly in the early work of three men', Gropius, J.J.P. Oud (1890–1963) and Le Corbusier that 'the inception of our new style' could be identified[20] [7.4]. Influenced by the abstract De Stijl paintings of Mondrian, Oud's projects became 'increasingly simple, rigorous and geometrical'.[21] But Le Corbusier was the decisive figure, for as early as 1921, his Citrohan project, wrote Hitchcock, 'was more thoroughly infused with a new spirit, more completely freed from the conventions of the past than any thus far projected'.[22]

The 'innovations' of the pioneers, 'the half-moderns' according to Hitchcock and Johnson, were independent and divergent, but the Stuttgart *Wiessenhofsiedlung* showed architects working in 'parallel' to develop an International Style.[23] The new style was characterised by volume 'felt as immaterial and weightless'.[24] Where traditional buildings responded to gravity, stresses in the new skin-like walls were both vertical and horizontal 'as in stretched textile'.[25] Nevertheless, horizontal emphasis had become 'the most conspicuous characteristic of the international style'.[26] In his later essay 'The International Style Revisited', Hitchcock summed up the new style: 'formal simplification', 'smooth rendered surfaces ... [and] platonic abstractions'.[27]

Architecture is the will of the age conceived in spatial terms. Living. Changing. New.

Mies van der Rohe,
Working theses

These aesthetic principles became canonical for the Modern Movement, although individual architects might not adhere to all. Ludwig Mies van der Rohe (1886–1969), for example, was acknowledged as one of the 'masters' of modernism, but his role was played down because his buildings emphasised interpenetration of space rather than 'volumetric enclosure'.[28] The Tugendhat House (1930) fitted the canon whereas his more well-known Barcelona Pavilion (1928–9) did not [7.5]. Frank Lloyd Wright was neither represented in the exhibition nor the book because of his emphasis on organic form and the varied appearance of his buildings, none of which met the criteria prescribed for the International Style.

In one of the earliest attempts to define the character of modern art, Ortega y Gassett characterised it as a 'pure art', which helps explain the form taken by the Modern Movement in architecture. Where modern painters eliminated the tradition of representation to concentrate on matters purely concerned with paint and the painted surface, so modernist architects, as portrayed by Hitchcock and Johnson, worked with only the essential elements that constituted architecture; space perceived as volume, engineering as the necessary bodily support, and function as the purely practical purpose of architecture. Oud's buildings, for example, they described as 'pure architecture'.[29] But Frampton has pointed out that architecture cannot aspire to cultural autonomy 'since it is too intimately involved in the processes of everyday life'.[30]

7.5 Ludwig Mies van der Rohe, Barcelona Pavilion

Tournikiotis includes Hitchcock in his set of 'pioneer historians', and describes how 'innovation' was made a pre-requisite of their characterisation of modern architecture. The International Style was most important, he says, in 'establishing its genealogy', which 'lay in the process of disintegration and reintegration';[31] pioneers reintegrated the nineteenth century's separation of building construction and engineering. Traditional materials, however, 'were ruled out ... in order to underscore the significance of innovation'.[32] With these precepts and the emphasis on abstraction, a modern architecture was able to escape from historicism, from the past, from traditional forms and details of building, and render itself totally new. But by aligning architecture with the rationalisation of production, the human experiential-psychological requirements of the built environment became overlooked. A brief review of the avant-garde movements will indicate the extent to which the language of architecture became removed from the existential, sheltering role of building. This was to be pointed out by the next generation of architects who challenged the by then tired platitudes of CIAM.

Without tradition – which selects and names, which hands down and preserves, which indicates where the treasures are and what their worth is – there seems to be no willed continuity in time and hence, humanly speaking, neither past nor future, only sempiternal change of the world and the biological cycle of living creatures in it.

Hannah Arendt,
Between Past and Future

Architecture must first of all come to terms with itself, that is, with its specific characteristics; but at the same time it must also come to terms with its social responsibilities.

Giorgio Grassi

FUTURISM, DE STIJL, CONSTUCTIVISM, EXPRESSIONISM AND THE BAUHAUS

The early years of the twentieth century were awash with 'isms', movements that defined new art concepts for a new era. Cubism, which emerged in Paris between 1905 and 1910 in the paintings of Georges Braque and Pablo Picasso, played a decisive role in radically transforming the representation of things and space. Although any direct application of Cubism to architecture remained problematic, nevertheless the aims of Cubism – transparency, layering, volumetric interpenetration, the rejection of perspective – played an important part in the architectural movements that followed.

* * *

Futurism was an Italian movement inspired by Cubism, but whereas that concerned itself with internal issues of art and perception, Futurism aimed at transforming the world.[33] The Futurist manifesto, written by Fillipo Marinetti (1876–1944), proclaimed that 'the world's magnificence has been enriched by a new beauty; the beauty of speed'.[34] Futurist architecture emerged from an exhibition entitled *Nuove Tendenze* (New Technologies) in Milan in May 1914, dominated by the drawings of Antonio Sant'Elia (1888–1916) and Mario Chiattone (1891–1957). 'Architecture is breaking free from tradition',[35] with its 'carnival decorative incrustations',[36] wrote Sant'Elia, which alerted Marinetti to its potential as a 'Manifesto of Futurist Architecture'.[37] In a resounding paragraph his words conjure up the fantastic character of the buildings shown in Sant'Elia's visionary drawings of power stations, transport interchanges, railway termini, and tall apartment buildings with exposed lifts, all drawn with very low vanishing points to emphasise dynamism [7.6].

7.6 Giuseppe Terragni, Monument to Sant'Elia, Como

> We must invent and rebuild the Futurist city; it must be like an immense, tumultuous, lively, noble work site, dynamic in all its parts; and the Futurist house must be like an enormous machine. The lifts must not hide like lonely worms in the stair wells … the lifts must climb like serpents of iron and glass up the house … of glass and iron.[38]

The technology hardly existed that could realise the Futurist vision. After World War I, a war the Futurists actively encouraged where machines played such a part in the terrible devastation of human life – including that of Sant'Elia who was killed in the war – there was little appetite for glorifying technology. Not until the 1970s did the 'white heat of technology' become so acclaimed again and finally given architectural expression in Roger's and Piano's Centre Pompidou (1971–7) in Paris, a building showing kinship with the Futurist vision. Underlying many subsequent hi-tech buildings is a similar exaggerated emphasis on technological possibilities to determine the built environment with little concern for human psychological needs.

* * *

De Stijl artists promoted the idea of 'aesthetic autonomy', in contrast to Futurists engagement. Its founders were the painter Pieter Mondrian (1872–1944) and the painter and architect Theo van Doesburg (1883–1931). The black-gridded paintings with rectangles of blue, red and yellow of Mondrian, who had worked in Paris and was influenced by Cubism, came to epitomise the abstract character of De Stijl. The journal *De Stijl* proclaimed that such a 'pure' art of painting should serve as a model for architecture.

'There is an old and a new consciousness of time', announced the De Stijl manifesto.[39] It called 'on all those who believe in the reform of art and culture to destroy those things which prevent further development', just as De Stijl painting had 'eliminated what stands in the way of the expression of pure art'.[40] The new consciousness of time was to be expressed through abstraction, which would emphasise the present by eliminating all reference to past art forms. Mallgrave describes Van Doesburg, the driving force of the movement, as seeing 'the appropriateness of abstraction as a spiritual means to rid art of its contaminating materialism'.[41] He was greatly influenced by Kandinsky's *Concerning the Spiritual in Art* (1910) and the De Stijl movement drew support from the Neo-Platonic and Theosophical philosophy of M.M. Schoenmaekers. These influences reinforced the idea that abstraction represented a purity that would cleanse art and architecture of the stifling influence of history.[42] Colour would be the expressive medium of painting and for architecture it would be purely space.

In our minute splicing of our lives into milliseconds, we live separated from everything that surrounds us.

Werner Herzog,
Cave Art in the Chauvet Cave

The publication of Frank Lloyd Wright's flowing house plans inspired De Stijl architects to produce dynamic compositions where a continuous space appears to flow between and around free-floating vertical and horizontal planes. Van Doesburg said that in 'this way architecture acquires a more or less floating aspect'.[43] The most complete expression of De Stijl architecture is the Schröder-Schräder house in Utrecht, (1924) [7.7]. Designed by the cabinet maker Gerrit Rietveld (1888–1964) in collaboration with interior decorator Truus

7.7 Gerrit Rietvelt, Schröeder house, Utrecht

Schröder-Schräder, it is an open composition of horizontal and vertical planes that overshoot and over-sail one another, where space flows almost unconstrained from room to room and from inside to outside. The house appears as a work of abstract sculpture in stark contrast to the traditional brick and tiled roof neighbour against which it abuts. It was actually built of brick and timber itself and this lack of constructional honesty led to criticism from new groupings of architects such as the 'Amsterdam School' and 'De 8', whose work was predicated on rationality of construction. By 1921 many original members had left the movement and the later grouping of De Stijl artists came increasingly under the influence of the *Neue Sachlichkeit*.[44] It was these more functional housing schemes at Keifhoek, Rotterdam (1925–7) and at the Hook of Holland (1924–7) that Hitchcock and Johnson chose to represent Dutch architect's contribution to the International Style.

* * *

Constructivism emerged in the immediate aftermath of the Russian October Revolution. Constructivism became a hold-all name for a number of groupings of radicals who produced few buildings but many revolutionary slogans. It 'is necessary to do away with all dying systems of the past', wrote Kasimir Malevich (1878–1935) in his Suprematist Manifesto (1924). 'Life must be purified of the clutter of the past, of parasitical eclecticism'.[45] Malevich, whose 'Black Square on a White Ground' was the first entirely abstract painting, defined Suprematism as a 'dematerialised and non-objective form of art'.[46] He founded a school for the 'Establishment of new forms of art' (Unovis) in 1919 where abstraction was to be complemented by technology. 'The forms of classical antiquity, they say, are important … But where then is the aeroplane, or even merely the motor car to be housed? How can modern technology be expressed in antique forms?' [47]

Several organisations arose, such as INKhUK (The Institute for Artistic Culture) and VKhUTMAS (Higher Artistic and Technical Studies) to proselytise and facilitate debate. The Association of Contemporary Architects (OSA) was formed in 1925 under the leadership of Mosei Ginzburg (1892–1946) and included the Vesnin brothers:

Leonid (1880–1937), Victor (1882–1950), and Alexander (1883–1959). Ginzburg had studied at the *Ecole des Beaux-Arts* and the Academy of Fine Art in Milan and was familiar with the Futurists and Le Corbusier's work, as well as the new aesthetic theories of Wölfflin and Worringer.[48] The OSA set out to end the 'artist/craftsman-like' relationship between architect and client and transform the architect into 'a new type of professional who was first a socialist, second a politician, and third a technician'.[49] The dynamic form of projects such as the Vesnin brothers' Pravda newspaper headquarters in Moscow, designed in 1923, expressed the architectural syntax of Constructivism. 'All accessories ... such as signs, advertising, clocks, loudspeakers and even the elevator inside, have been incorporated as integral elements', wrote El Lissitzky, capturing the dynamism of the project. 'This is the aesthetic of Constructivism.'[50]

A member of the 'Association of New Architects' (Asnova), El Lissitzky was the first to translate abstract painting into three-dimensional abstract forms called 'Prouns' (Project for Affirmation of the New). This group aimed to free architecture from the 'atrophied forms' of historic styles. Konstantin Melnikov (1890–1974) was a member and perhaps the best known Constructivist architect as some of his designs – the Zuev Workers' Club (1926) and the Rusakov Worker's Club (1927–8) – were actually built. They show the interplay of formal abstraction and technological expression that sat at the heart of Constructivism.

The spiralling monumental tower by Vladimir Tatlin (1885–1953) for a Monument to the Third International (1919–20) became the iconic structure of Constructivism [7.8]. The group, centred on Tatlin, preferred to be called Productivists and one of their slogans, typical of the period, was, 'Down with Art! Long live technology! ... Long live the Constructivist Technician'.[51] Constructivists saw the engineer as the generator of form, whereas for Suprematists form was created first through art.

7.8 Vladimir Tatlin, Monument to the Third International

Constructivist architecture set itself against all historical styles and theories, turning instead to the material of engineers, constructors of a wholly new world-order. Artists were bidden to 'go into the factory where the body of life is made'.[52] But this attempt to make a visionary architecture entirely free from history was short-lived. Lenin, the leader of the revolution, died in 1922 and ten years later Stalin issued his decree *Concerning the Reorganisation of Literary-*

Artistic Societies, which directed architects to 'socialist realism', thus ending revolutionary experiment by prescribing the stripped, overbearing Neoclassicism that became synonymous with twentieth century dictatorships.

* * *

The story of the Bauhaus is so well known that it hardly needs recounting here. Its *Vorkurs* (preliminary course), with its aim of liberating the creative potential of students, became emulated in art school foundation courses everywhere. The aims of the Bauhaus were radically transformed between the beginning and the end of its short life and the conflicting issues promoted by its personalities throw into stark relief the concerns raised here. In broad outline, the Bauhaus shifted from an Arts and Crafts ethos to become a school of industrial design via the Werkbund and Expressionism, the fading force of which shaped its early design teaching.

Expressionism is a problematic term as it has been applied in different ways to art and architecture, and Expressionist architects, unlike painters, formed no single grouping. But the Bauhaus manifesto (1919) was couched in Expressionist sentiment, which Lyonel Feininger's woodcut frontispiece entitled 'Cathedral' – a steepled church crowned with stars – well illustrates.

> Let us then create a new guild of craftsmen without the class distinctions that raise an arrogant barrier between craftsman and artist. Together let us desire, conceive and create the new structure of the future, which will one day rise toward heaven from the hands of a million workers like the crystal symbol of a new faith.[53]

The Bauhaus manifesto was written by Gropius, who became its director in 1919, four years after succeeding van de Velde at the Weimar Academy of Fine Art. Van de Velde's *Werkbund* Theatre fitted the Expressionist mould, as did Taut's Glass Pavilion at the Cologne exhibition. The Observatory and Astrophysics Laboratory (1917–21) at Potsdam (better known as the Einstein Tower) designed by Erich Mendelsohn (1887–1953), perhaps best exemplifies van de Velde's plea for the creative freedom of the artist to find expressive form, a defining characteristic of Expressionism [7.9].

Expressionists reacted against the forward-looking drive of modernism in early twentieth century Germany.[54] After the horrors of the first industrialised war, radical artists and intellectuals formed associations such as the *Novembergruppe*. Architects including Taut, Gropius, Adolph Behne (1888–1948) and Heinrich Tessenow (1876–1950) formed the *Arbeitsrat für Kunst* (Working Council for Art), whose circular entitled 'Under the wing of a great architecture' (1919) anticipated the Bauhaus programme: 'Art shall no longer be the enjoyment of the few but the life and happiness of the masses. The aim is an alliance of the arts under the wing of a great architecture.'[55]

The hardship that fell upon a defeated Germany, however, made the realisation of such a programme impossible. Architects turned instead to drawing a visionary architecture of glass and crystal typically set in Alpine mountains, a utopian dream in the midst of what was a dystopian reality. Taut initiated the *Glaserne Kette* (Crystal Chain) to exchange letters and drawings that postulated a world that had turned its back on rationalisation and industrialisation, emphasising instead *Geist* (spirit), and the new art theory concepts *Fühlen* (feeling) and *Wollen* (will).[56] Taut's drawings published as *Alpine Architecture* (1919) remain the most suggestive of this aspect of Expressionism, the crystalline structure underlying natural rock forms.

Gropius' brief was to transform the Weimar Academy of Fine Art into a school of craft-based instruction.[57] He changed its name to *Staatliches Bauhaus*, thus evoking the *bauhütte* where the various crafts worked on a medieval cathedral. The major influence in the school's first years was the painter Johannes Itten (1888–1967), who designed and taught the *Vorkurs*, which every student passed through upon entering the school.

Itten's teaching – playful exercises in texture, colour, tones and forms, and analysis of the expressive content of works of art in terms of line and rhythm, light and dark – were inspired by his philosophy, Mazdazaan, one of several esoteric, pseudo-religions popular at the time. In this we see the influence of Nietzsche, for Ahura Mazda represented 'Good' as spoken by Zarathustra.[58] Where the gnomic utterances of Nietzsche's *Thus Spoke Zarathustra* made the book open to misunderstandings, the simplified form of Mazdazaan emphasised the duality of good and evil, the light and dark that featured large in Itten's teaching: 'Mazdazaan saw the world as a battle field on which

7.9 Erich Mendelsohn, Einstein Tower, Potsdam

We must necessarily demonstrate that the young forces in architecture draw their architectonic experiences not from history nor from heaven, but solely from the fertility of their own visions of space.

Erich Mendelsohn,
The problem of a new architecture

The surface of the Earth would change greatly if brick architecture were every where displaced by glass architecture. It would be as though the Earth clad itself in jewellery of brilliants and enamel.

Paul Scheerbart,
Glass Architecture

evil continuously challenges good for supremacy.'[59] Itten equated the artist with Nietzsche's *Übermensch* who would overthrow the materialist civilisation that was emerging under industrialisation, whether capitalist or communist.[60] He transmitted his doctrine to students, not only by his teaching but also by promoting a lifestyle of vegetarian diet, monk-like attire and both physical and mental exercises.

Itten's influence became all-pervasive and soon ran against the direction that Gropius' own ideas on art and design education were taking. Awareness of Soviet art – El Lissitzky came to live in Berlin in 1921 – and Dutch developments – van Doesburg was invited to Weimar in April 1921 and stayed for nine months – played a part in this. Responding to Taylorism and Ford's project for rationalisation of production, Gropius turned the Bauhaus towards industry and mass production. His determination to transform the school from craftsmanship to designing for industrial production led to a rift with Itten, who opposed 'solving practical tasks' and resigned. He was replaced by the Constructivist László Moholy-Nagy (1895–1941). Wearing overalls in contrast to Itten's wine-red robes, he took over the *Vorkurs* and directed students to making collages assembled from materials associated with industrial production.

This change of direction was starkly apparent in the title of a lecture Gropius gave in 1923 entitled 'Art and Technology: A New Unity'.[61] Political changes in the regional parliament early the next year, however, led to the closure of the school in Weimar. But in 1925 the mayor of Dessau invited the Bauhaus to move there and Gropius' *Principles of Bauhaus Production,* written to coincide with this new phase of the school, shows its complete transformation from a 'guild of craftsmen' to place of research and development.

> The Bauhaus workshops are essentially laboratories in which prototypes of products suitable for mass production and typical of our time are carefully developed and constantly improved ... The crafts of the past have changed, and future crafts will be merged in a new productive unity in which they will carry out the experimental work for industrial production.[62]

It was from this phase that the 'classic' Bauhaus designs were produced: Marcel Breuer's tubular steel chairs; Herbert Bayer's typography, book and poster designs; Wilhelm Wagenfeld's vases, metal pots and his

A breach has been made with the past, which allows us to envisage a new aspect of architecture corresponding to the technical civilization of the age we live in.

Walter Gropius,
The New Architecture and the Bauhaus

much imitated table lamps; Marianne Brandt's brass, chrome-plated and silver ware; Mies van der Rohe's 'Barcelona Chair'.

The move to Dessau gave Gropius the opportunity to design the Bauhaus building, making it possible for him to realise his conception of a modern architecture [7.10]. The Dessau Bauhaus (1925–6) was very different from his formally planned Fagus Factory and the Model Factory at the Cologne Werkbund Exhibition. The new building was 'freely planned with wings' shooting off in three directions, showing the ascendancy of functionalism at the Bauhaus, the impact of Suprematism, De Stijl paintings, and Frank Lloyd Wright, whose designs Gropius was carefully studying at this time.[63] The student housing, a tall white cube with expressed balconies, exemplifies the International Style [7.11]. A glazed bridge walkway joins the student residence to the workshop block which, dominated by its three-storey-high fully glazed wall, Martin Kierien described 'as a symbol of the "Bauhaus community", whose spirit was to gather, cluster and, so to speak, crystallise here'[64] [7.12].

This was far from the 'crystal cathedral' envisaged by Gropius at the outset of the Bauhaus. *Neues Sachlichkeit* had come to dominate thinking and teaching. Functionalism became even more the watchword when Gropius was succeeded by Meyer in 1928. 'Everything in the world is the product of the formula: function times economy,' he wrote. 'Building is not an aesthetic process.'[65] And architectural form was simply a '"calculable" product of the … logic of "scientific" design'.[66]

Nietzsche detested the dominant functionalism of the nineteenth century, and Itten's view of Mazdazaan reveals why he had no choice but depart a Bauhaus heading in this direction. 'Mazdazaan … constitutes a system of teaching and upbringing', wrote Itten, 'the goal of which is man's basic pre-servation and higher development.'[67] The Bauhaus helped propel architecture on its highly technological path, which ran counter to Itten's hopes for mankind's 'higher development'. In this turn to a scientific/technological process for design we see more clearly than ever before the process of rationalization underlying the rise of modernity, which stealthily came to dominate over the higher life-goals sought by Itten, the process that Habemas came to call the total 'rationalisation' of society.

7.10–7.12 Gropius,
The Bauhaus, Dessau

AMERIKANISMUS

'*Amerikanismus*' became a widespread interest in a 1920s Germany trying to put its troubled immediate past behind. It was a fascination with the many cultural manifestations that spread from the new world: film, music, dance crazes, industry and the modern city.[68] Where much of this simply brightened and relieved the economic difficulties of the present, it also pointed the way forward to a future set free from history coinciding as it did with Taylorism and Fordism. As Vincent Scully has written, 'of all … Western civilisation, America was the one to which the future seemed most open'.[69] This helps explain the appeal of *Amerikanismus* to European architects breaking free from historicism, continues Scully:

> The cataclysmic modern shift from the small, pre-industrial world to a new world of mass population and industrialisation did not begin in America, but when it came to these shores it developed faster and more completely in the United States than anywhere else in the world … So the American became the first mass man, the first modern man, trampling all over the earth and all old things.[70]

He traces a line of development from the open, Shingle Style houses of H.H. Richardson (1838–86) through the early skyscrapers of William le Baron Jenny (1832–1907) – such as the Home Life Building of Chicago (1884–5) which is credited with first giving expression to the steel frame and cladding[71] – to those of Louis Sullivan (1856–1924). His Wainwright Building (1890–1), for example, was not 'of an open steel cage but that of a physical force, contained but vertically standing'.[72] Scully reads Richardson's and Sullivan's architecture as 'democratic' and humanist, attributes that aimed to ameliorate the rampant technological materialism of late nineteenth century America.

The first European architect to visit America and reflect upon these developments was Loos. He left Vienna for the United States in 1893 and remained there for three years. The timing of his departure may have been influenced by the World's Columbian Exposition held in Chicago that same year.[73] 'How this has changed … me', he wrote. His critical attitude towards ornament sprang from the contrast between unornamented American products and those of Austrian applied art, which he described as 'nothing but a Philistine lie'.[74] America 'symbolised the future' for Loos, wrote Joanna Drew, in contrast 'to the thoroughly historicising atmosphere of Central Europe and Vienna'.[75] Loos wrote little about contemporary American architecture in articles sent back from the United States, although he did later write an insightful article on 'The Principle of Cladding'. But he was clearly affected by his time in Chicago, Philadelphia, St. Louis and New York, where a skyscraper boom was underway. It is from this experience that he stated: 'the engineers are our Greeks. We receive our culture from them; the entire globe is covered by their culture.'[76]

Scully argues that by 1914 the invention and leadership that America held in architecture's embracing of modernity passed to Europe. For an increasing air of fantasy pervaded American skyscrapers in the first decades of the twentieth century with eclectic borrowing from historical forms as the steel frame and electric lift saw buildings soar higher and higher. Lines of thought that had begun in Europe returned from the United States, transformed and stimulating, in turn, ideas pursued by European 'Pioneers'. In his book *America,* for example, Mendelsohn wrote that 'America therefore only means the extension of the horizon of our own thought.'[77]

Scully argues that the early work of Wright 'grew to culminate, integrate, and, in one sense, to complete the American nineteenth century development'.[78] The *Wasmuth* publication of Wright's buildings, accompanied by an exhibition of his work in Berlin in 1910, became the source of his influence on Europeans, particularly his assertion that 'the new reality … is *space* instead of matter'.[79] His influence on De Stijl has been noted, and Scully points to the striking formal resemblance between Wright's Mason City National Bank (1909) and Gropius and Meyer's Model Factory at the 1914 Werkbund Exhibition. And as we have seen, Gropius drew inspiration from Wright's planning when designing the Dessau Bauhaus in 1925–6. The plan for Mies van der Rohe's project for a Brick Country House (1923), the forerunner of his Barcelona Pavilion, reads as a didactic elaboration of a Wright 'Prairie House' as transmuted through the prism of De Stijl. Mies' early un-built skyscraper projects show the impact of American skyscrapers combined with Nuam Gabo's Constructivist sculpture. Writing about the period immediately before World War 1, Mies described how 'the potential vitality of the architectural idea of the period' had been lost. 'At the moment, so critical for us, the exhibition of the work of Frank Lloyd Wright came to Berlin.'

Frank Lloyd Wright, Mies van der Rohe, and Le Corbusier have been hailed as the 'masters of Modernism', with some historians adding Gropius and more recently Alvar Aalto (1898–1976) to the pantheon. In his essay 'Wright vs. The International Style', Scully argues that the influence of Wright on European architecture in the 1920s was reciprocated and contributed to his 'renewed burst of achievement in the later 1930s.'[80] His greatest works are, perhaps, the 'Prairie Houses' [7.13] and house known as Falling Water (1936), where the use of horizontal metal windows and the floating white forms suggested to Scully the influence of Le Corbusier's Villa Savoye. But Wright transformed 'the creative assimilation of a host of influences' into something uniquely his own, organic and open to the landscape. Wright became very hostile to the abstract formalism of the International Style which he dubbed 'collectivist' and 'un-American'.[81] For 'every place an appropriate formal language', he argued.[82] In *An American Architect* (1955) he wrote that building should be 'parallel to the earth [and] belonging to the ground.'[83] Wright's renewal grew from his own return to origins and traditions. The compacted forms of Mayan temples influenced his Barnsdall House (1917–20) and Taliesin West (1937) in the Arizona desert,[84] where he retreated with disciple-assistants to live out his own version of the American dream – 'the myth of the Pioneer' – his vision wholly at odds with the consumer culture that arose in the United States after World War II.[85]

7.13 Frank Lloyd Wright, The Robie House, Chicago

Let us not … overestimate the question of mechanization, standardization and normalization. And let us accept the changed economic and social conditions as fact … The decisive thing is which of these facts we choose to emphasize. This is where spiritual problems begin. What matters is not 'what' but only 'how'.

Mies van der Rohe,
The new era

Mies van der Rohe emigrated to the United States in 1937, four years after the Nazis closed the Bauhaus where he had been director since 1930. Before this he had directed the *Weissenhofseidlung* in Stuttgart (1927), where his housing, white and abstracted, played a prominent part in determining the character of the International Style. For the Barcelona Pavilion he adapted the Wright/De Stijl interest in a fluid arrangement of spaces. But already it shows the refinement of details in the steel and glass vocabulary that was to become his trademark. Invited to teach at the Illinois Institute of Technology, he was given the commission to design the campus plan and its new buildings where the central theme of his American work became established [7.14]. In place of the flow and asymmetry of the Barcelona Pavilion, his buildings became simple, cubical volumes articulated by an exposed metal frame.[86] Replacing his former spatially complex designs with box-like buildings meant that he could concentrate on refining the details – 'God is in the details', he is reputed to have said. The Farnsworth House (1946–50) illustrates Scully's observation that, ideally, 'Mies would have one cool, static pavilion for all functions … defined by a structural frame'.[87] For the Lakeshore Drive Apartments in Chicago (1950–1) he emulated Sullivan's achievement of stressing the vertical unity of the building, which he did by welding vertical steel I-beams to the window mullions [7.15].

7.14 Mies van der Rohe, Illinois Institute of Technology

Mies' influence on American architects of the next generation was enormous. But his own Schinkel-school background, stemming from his time working for Behrens, gave his work a classicising elegance that few could match. But Scully describes the negative aspect of his legacy; 'this classicising limitation of himself to a few simple shapes, to "almost nothing", was at first a virtue but it had certain dangerous restrictions in it, since it answered all problems by ignoring most'.[88] Mies' legacy can be seen everywhere in the faceless glass skyscrapers by lesser architects that dominate city financial centres. Less obviously, his legacy of the elegantly detailed box can be seen as one factor in the proliferation of high-tech 'sheds', where his elegant detailing is often replaced by rhetorical structure.

7.15 Lakeshore Drive Apartments, Chicago

The various 'isms' became synthesised at the Bauhaus, where the new art concepts had played a part in transforming craft methods of making objects of everyday use into industrial prototypes. But where such objects remained recognisable from their familiarity in everyday use, Modern Movement buildings became unrecognisable in relation to traditions of dwelling and built form. Modern art set out to shock and challenge an accepted reality, but it is questionable whether humans can inhabit a constantly changing world. Buildings came to look like rational containers of 'functions' or elegant 'packaging'. This led to a crisis of meaning, which played a part in the Modern Movement's ultimate failure. The legacy of that other great 'master', Le Corbusier, is much more complex. Not only was he a master of modernism, he was also a master of ambiguity, including his attitude to history and is therefore best considered separately.

Chapter 8: Le Corbusier: for or against history?

To celebrate the centenary of his birth, the Arts Council of Great Britain staged an exhibition entitled 'Le Corbusier, Architect of the century'. Few would dispute this claim. Not only was he a great architect but also a prolific polemicist whose writings had an unrivalled and world-wide influence from the Soviet Union to South America. An immense amount has been written about his work and little new can be added here. But much recent scholarship has focused on the changed character of his later buildings. In contrast to the earlier rationalist pronouncements in *Vers une architecture* (1923), for example, a distinctive poetic approach became manifest. The aim here is to explore the dramatic change that took place in his work around the time of World War II. This shows how a latent interest in history became deepened by Le Corbusier's growing intellectual and artistic involvement with ideas of time and mythical themes. This phase in his intellectual life is well conveyed in his less well-known book *Le Poème de l'Angle Droit* (1958). In the context of the narrative set down here, this makes a significant point in the turning away from the pure rationalism that drove the early Modern Movement. From here on in we will see how history and tradition emerged as both critique and inspiration.

PURISM AND THE ENGINEER'S AESTHETIC

The first of Le Corbusier's seminal sequence of white villas was his project for the Maison Citrohan (1920). Its white, cubical form with external stair to a roof terrace may have been inspired by the whitewashed villages of Greece that he witnessed on his *Voyages d'Orient*, his 1911 tour of the Balkans, Greece, Italy and Turkey. But underlying his choice of abstracted form was his youthful education under the neo-platonic guidance of Charles L'Éplattenier, whose early influence cannot be overemphasised.

During the period 1918 to 1925, Le Corbusier collaborated with the painter Amédée Ozenfant (1886–1966) to form an artistic movement they called 'Purism'. Launched in a joint exhibition at the end of 1918, this was followed by their book *Après le Cubisme*,[1] a critique of Cubism, which they considered broke up the integrity of objects for pictorial or visual effects.[2] Purist paintings, in contrast, depicted everyday objects – 'vases, glasses, bottles, plates' etc. – as flattened silhouettes overlapping one another on a perspective-less canvas.[3] Contours and colours were selected to 'reinforce the formal relations that unite the objects within a precise clear structure' to create a harmony appropriate to the significance they gave to these objects of everyday use.[4] Colin Rowe (1920–1999) compared this implied or 'phenomenal' transparency with Cubism and contrasted it with the literal transparency of a glass wall; Le Corbusier's Villa Stein is the former, the Bauhaus the latter.

In their essay 'Le Purisme' (1920), Le Corbusier and Ozenfant made an analogy between Darwinian natural selection and 'mechanical selection', which they argued made traditional objects of everyday use significant because they were 'extensions of human limbs'.

> Man and organised beings are products of *natural selection*. In every evolution on earth, the organs of beings are more and more adapted and purified, and the entire forward march of evolution is a function of purification … When examining these selected forms one finds a tendency toward certain identical aspects, corresponding to constant functions, functions which are of maximum efficiency, maximum strength, maximum capacity, etc., that is maximum economy. ECONOMY is the law of natural selection. It is easy to calculate that it is also the great law which governs what we will call 'mechanical selection'.[5]

From his earlier experience of working for Behrens and Perret, Le Corbusier was disposed to uphold the achievements of engineering in shaping a modern culture. But Purism and his neo-Platonism were equally important for the formal development of his white houses of the 1920s. In his *Vers une architecture*, for example, he significantly illustrated smooth, cylindrical American grain silos on the title page of a chapter called 'Three Reminders for Architects'.

I hoisted engineers up the flagpole. Towards an Architecture was dedicated to them.

Le Corbusier,
Precisions

TOWARDS A NEW ARCHITECTURE

Le Corbusier had access to state-of-the-art reinforced concrete design during his time working for the Perret brothers in 1908–9. From this

8.1 Le Corbusier, Maison La Roche, Paris, approach view

8.2 Ground floor plan

background knowledge he designed what he called the 'Dom-ino' system in 1915, which was to become the armature for the early houses. It's reinforced concrete-frame structure had columns set back so that walls could be built flush with the face of the floor slabs. This enabled the houses that followed to have the platonic pure form he desired.

The awkward configuration of the site for the Maison La Roche (1923) made it impossible for Le Corbusier to develop the ideal plan he perhaps had in mind for this early house; nevertheless it incorporated characteristically white and platonic forms. In planning the entrance Le Corbusier inverts a typical historical device for resolving an axis. In place of a concave form to receive and terminate a line of movement, there is the convex form of the picture gallery (on *pilotis*) which helps deflect movement to the entrance set to one side [8.1]. Entrance is into a triple-height space with a projecting first-floor balcony which marks a stage in an architectural promenade that is set up, and leads to the principal salon [8.2, 8.3 and 8.4]. In developing the complex entrance sequence to the Maison La Roche, Le Corbusier adapted the plan of the 'Roman House of the Tragic Poet' at Pompeii, which he sketched in his *'Voyage d'Orient'*[6] and illustrated in *Vers une architecture.*[7] In his essay 'A paradoxical avant-garde', Richard Etlin traced what might be borrowings and transformations of this kind in several villas of the 1920s.[8]

8.3 (Above) Entrance Hall
8.4 (Right) Salon

The Maison Plainex (1924–8) has been interpreted by William Curtis to show Le Corbusier's historical understanding of the differences between a Parisian townhouse – *hôtel particulier* – and a *pavilion* in a landscape.[9] The house presents a formal façade to the busy Avenue

Masséna with a central balcony projecting from the piano nobile [8.5]. A central atrium is derived from the precedent of the Roman atrium, says Curtis, perhaps the Casa del Noze in Pompeii which had impressed Le Corbusier. Despite these historical underpinnings, Le Corbusier remained intent on forging an aesthetic poised between abstraction and the machine, an aesthetic for the modern world. At the Maison Cook (1926) he brings this to a pitch of perfection with two floors lifted on *pilotis* and with full-width strip windows, the house topped by a canopied balcony on thin, fragile supports that evoke the Farman Goliath biplane illustrated no less than six times in *Vers une architecture*. Beneath the under-croft of the house is a lobby shaped like the nose of the Farman Goliath complete with pilot's windscreen and entered by a cabin door at the side. The Maison Cook exemplifies Le Corbusier's vision of 'a house as a machine for living in', an expression given prominence in *Vers une architecture*.

In this same year, 1926, Le Corbusier published his 'Five Points of a New Architecture'. These clearly aimed to emulate and replace Serlio's 'Five Orders of Classical Columns'. The 'Five Points' were: 1) *pilotis*, 2) roof-garden, 3) the free plan, 4) strip windows, and 5) the free façade. In combination with his 'Maison Dom-ino' structural frame, the 'Five Points' formed the template for this group of early villas.

In the chapter on 'Automobiles' in *Vers une architecture* Le Corbusier describes the Greek temple as 'a product of selection applied to an established standard', and on the following two pages photographs of the Parthenon are placed immediately above photographs of automobiles, including the Delage 'Grand Sport' of 1921, which demonstrated his belief in progress through 'mechanical selection'.[10] The Villa Savoye (1929–31) marks the climax of Le Corbusier's pursuit of the house as machine, although here overt references to machine forms are less apparent [8.6]. Instead the Villa is a platonic form, a pure white box raised above the crest of a hill on *pilotis* and appears as some unearthly machine poised for lift-off, an impression reinforced by the ship's bridge-like strip windows and the control tower-like forms above.[11] A sketch by Le Corbusier strikes a lyrical chord; the house as delicate machine landing upon an Arcadian nature across which a car traverses, the car

8.5 Maison Plainex, Paris

The house is not an object, a 'machine to live in', it is the universe that man constructs for himself by imitating the paradigmatic creation of the gods, the cosmogony.

Mercia Eliade,
The Sacred and the Profane

8.6 Villa Savoye, Poissy

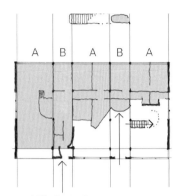

8.7 Villa Stein, Paris
ground-floor plan

8.8 Entrance portico
8.9 Front view

brought into harmony with nature by mechanical selection, an image inspired perhaps by Ledoux's House for the Rural Guards.

His most well-known use of history came in the Villa Stein (1928) at Garches, which Rowe's seminal essay 'The Mathematics of the Ideal Villa' (1947) shows to be informed by Palladio's Villa Malcontenta.[12] Rowe demonstrates that the structural grid of the Villa Stein corresponds almost exactly to that of Palladio's villa with its A:B:A:B:A rhythm of major and minor bays.[13] Le Corbusier differs from Palladio in having rectangular bays throughout whereas those of the Villa Malcontenta are mainly square [8.7]. This shifts the emphasis of the plan from the centre to one of layered frontality in the Villa Stein, an effect emphasised by the shallow cantilevered bays at the front. Le Corbusier seems to be taking delight in demonstrating his knowledge of classical tradition – stable neo-platonic geometry for a fragmented world – but, more significantly, showing how a modern conception of space – the free plan – transforms the experience of living. Where Palladio has, for example, his porticoed entrance on the central major bay, Le Corbusier sets up the axis of the driveway approach on the left-hand minor bay (the servants' entrance) and the entrance itself on the right-hand minor bay (beneath an aeroplane wing canopy) [8.8]. Facing the entrance door is a smaller version of the concave wall we saw at Maison La Roche which deflects movement sideways, up and across the first-floor plan through layers of space that have been compared with a compositional device in Le Corbusier's Purist paintings.

But the Villa Stein also presents itself as a most overt example of his conception of 'the house as a machine for living in'. The front façade appears almost literally as the rear pleasure deck of the ocean liner Aquitania, which is illustrated in *Vers une architecture*[14] [8.9]. (M. Stein made his fortune in building the tram system in San Francisco, so would have been familiar with pleasures of a sea voyage.) A carefully composed photograph in Le Corbusier's *Oeuvre Complète* shows the owner's car pulling in from Paris, as if suggesting that, thanks only to machines, the new captains of industry could retreat from the city and inhabit this appropriate fragment of ship's bridge, or pleasure deck, beached here in the midst of nature. So history is used, inverted and commented upon in this extraordinarily rich summation of his working method at this time. But a major change in his ideas and work began to take place shortly after this.

GOING TO GROUND

At about the time the Villa Savoye was nearing completion, a distinct shift is detectable in Le Corbusier's work. The fragile, white architectural machines of the 1920s became replaced by muscular, textured buildings. A first indication of this appears in his Cité de Refuge (1929–33) where sturdy, black-painted columns and exposed beams replace the former delicate *pilotis* and flat slabs. This change becomes more apparent in his Pavillon Suisse (1930–1) at the Cité Universitaire in Paris, where massive, muscular columns with a bone-shaped profile support the building [8.10].

8.10 Pavillion Suisse, Paris bone-shaped pilotis

Painting became of central importance to his creativity in architecture and a change in his subject matter at this time is further evidence of the shift from a mechanical to an organic conception of building. In place of *objet-types* his source material now became what he called *objets à réaction poétique*. His painting became preoccupied with bones, shells, pieces of wood and other natural material often set in a fragment of landscape amongst enigmatic images of ropes and other objects from a pre-industrial world.[15] Le Corbusier was by now a world-famous figure and a trip to South America in the autumn of 1929 seems pivotal in strengthening his feeling for nature.[16] He began to paint images of large, stocky women and these indicate an important aspect of his changing ideas. On the return voyage he developed an intimate relationship with the Afro-American dancer Josephine Baker.[17] These events, revealed by the change in his painting, mark a significant shift in his ideas where a half-hidden history became replaced by a burgeoning interest in the 'primitive' and the mythical underpinnings of time.

How his built work was about to change is indicated by his little book *Une Maison – un palais* published in 1929. On the cover is a curious juxtaposition of an axonometric of his design for the League of Nations building (1927) – a sophisticated layered composition of slab-blocks on *pilotis* – and a fisherman's hut built of the poorest natural materials. The central theme of the book was the significance of the 'primitive'; architecture had to satisfy more than simply material needs and express advanced technology, Le Corbusier seems to be saying it had to nourish deeper layers of the human psyche.[18]

His first building to show the effects of this was La Petite Maison de Weekend (1934–5). In stark contrast to the Villa Savoye floating above the ground, this tiny suburban retreat is semi-buried in the earth and covered with a turf roof. A vaulted concrete roof and earthy handmade bricks enclose the rooms which look out onto a garden where a pavilion in the form of a detached section of the structural frame sits like a reincarnation of Laugier's primitive hut.

The 1930s were a lean time for architects, and with very few commissions Le Corbusier busied himself with projects and travel. He made a lecture tour of the United States where he hit the headlines by declaring that American skyscrapers were too small and too close together![19] He proposed to remedy this with what he called 'Cartesian skyscrapers', immensely tall buildings on a Y-shaped plan surrounded by green open space, a local variant of his rationally organised earlier concept for a *Ville radieuse* (Radiant City, 1930), or his Plan Voisin for the Latin quarter of Paris (1922–5).

After World War II his buildings persisted with the rugged, muscular vocabulary seen emerging at the Pavilion Suisse and La Petite Maison de Weekend. The Maison Jaoul (1952–4) pursued the latter idiom but introduced the rough-cast concrete which became a feature of his post-war buildings and launched the style that became known as Brutalism[20] [8.11]. When he came to design the Unité d'Habitation (1946–52) in Marseilles it was not a tall, 'Cartesian' tower block, but a long, horizontal slab block in rough boarded concrete – 'man-made stone', he described it. Raised on massive columns and with the fragile and recognisable scaled elements – windows and doors – set back from the heavy balcony balustrade and *brise-soleil,* the building transcended the scale of more typical tall, steel-framed structures.

In his essay 'Battered Bunkers', John Farmer argued that Le Corbusier's rugged Brutalist vocabulary was partly a response to the destruction wrought by machines–particularly aircraft–in World War II; built form as a psychologically protective carapace informed by memories of actual military bunkers.[21] Suitably transformed by Le Corbusier from dark redoubts to magical spaces of light and shadow, the Unité presents what Scully describes as 'a new mid-twentieth century image of the embattled human presence in the world'.[22]

The intellectual life of post-war Paris was dominated by the Existentialism of Sartre and Camus, whose writings explored the meaning of human existence in a traumatised world. Le Corbusier would have been aware of these currents and also, perhaps, the anthropology of Levi Strauss, the phenomenology of Merleau-Ponty, and the comparative mythology of Eliade, all of whom were in Paris at this time. This gathering of research into meaning, the 'primitive', the sacred and myth clearly affected Le Corbusier's ideas at this time and are best broached through a discussion of his *Le Poème de l'Angle Droit* published in 1958.

8.11 Maison Jaoul, Paris

It is as if Le Corbusier's level of maturity was such that he alone, out of the modern pioneers, was able to work in such a way as to achieve multiple levels of meaning in any given building.

Kenneth Frampton

LE POÈME DE L'ANGLE DROIT

Le Corbusier described painting as his 'secret labour', a solitary, patient research of fundamental importance. Written between 1947 and 1953, 'The Poem of the Right Angle' combines line drawings, twenty colour lithographs and a handwritten prose poem. 'The experience of his life is in the thickness of this book', Le Corbusier announced in his *Oeuvre Complète.*[23] The contents of the book are organised thematically and Le Corbusier conceived the twenty lithographs, which summarise the themes, as an iconostasis, like icons set in tiers arranged in the form of the 'true cross' as used in the Greek Orthodox church. The central spine emphasises key elements of his creativity and personal life, with the horizontally arranged lithographs elaborating the source of his ideas at this time. Much recent scholarship has followed Daphne Beckett in exploring the meaning of the enigmatic imagery depicted by Le Corbusier, but the concentration here will be on interpreting the *Poème* in relation to how his evolved, mature ideas, which centre on notions of primordial time, move beyond history and into the deeper, mythical and human sub-conscious past, to inform his post-war buildings.[24] At the apex and base of the central spine of the iconostasis of images is a lithograph of the right angle, which reflects Le Corbusier's 'pact with nature'.[25]

A mark of the change in Le Corbusier's thinking is that the house is no longer considered a 'machine for living in'; rather, he says, that: 'To make architecture is to make a creature'.[26] His primary design intentions shift from the formal systems of the 'Five Points' to creating experiential moments in a building that evoke ideas about mankind's relationship to the cosmos. The 'elements of a vision', Le Corbusier wrote, had been triggered for him by 'a stump of dead wood and a pebble both picked up in a sunken Pyrenean lane'.[27] This marked a personal recognition of the 'sacred' in nature, a notion underlying all mythology and religion being expounded by Eliade at this time.[28] The opening page of the *Poème* has a drawing of what appears to be islands rising from water, a widespread mythical image of earth's creation from the primordial ocean. But, on a closer look, it is a self-portrait of Le Corbusier's body in a calm sea or a bath, his knees and feet protruding like islands from the water, a suggestive image of his own re-birth to the sacred.[29]

The upper layer of lithographs, which open the book, are on the theme of Environment (*Milieu*) where Le Corbusier introduces the sun as 'master of our lives'.[30] He remarks upon its 24-hour cycle, the 'immemorial' daily cycle, but emphasises the drama of 'night and day – these two phases rule our destiny'.[31] This section on Environment ends with Le Corbusier stating that 'Between poles reigns the tension ... of opposites' which become reconciled in a 'proposed union'.[32] The idea that all human cognition was organised by such polarities as light/dark, hard/soft, the raw and the cooked, was expounded by Levi-Strauss and taken up in the movement known as Structuralism, a popular intellectual current of post-war Paris and increasingly world-wide. Le Corbusier opens the book by saying that not only men and beasts affirm the reign of the sun but 'also ... the plants perhaps'. Lithograph 4 shows a simplified section of the Unité with the sun's mid-summer and winter trajectory inscribed upon it, and in the dark earth beneath a plant bulb is opening [8.12]. He seems to be describing the reciprocity between light and dark as fundamental to the creation of life-forms and an expression of the sacred. On the spine of the second layer of lithographs, just before the image of the Unité, is an approximation of the 'Five Points' diagram, to which has been added *brise-soleil*. In stark contrast to the strip window of his early houses, designed to cast maximum light onto floors, the *brise-soleil* was not only conceived as an environmental device to reduce solar gain, but also to cast shadows, to heighten the sense of light and dark that lay at the heart of his interpretation of the idea of the sacred.

The pilgrimage chapel of Notre Dame-du-Haut (1950–4) at Ronchamp can be read as an expression of this, which seems to me more fruitful than chasing after sources for its unique sculptural form. The site's long history beginning as a pagan sun temple appealed to Le Corbusier. Pilgrims approach the chapel sitting on top of a hill by a steep path, leaving the forested, shadowed world of the valley behind as they climb towards the light. As one approaches the chapel, the sky brightens as the horizon recedes below, the battered angle and concave form of the white-washed south wall reflects sunlight intensely upon the eyes [8.13].

Entering the chapel, instead of the conventional bright illumination from on high, the visitor is plunged into a world of semi-darkness [8.14]. A horizontal strip of light that separates roof from wall evokes the idea that this might be a subterranean space. Le Corbusier seems to be inverting the received Christian symbolism of spiritual light emanating from on high, in a similar way to how he inverted, experientially and phenomenologically, formal devices in his early houses, and here inviting people to re-think the origin of the sacred – how Christianity transmuted pagan sources – in the reciprocity of light and dark, an idea disseminated by Eliade at this time.[33]

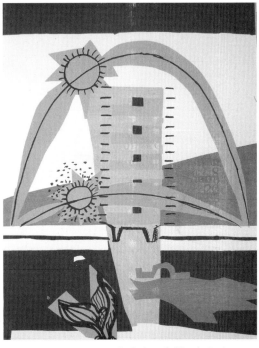

8.12 *Le Poème de l'Angle Droit*, B4 Environment. © FLC/ADAGP and DACS, London 2012

8.13 Notre Dame-du Haut, Ronchamp

8.14 Notre Dame-du-Haut, interior

For Le Corbusier the sacred is not some metaphysical abstraction or otherworldly realm, it stems from the material facts of primordial existence. The first layer of the *Poème* recounts the familiar water cycle – clouds, rain, river, sea, water vapour, clouds – which he had witnessed dramatically on a long flight over South America.[34] In the second layer he illustrates how a river meanders but then cuts through its banks to form a straight line, as 'life must force a passage, burst the dam of vicissitude'.[35] The river then runs on down and the 'level is fixed where the waters stop flowing to the sea'.[36] At the top centre of the section on Environment is an image of a man standing against a horizon and inscribed on the ground is a cross within a circle, an archetypal symbol of orientation, which corresponds to Le Corbusier's aim, as he explains in the *Poème*:

> The universe of our eyes rests
> Upon a plain edged with horizon
> Facing the sky
> Let us consider the inconceivable space …
> Erect on the terrestrial plain
> Of things knowable you
> Sign a pact of solidarity
> With nature: this is the right angle …[37]

The image Le Corbusier paints of his man erect against the sea is diametrically opposed to the meaning implied in Casper David Friedrich's well-known painting 'Monk against the Sea' (c. 1809). Where the monk turns to face a vast oncoming storm cloud as a metaphor for the overwhelming of his Christian faith, Le Corbusier paints his man facing the sun and signing 'a pact of solidarity with nature'. He intuitively grasped a conception of the poetic as an expression of humankind's original relationship to the cosmos as expounded by contemporary Existentialists. The lithographs are full of images of fertility and fecundity that have their source in natural processes. Alongside a depiction of his symbol of 'Offering' (the Open Hand) he writes:

> The waters flow
> The sun provides light[38]

In a more personal section dominated by erotic images, is what might appear to be a menhir – the first monumental art – against the sea, but it is, in fact, a self-portrait of his supine torso with an erect penis as he watches a large, naked woman on the shore.[39]

The closing lithograph is called 'Instrument' and shows a hand inscribing a cross within a flattened circle. Where his initial rendering of the right angle depicted man's existential condition, this version suggests the intellectual means by which the creative act of building can reconcile humans with their environment. Drawn with charcoal – material transformed by fire from a tree drawn forth from the dark earth by the sun – the image evokes Jung's conception of the mandala, an archetypal symbol of choice and orientation, a cross bounded by a never-ending circle, symbolic of the cyclical life of plants and the seasons. In this way, Le Corbusier re-established the existential dimension to geometry.

As a young man Le Corbusier had read and annotated *Thus Spoke Zarathustra,* where the description of an eagle soaring and circling the sun has been interpreted as one expression of Nietzsche's demand for a living culture founded upon the idea of the eternal return.[40] The *Poème* shows how far Le Corbusier had departed from his earlier mechanistic world-view to embrace a conception of architecture rooted in the primordial rhythms of the natural world, the world of Eliade's eternal return. Le Corbusier's recourse to this has been described as a synthesis of 'modernism's promise and a primitivism that embodies fundamental human values'.[41] His early buildings are object-like precise prisms, 'the magnificent play of masses … in light'.[42] His later work, in contrast, is created from a fundamentally mythical mindset, history beyond history, a world of light and dark, illumination and shadow. In this Le Corbusier gave a deeper meaning to how history and traditions can inform architecture and embody human values in a fast-changing, technology-dominated world.

> With Carbon
> we have
> traced the right angle
> the sign
> It is the answer and the guide…[43]

Chapter 9: Regional resistance to the International Style

ASPLUND, AALTO AND THE NORDIC RESPONSE

International modernism reached the Scandinavian countries in the 1920s and was given a major impetus by the Stockholm Exhibition in 1930. The preceding decades had seen an architecture of National Romanticism followed by an idiosyncratic Nordic Classicism, the combined legacy of which led to a subsequent questioning of the appropriateness of an International Style for Scandinavia. In this we witness a first challenge to the slogan 'form follows function', which, as Christian Norberg-Schulz (1926–2000) says, 'pretends to be universally applicable'.[1] Not only was it deemed applicable everywhere, transcending matters of place, but also history.

[The] social manifestation which the Stockholm Exhibition wants to be has been clad in an architectural language of pure and unconstrained joy ... Asplund's architecture explodes all boundaries.

Alvar Aalto

The chief architect of the Stockholm Exhibition was Erik Gunnar Asplund (1885–1940), who has been aptly described as 'the inspiring architectural personality in the Nordic countries'.[2] Shortly before the Exhibition, Asplund's Stockholm City Library (1921–7) had been completed and nothing could be more different from the light, modern vocabulary of the Exhibition buildings than this monumental expression of Nordic Classicism.

A critical review of the newly completed library stated that 'New classicism is dead', replaced by a functionalism that represented a 'fundamental difference in mentality'.[3] In preparing for the Exhibition, Asplund took note of this and toured Europe, where he visited the Stuttgart *Weissenhofsiedlung* and met Giedion, Hoffman and Pierre Jeanneret (Le Corbusier's engineer cousin in the architect's absence).[4] The Stockholm Exhibition showed a sure grasp of the International Style, but Asplund introduced a festive lightness that was entirely new. Wood and steel columns braced with wires supported laminated timber trusses, and an array of flags, canopies and neon signs added a playful air, aided by a Constructivist-inspired advertising mast. Quite different from the park-like setting of the Weissenhofsiedlung, or *Neue Sachlichkeit* rational planning, here the buildings were grouped to make a more traditional pattern of streets.

In contrast to the architecture of the Exhibition, the City Library is dominated by a tall cylindrical volume containing the book collection, which shows the influence of Ledoux's *Barriere de la Villette* [9.1].

But Asplund's only overt historical reference is an Egyptian door surround to the gigantic entrance, a reference to Thorswalden's Museum (1839–48) in Copenhagen, a building devoted to the acclaimed Scandinavian Neoclassical sculptor. The Library's sense of heavy, massive form is reinforced by the Nordic Classicism practice of applying a thin layer of stucco over roughly laid brickwork or stone such that the texture can be seen through, as indeed can also the colour when the finish was a thin colourwash.[5] This desire for an intense materiality sprang from the teachings of P.V. Jensen-Klimt who, at the beginning of the twentieth century, argued for 'a regional sense of style and awareness of materials', which led him to point, not to Laugier's primitive hut as the origin of Scandinavian architecture, but to dolmens, the massive exposed stones of prehistoric burial mounds.[6]

9.1 Erik Gunnar Asplund, City Library, Stockholm

Asplund's earlier Lister County Courthouse (1917–21), Solvesborg also shows the influence of Ledoux with its exaggeratedly wide gable front suggesting a vernacular origin, but one overlaid with classical motifs – swags and suggestions of broken pediment [9.2]. There is a hint of *architecture parlante* in the semi-circular arched entrance that opens like a devouring mouth to the accused brought to the courthouse. A bell and large clock on the gable draws attention to time, time that would be taken away from the guilty.

A deep interest in a narrative architecture responding to regional traditions was shown at the very beginning of Asplund's career when he combined with Sigurd Lewerentz (1885–1975) to win the competition for the South Stockholm Cemetery in 1915. A rapid rise in the city's population created the need for more cemetery space for which seventy-five hectares of forest were acquired. In contrast to the other fifty-two entrants, Lewerentz and Asplund eschewed the formal landscape planning more typical of the period and arranged graves informally beside narrow paths wandering through the undisturbed forest.[7] This imagery and a prominently displayed tall wooden cross in the pine forest – 'The Way of the Cross' – evoke archetypical Nordic

9.2 Lister County Courthouse, Solvesborg

In the ritual of burial we silently bear witness to a deep-seated belief that in every present moment there is always the possibility to remember the past and to imagine a future.

Robert Romanyshyn,
Technology as Symptom and Dream

landscape symbolism, not unlike that depicted in the paintings of Casper David Friedrich, or more recently Ingmar Bergman's film 'The Seventh Seal'. 'The deep respect that Swedish people feel for death' has been remarked upon,[8] and the configuration and symbolism of the Woodland Cemetery tapped into a profound aspect of this at a time when industrialisation had brought people from the country to the city. But in death they were returned home to the primordial forest landscape.

9.3 The Woodland Chapel, Stockholm

This diffuse symbolism is concentrated in the image of Asplund's Woodland Chapel (1918–20). Subservient to the woodland setting in which it sits, the chapel appears as a pyramid floating above the ground on slender, white-painted Tuscan columns [9.3]. But the pyramidal roof is covered with timber shingles, and the building resembles a small vernacular wayside chapel often seen in Scandinavia. In the Woodland Chapel, as in the Cemetery as a whole, we see Asplund combining Romanticism and Classicism with an archetypal sense of the origins and deepest meaning of death as well as intensifying a regional tradition of building.

This deep-seated interest in such themes led Asplund to renounce the straightforward application of the International Style. In a lecture titled 'Our Architectonic Concept of Space' (1931) delivered the year following the Stockholm Exhibition, he declares a significant influence that helps to explain both his change from Nordic Classicism to functionalism and why he tracked back to explore an idiom more appropriate to Nordic traditions.

He begins by referring to 'the views of a philosopher of my subject; Oswald Spengler.'[9] Spengler's book *Der Untergang des Abendlandes* (The Decline of the West) described the disintegration of Western civilisation and was an immense public success, capturing the widespread pessimism at the end of World War I. Like Vico, and in opposition to Hegel, Spengler wrote of a succession of cultures each of which, 'like nature, has flowered, withered and died'.[10] Spengler attributed to each culture what he called a 'prime symbol' that became manifest in what Asplund translated as a 'space concept'.[11] Spengler traced a historical development of spatial conceptions from

Chinese and Egyptian to the modern 'Western infinitely wide and infinitely profound three-dimensional space'.[12]

At the time of designing the Stockholm Exhibition, Asplund took a positive message from Spengler, seeing 'in the dissolution of architectonic space', such as the flowing inside-outside space of Mies van der Rohe's Barcelona Pavilion, a new space concept expressive of the modern world. Asplund saw 'the new concept of space in polemical opposition to an older tradition', he said. 'I have also used the term 'dissolution' of space – it sounds almost like decay. But it is not a de-generation, it is a regeneration of architecture'.[13] But it was the decline of Western civilisation that Spengler described, of which he believed no foreseeable salvation to be at hand.[14] He foresaw the West's 'inevitable *destiny* ... [as] ... death following life ... an end, irrevocable'.[15] To emphasise his point, he compared modern Western civilisation with the Romans who, he said, had '*closed* a great [Classical] development'.[16]

In the preface to a revised edition Spengler wrote: 'Those to whom I owe practically everything: Goethe and Nietzsche'.[7] He labelled Western culture as 'Faustian', seeing in the character faults of Goethe's Faust analogies with a declining Western civilisation; 'A restless groping for power', over-reaching egoism, and in Faust's 'compact with Mephistopheles', an all-too-ready willingness to sell his soul to the devil for 'unprogressive satisfactions'.[18] Spengler contrasted 'Faustian' with 'Apollonian'. By replacing Dionysus with Faust, he indicates that he did not share Nietzsche's hopes for rejuvenation. Spengler disparaged the idea of 'linear progress', which he portrayed as the chauvinism of Western civilisation and which, like Nietzsche, he saw as stemming from Hegel's view of history. Spengler described this linear view of history 'as a sort of tape-worm insidiously adding to itself one epoch after another'.[19]

It may be that Asplund later came to grasp Spengler's pessimistic reading of civilisation with its ambitions for world-wide industrialised hegemony. For a closer reading of *The Decline of the West* would have suggested to Asplund how an overbearing, homogenous global culture might be deflected.

> I see in the place of that empty figment of *one* linear history ... the drama of a *number* of mighty Cultures each springing with primitive

strength from the soil of a mother-region to which it remains firmly bound throughout its whole life-cycle, each stamping its material, its mankind, in *its own* image.[20]

Spengler here identifies a way to avert terminal decline. He probably drew this from Herder who earlier had 'insisted upon and celebrated the uniqueness of national cultures' and 'passionately believed that every culture has its own irreplaceable contribution to make to the progress of the human race'.[21] Having designed the Bredenburg Store (1933–5) in the International Style, Asplund's later designs explore an idiom that reconnects buildings with aspects of his national culture [9.4]. The Gothenburg Law Courts Annexe and the Woodland Crematorium are good examples. In a lecture, 'Art and Technology', delivered in 1936, he announced that he was 'virtually withdrawing to the intangible realms of art'.[22]

9.4 Bredenburg Store, Stockholm

Asplund won a competition for extending the existing Law Courts building in 1913 and reworked his initial Romantic Classicism design many times before construction began in 1936.[23] His final design attempts to meld modernism with classicism [9.5]. An expressed steel frame structure echoes the pilastered façade of the nineteenth century Neoclassical law courts. Traditional vertically proportioned windows, asymmetrically located and idiosyncratically detailed in Asplund's later manner, are used rather than International Style strip windows.

9.5 Law Courts extension, Gothenburg

But it is in the interior of the annexe where Asplund shows how a modernist architectural vocabulary could be recast to evoke a more particular, regional feeling [9.6]. Arranged around a top-lit atrium, a fully glazed wall opens to the courtyard of the existing law courts. The curved walls of two plywood panelled courtrooms thrusting into the atrium contribute most to an organic feel of the space. Details such as curved balconies, the semi-circular opening and the half-landing to the free-standing stair rising from the principal first floor, its kidney-shaped first tread, and the bone-like profile of fire-proofing to the steel columns all add to the softer, organic

9.6 Law Courts extension, main hall

feel. In exploring Spengler's role in the transformation of Asplund's work from Nordic Classicism to this unnamed, regionally orientated modernism, Stuart Knight ventures that: 'Asplund seeks to locate "functional theory" not within the context of a machine aesthetic, but within one sanctioned "organically" by history.'[24]

The crematorium for the Woodland Cemetery (1935–40) was the last project that Asplund saw through to completion. Strategic decisions were made with Lewerentz in a joint plan of 1932, but the executed project was Asplund's alone. As in the earlier Woodland Chapel, building is subordinate to landscape. A long, low wall holds back the forest-edge, locating and partially screening the buildings, at the same time as directing movement to the crest of the hill on which sits the loggia to the principal chapel [9.7]. Silhouetted against the sky like an abstracted classical temple, the loggia is read as the sole built element, along with a tall wooden cross and 'meditation knoll' suggestive of a burial mound, a melding of biblical and archetypal Nordic landscape.

9.7 Woodland Cemetery, Stockholm

Two small chapels, entered via a courtyard, are partly hidden by the long wall. The main chapel is set back asymmetrically behind the great loggia, the combination of the two forms marking the symbolic heart of the project. A temple-like form seen from a distance becomes in fact a light, open shelter for the gathered mourners. The subtly tapered stone-clad columns have no classical trimmings and the wide inter-columnation reads as modern whilst retaining a vestige of the sacred aura associated with Greek temples. But where there would be a closed box-like *cella* in the classical temple, Asplund opens up the loggia to the sky at its centre where a striking Resurrection monument reaches up to the light [9.8].

9.8 Woodland Cemetery, loggia to chapel

The chapel also mixes a vestigial classicism with Christian and more archaic or primordial forms. The basilica-type nave is flanked with primitive Tuscan columns that support a shallow vaulted roof, the curves of which are taken up in the apse. Curved both in plan and section, the space of the chapel becomes suggestive of a cave or womb. The furniture and detailing in these chapels is considered to be Asplund's finest and a major contribution to the emergence of Scandinavian modern design. Asplund's organic detailing combined with fluid modernist space became taken up by Alvar Aalto (1898–1976) and paralleled, to some extent, the work of Hugo Häring (1882–1958) and Hans Scharoun (1893–1972) in Germany.[25] In his obituary notice, Aalto wrote that Asplund's 'immediate feel for nature' underpinned all his 'various stylistic periods', and that 'rootless technocratic constructivism' was 'alien to his spirit'.[26]

Closely involved with Asplund, and party to discussions on the Stockholm Exhibition, Aalto followed his mentor in coming to reject international modernism as appropriate for Scandinavian culture and climate. Aalto became a lifelong friend and continued Asplund's development of a modern architecture that responded to regional traditions. His earliest work was in the Romantic Classicism idiom followed by his sole experiment with the International Style at the Paimio sanatorium, designed in 1928 when he was only thirty. Aalto was perhaps doubly fortunate in inheriting the rich tradition of Nordic Romanticism whilst being able to react against 'zero degree functionalism'. Aalto turned for inspiration to the indigenous buildings of the thickly forested region of his native Finland, called Karelia. These were works of the 'people', he argued, that paralleled the Finnish founding myths collected in the Kalevala.[27] He suggested that there were 'laws that organically link tradition and impulses from the past with contemporary creative work'.[28] Karelian architecture had, he continued, 'special value as a tool for analysing ways in which human life can be harmoniously reconciled with nature.'[29]

The key to this all-important aim, according to Aalto, would be 'to extend our definition of rationalism'.[30] This could only be achieved, he considered, by shifting the focus from the sciences shaping technology to the relatively new human sciences, in particular psychology. His Villa Mairea (1937–8) illustrates this and can also be read as an explicit critique of Le Corbusier's Villa Stein. Where Le Corbusier announces entry to the Villa Stein with a canopy that looks like an aeroplane wing – the house as machine – Aalto designed a porch supported on un-sawn timber poles tied together with rope and resting on boulders, an entrance that links the house with the forest in which it sits [9.9]. Immediately on entering, a balustrade with an irregular rhythm of full-height balusters evokes the random pattern of birch trees in the surrounding forest. Although white like the Villa Stein, the Villa Mairea has wood box-framed windows that orientate bedrooms to the rising sun in contrast to Le Corbusier's strip-windows

The tubular steel chair is surely rational from technical and constructive points of view; it is light, suitable for mass production, and so on. But steel and chromium are not satisfactory from the human point of view. Steel is too good a conductor of heat. The chromium surface gives too bright reflections, and even acoustically it is not suitable for a room.

Alvar Aalto,
The Humanising of Architecture

9.9 Aalto, Villa Mairea, Noormarkku, entrance porch

[9.10]. These details and more, draw attention to correspondences between the architecture and the specific nature of Finland.

Aalto became increasingly concerned at the overwhelmingly large buildings generated by twentieth century institutions. Once again he found the answer in the Karelian village with its informal grouping

9.10 Villa Mairea

of buildings around a courtyard. He compared this to a 'biological cluster of cells'.[31] He applied this lesson to many of his larger buildings, of which the Säynätsalo Town Hall (1949–52) is a good example. The various parts of the building are grouped around a raised courtyard approached by two stairs, one with turf treads [9.11]. Raising the courtyard allows the enclosing buildings to be single storey, an unexpected small scale for such an institution [9.12]. Thin timber poles

over window mullions take up the rhythm of the surrounding trees. In his competition report, Aalto wrote that he used the courtyard form because of its associations with parliaments through history 'from Crete … to the Renaissance'.[32] In addition to the regional traditions on which he sought to ground his architecture, he had particular regard for history: 'I am inclined to believe that history offers a kind of statistics on how human beings react to their surroundings.'[33] Aalto points here to how tradition is related to but subtly differs from history.

9.11 (Left) Säynätsalo Town Hall
9.12 (Above) Säynätsalo Town Hall, courtyard looking towards entrance and council chamber

Tradition demonstrated how building had responded to regional conditions to provide physical and psychological protection. Up until the Modern Movement, historical styles of architecture had been adapted to local circumstances, as in Nordic Classicism. But the focus on style that shaped the International Style proved incapable of dealing with Scandinavian needs. It is perhaps not surprising that the harsh climate of Nordic countries would be the first to reveal this more general shortcoming. Nevertheless, as Aalto said, the history of architecture did provide him with a wealth of material to work from.

TERRAGNI AND ITALIAN RATIONALISTS

In a similar way to Asplund's and Aalto's acknowledgement of regional traditions, Giuseppe Terragni (1904–43) insisted upon an Italian character for modern architecture, although his earliest designs belie this. His project for an Officina per la Produzione del Gaz (1927), for example, shows overt influence from Russian Constructivism, as does his first building, the Novocomum Apartments (1927) in Como [9.13]. A glazed cylinder capped by an over-sailing top storey at the corners of the building is clearly derived from Golosov's Zuyer Club in Moscow. Strip windows on the top floors, continuous balconies, and horizontally proportioned windows show a more general influence from international modernism. At a distance the building appears to be in the white-painted stucco favoured by the International Style, but on closer inspection it is white terrazzo, an early indication of Terragni's interest in materials and craftsmanship.[34] The *Novocomum* Apartment building caused great controversy not only because of its new style, but also because the elevation drawing submitted for approval depicted a full range of classical elements.[35]

9.13 Terragni, Novocomum apartment building, Como

Critics pointed to the foreign influences on the completed building, but this was not Terragni's aim. For upon graduating from Milan Politecnic in 1926, he and six others formed the *Gruppo 7* and wrote a series of articles (that became known as the *Gruppo Sette* Manifesto) in which they 'announced the Italian character of their architecture'.[36] They had grasped the international dimension of the new movement for they referred to 'Behrens, Mies van der Rohe, Mendelsohn, Gropius, Le Corbusier'.[37] But they also insisted upon 'a distinct nationalistic character' discernible in the countries where modernism was pioneered – 'Germany and Austria', 'Holland', 'the Nordic countries'.[38] A measure of chauvinism creeps in as they discuss how the movement might develop. 'Italy, because of its nature, tradition, and most of all because of its victorious period it is passing through, is the most worthy of the mission of renewal.'[39] (The 'victorious period' alluded to the *Risorgimento* and also Mussolini's Fascist movement, in its ascendancy at this time). 'It remains for Italy to give maximum development to the new spirit, to carry it to its logical conclusion, until it dictates a *style* to other nations, as it has in the great periods of the past.'[40]

The group criticised Futurists for their 'systematic destruction of the past'.[41] They were equally damning 'of taking inspiration for architecture from the machine', or copying 'the aesthetics of the airplane'.[42] After a comprehensive demolition of these pioneers and their total disregard for history, the young Italians aligned their movement's architectural aims firmly with their native traditions.

> Here, in particular, there exists a classical foundation. The spirit (not the forms, which is something different) of tradition is so profound in Italy that evidently, and almost mechanically, the new architecture will preserve the stamp which is typically *ours*. And this is already a great force, since tradition, as we said, does not disappear, but changes appearance.[43]

Terragni's group became known as the Rationalist movement following the *Espozione dell'architettura razionale* of 1928. For as well as national, the new Italian architecture was also to be rational; the 'new architecture, the true architecture, must result from a rigid adherence to logic, to rationality'.[44] The logic that engendered technology was to be celebrated, not the machine itself. The emphasis on rationality suggested that a rigorous aesthetic would be their way to adapt the modernist grammar of architectural forms to Italy's classical history. The canonical building of Italian rationalism is Terragni's Casa del Fascio (1932–6), where his particular conception of rational architecture became most clearly made manifest.

A word should be said for Italian fascism before we discuss the building. At this early stage it was largely an emancipatory, populist movement for workers and the 'people'. It all too quickly descended, however, into imperial ambition and dictatorship. Along with many intelligent, creative men, Terragni was drawn into its heady brew and his Casa del Fascio celebrated its achievements. It has been argued that his early death may have been suicide and that he regretted, but too late, that his own grasp of fascism was a misunderstanding of its ultimate aims.[45]

9.14 Casa del Fascio, Como

Mussolini had written that 'Fascism must be a glass house into which everyone can see.'[46] Terragni acknowledged this and the Casa del Fascio can be seen as a translation of a traditional courtyard house, or palazzo, into a modernist, transparent architectural idiom. The form and composition of the building is determined by rigorous geometry and a proportional system, which Terragni argued made the process of his work essentially the same as his Renaissance predecessors, hence reflecting both regional and historical traditions [9.14]. Its extremely complex composition has been much studied and it would divert us from the task here to analyse it in detail. Sufficient to say that Terragni manipulates an interplay between symmetry – the central three bays of the top floor – and asymmetry – the blank two bays on the right of the front façade – and in plan between the axiality of the central hall and a rotational, layered cross-circulation.

9.15 Casa del Fascio, corner detail

An exposed structural frame shows Terragni stating his opposition to Le Corbusier's machine aesthetic, for the grid of the frame can be read as a modern translation of pilasters and string courses. As Bruno Zevi writes, 'the main volume is not on "pilotis" and the facades are not free from the structural framework, in fact they are involved with it, so as to achieve a layered depth' [9.15]. 'The pulling back of the entrance and breaking up of the top make certain that the building attains a transparency.'[47] The open structural framework on the top floor 'captures' what Terragni described as the 'spectacular setting with the steep slope of the [Brunate] mountain' behind and showing through.[48]

Thomas Schumacher has pointed out how the circulation along one edge of the hall reflects traditional Como courtyard houses where the entrance is to one side.[49] He also suggests that the long, through hall of the Casa del Fascio resembles the Venetian palace type.[50] He argues further that the façades of these, with their open loggias – from the 'Byzantine to the baroque' – show how the inside–outside relationship central to Terragni's concerns has a historic precedent.[51]

Notwithstanding this, Terragni wrote that a 'casa for the masses is not, and cannot be, public housing in the way we typically understand this type of construction'.[52] Rather, he continued, 'it had to become a House, a School, a Temple'.[53] The Casa del Fascio had to represent the aims of the movement and this is most clearly seen in the main hall, which Terragni described as 'the spiritual and ceremonial centre of the entire building'.[54] With its highly polished marble floor, glass block side wall and ceiling, double-height glazed front wall, and reflective details such as the glass balustrade to the stairs, all combined with the clarity of the expressed structure, the hall does evoke the impression of a 'glass house' into which everyone can see' [9.16]. A notable innovation was the sixteen linked glass front doors opened 'by simply pushing a button', which Terragni designed to facilitate a mass exodus for the 'flanked rows of Fascists' onto the streets after listening to the exhortations of the leader.[55]

9.16 Casa del Fascio, Main Hall

Terragni and the Rationalists eventually lost their battle to convince Mussolini that their architecture represented the Fascist movement, which adopted instead a stripped-down Neoclassicism with a more overt appeal to Roman grandeur championed by Piacentini (1881–1960) and others [9.17]. Bruno Zevi summarised the Casa del Fascio in such a way as to exonerate Terragni and, as the building is now a Casa del Popolo, his reading does indicate how a Modern Movement vocabulary, given underlying references to history, tradition and other ideas, can provide a framework for a liberal, humane architecture.

9.17 Guerini, La Padula and Romano, EUR, Rome

> The rationalist framework is being continuously animated through inventive outbursts ... The intransigent aspiration towards perfection has a political connotation, it is the antithesis of a fascist reality. It personifies a desperate rejection which stems from within the corrupt system.[56]

9.18 Terragni, Casa Giuliana, Como

Peter Eisenman, amongst others, has exhaustively analysed Terragni's buildings – in particular the Casa Giuliana (1939–40) in terms of the formal manipulations he used in the design: layering, rotation, excavation, subtraction, addition, etc. [9.18].[57] Eisenman focused solely on the process, however, and exploited this to generate designs of his own that are purely self-referential and abstract. Nothing could be further from Terragni's aim. For as his assistant Zuccoli stated: 'Architecture is never merely a composition of elements in certain relationships.'[58] For Terragni geometry, proportion and number carried meaning and connected him to regional-historical traditions of architectural practice. Geometry and number were neither purely abstract nor instrumental. His un-built project for the Danteum shows this most clearly.

The spiritual reference ... of the Poem must be expressed in unmistakable signs by an atmosphere that influences the visitor and appears to weigh upon his mortal person so that he is moved to experience the 'trip' as Dante did.

Terragni,
Relazione Sul Danteum

A tripartite Temple of rooms disposed at different levels establishes an ascending route. Constructed in different ways, these rooms are integrated to gradually prepare the visitor for a sublimation of matter and light.

Terragni,
Relazione Sul Danteum

The Danteum (1938) was conceived as a building to house all editions of Dante's works and commentaries within a series of rooms that evokes the poet's mystical journey. In his *Divine Comedy*, he described a fall from grace followed by ascent to paradise, what Terragni called 'the extra-terrestrial trip' described in the poem.[59] In the *Relazione Sul Danteum* (1938) that he wrote to explain the project, Terragni states the necessity for an 'absolute geometric beauty' to pervade the design as in 'the exemplary architectures of the great historical epochs'.[60] He insists upon the golden section rectangle as the only appropriate geometry for the Danteum because it 'expresses the harmonic law of unity in trinity'; i.e. the short side is to the long side as the long side is to the sum of the two sides.[61] This is no arbitrary choice. Terragni explains how Dante's *Divine Comedy* is structured by 'certain symbolic numbers – 1, 3, 7, 10 and their combination – which happily can be synthesised into *one* and *three* (unity and trinity).'[62] The golden section generated the Danteum plan, as it had the adjacent Roman Basilica of Maxentius, hence providing a historical precedent, and early cinema screens provided a modern equivalent. Subsidiary aspects of the design, said Terragni, were 'spiritually chained to Dantesque compositional criteria.'[63] The building if realised would have appeared as a massive, stone-walled enclosure entered single file through a narrow passage to induce an aura of pilgrimage. An architectural promenade is then set up, which, through the character of spaces, their 'feel' or 'mood', makes analogies with Dante's mystical journey.

A courtyard represents the *atrium* of the traditional Latin house where Dante lived before the redemptive journey described in his poem.[64] Beyond is a 'forest' of 100 marble columns which symbolises the forest where, Dante says, 'I found myself in a dark wood for the straight way was lost'.[65] Three sets of three steps descend to the 'Inferno', an oppressive, columned hall whose floor steps down and corresponding cracks in the ceiling symbolise the fractured earth's crust where Lucifer fell into Hell.[66] Another three sets of three steps ascend from this space to Purgatory, a counter-pointed space of stepping ascent with large, rectangular openings in the ceiling.[67] Dante's Purgatory is a place of penitence with some 'sweetness', from which a glimpse of Paradise is seen. A space of 33 glass columns – representing the transparent angels of Dante's vision – supporting an open grid, is gained by another flight of three sets of three steps. Schumacher summarises the character of the architectural sequence as a 'progression from *dense to framed to open* – Inferno, Purgatory, Paradise – following a scheme of ascent toward the most holy and sacred [that] leads the visitor finally to the room dedicated to the new Roman Empire'.[68] Terragni calls this the *Imperio* and, as Schumacher says, it continues his infatuation with Fascist aims. But it also symbolises Dante's concept of a Holy Empire, the column-lined longitudinal space suggestive of an Early Christian basilican church. The Danteum acts as final confirmation of Terragni's belief in the meaning inherent in the geometrical practice of architects from his own historical culture, as well as drawing upon the archetypal significance of sacred mythology, and given new life by the character of the spatial narrative.

THE OTHER TRADITION

The doctrinaire pioneer modernism of CIAM and the International Style promoted by 'operative' historians as the only legitimate twentieth century architecture became challenged more recently by what Colin St John Wilson (1922–2007) called *The Other Tradition of Modern Architecture* (1995). The first chapter of his book is entitled 'The Battle of La Sarraz' where, Wilson writes, the first CIAM gathering 'was dominated by Le Corbusier'.[69] An important aim of the gathering was to 'affirm a unity of viewpoint on the fundamental conceptions of architecture', which were framed in purely technological/economic terms, as we have seen.[70] However, the formalism implicit in Le Corbusier's 'Five Points' and the prescriptions of the International Style were not accepted by some architects close to the movement's centre, who, although acting independently, Wilson groups together as the 'Other Tradition'. Written long after the event, the book describes how dissenting voices became excluded and, in what is essentially a critical and revisionist history of the modern movement, he argues that a more humane modern architecture emerged from amongst the architects who became marginalised.

Hugo Häring is the central figure in this challenge to what he calls a 'Cartesian', 'mechanistic' hegemony. In opposition to Le Corbusier's white abstraction and 'machine like imagery', Häring opposed a concept of 'the new building' whose ancestry he claimed to lie in a 'tradition, older by far, of building organically'.[71] The flowing forms of Häring's farm at Gut Garkau (1922–6) is Wilson's exemplary illustration of this 'Other Tradition', which he contrasts with Le Corbusier's box-like Radiant Farm (1938). To these he adds Scharoun's Moll House (1936) in Berlin and the later Berlin Philharmonie (1956–63). Amongst other architects he includes Loos, Asplund, Lewerenz, Aalto, Rudolf Schindler, Johannes Duiker, Taut, Mendelsohn and perhaps surprisingly, Eileen Gray (1878–1976), surprising only because she is the first woman we encounter in this history of architecture.[72]

> It still seems to many people inconceivable that a house too may be evolved entirely as an 'organic structure', that it may be 'bred' out of the 'form arising out of work performance', in other words that the house may be looked upon as a 'man's second skin' … The work of the engineer has as its goal merely the performance of material work within the limits or in the domain of economic effects …
> The architect, on the other hand, creates a Gestalt, a total form, a work of spiritual vitality and fulfilment, an object that belongs to and serves an idea, a higher culture.
>
> Hugo Häring,
> *The house as an organic structure*

Although Wilson acknowledges Le Corbusier's inventiveness and mastery – 'this brilliant but wrong-headed man' – he identifies him as the leading figure in a 'Dictatorship'. He describes and illustrates Le Corbusier's 'cruel caricature' of Häring whom he depicted, punning on his name, as a herring with a priest's hat, a halo and an umbrella in full flight after his expulsion from CIAM.[73] Häring's 'crime' was to oppose the Modern Movement's a priori rationalism and machine analogies with an approach to design which Wilson describes as 'based upon the fulfilment of purpose rather than … a preordained language grounded in geometry'.[74] In a lecture delivered in 1925, Häring himself stated that, 'we want to examine things and allow them to discover their own forms. It goes against the grain to bestow a form upon them from the outside.'[75] Wilson sums up Häring's approach – which defines the 'Practical Art' that he opposed to the ideologically driven International Style – as follows: 'Instead of rationalism he sought an understanding of life's complexity; instead of order, participation.'[76] It seems clear that Häring's commitment to what he called 'the new building was informed by calls for the 'art of building' to replace 'style architecture', which arose early in the twentieth century.[77]

The last section of the book is a series of case studies where Wilson contrasts a building by an architect of the 'Other Tradition' with one associated with mainstream modernism. The most telling is his comparison between Aalto's North Jutland Art Museum (1958–72) in Aalborg and Mies van der Rohe's National Gallery (1962–8) in Berlin [9.19 and 9.20].

He chose art galleries for it is a building type where the purpose to be fulfilled is clear: 'the display of works of art [requiring] the control of light sources'.[78] He contrasts Aalto's meticulous attention to qualities of daylight through a studied use of the section and a variety of rooms with Mies' flat-ceiling National Gallery in Berlin with its fully glazed walls, the glare from which makes it difficult to view paintings [9.21].

9.19 Mies van der Rohe, National Gallery, Berlin

The intellectual crux of his argument comes in a historical review of how the term 'function' – central to the functionalism of the Modern Movement – had become distorted by the Positivism of the nineteenth century. He cites Hannes Meyer (who stated that 'architecture = function × economics') as saying that he taught his students 'to come to grips with the only reality that can be mastered – that of the measurable, the visible, the weighable'.[79] Wilson counters this narrow definition of function by showing how differently it was defined in classical thought. The break with the classical conception of function came with the rise of aesthetics in the eighteenth century when Kant defined art as 'purposefulness without purpose' and architecture became identified as a 'Fine Art'. In separating architecture, as an art, from building, eighteenth century aesthetics contributed to a narrowed meaning of function. Only from this position could Meyer assert that building has 'nothing to do with art at all'.[80] Wilson counters this by referring to Aristotle's distinction between two kinds of art: 'Fine Art' – 'whose end is to serve only itself' – and 'Practical Art' – 'that serves an end other than itself'.[81] As Aristotle says, the end or aim of a 'Practical Art', is that 'the virtue of a thing is related to its proper function'.[82]

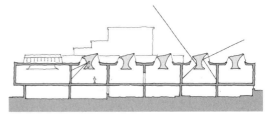

9.20 Aalto, North Jutland Art Museum, Aalborg
9.21 Section

Wilson goes on to explain that this required 'a clear apprehension of the ultimate end, or *causa finalis*, that the work is to serve'.[83] This was bound up with the Greek concept of *telos* (which we encountered in Hegel's historicism) that saw 'a unique purposefulness inherent in all created things and that it is the flowering and fulfilment of its potential powers that is the moving force in nature and in all human enterprise'.[84] From this more subtle definition of 'purpose' – 'the proper end to be served in a particular context of desires and necessities'[85] – the form of things would be derived through 'the art of making (*poiesis*)', which for building 'took the form of *tektonik*'.[86] How different from Meyer's purely 'measurable' was this classical definition of purpose or function! Wilson concludes that this broader definition of architectural design required:

> a strict linear sequence that proceeds from the discovery of what is desirable to the invention of an appropriate form, and thence to the elaboration of the technical means to make it possible. Pursuing that living sequence it can bring a form of life to its full identity for the first time, vivid and memorable.[87]

That is, architectural design should be a rounded understanding of a building's usefulness, its purpose and how it is made, not a forecast of future forms. Wilson is more Semper than Hegel. He sees the division between architecture and building as being consolidated with the rise of the *Beaux-Arts* schools – which taught and disseminated architecture – and the *Ecole Polytechniques*, where traditions of building architecture became influenced by the science of engineering, a process we saw beginning with Durand.[88]

Wilson had been inspired to pursue the 'Other Tradition' by Aalto's call for an expansion of the concept of rationalism to encompass the factors that affect the psychological experience of the built environment. Writing more than fifty years after the Modern Movement became established, Wilson gave vent to the disaffection felt by many of his generation of architects. Followers of the first generation of modernists pursued somewhat hermetic design processes that stressed ergonomics, new materials, structure and programme, with the result that a building's appearance was determined by its functional and technological organisation – form crudely following function, or an aestheticisation of form. The outcome of Wilson's historical review of architecture as a 'Practical Art' with its origin in classical philosophy/

theory was, he said, that 'we have paradoxically come to retrieve the concept of "function" from "Functionalism"'.[89]

In the 'Other Tradition', Wilson brings together architects who embraced the material conditions of modernity but who refused to be led by the future-forward technological bias and away from the deep-rooted needs and desires of humanity in the buildings they designed. Asplund's turning away from the International Style was an early indication of responses to incipient globalisation. With buildings throughout Europe and the US, Aalto became the most well-known architect in suggesting an alternative way forward. By expanding a definition of rationalism and by assembling discrete, identifiable elements around a residual courtyard, as at Säyänatsalo, he showed how to humanise the scale of ever-larger institutional buildings. Frampton later picked up and developed these themes into what he called a 'Critical Regionalism', to which we will return.

In *Court and Garden; From the French Hôtel to the City of Modern Architecture* (1986), Michael Dennis wrote of 'two traditions': the pre-modern ('would pre-Enlightenment be more accurate?', he asked) and the modern, an urban tradition where space took precedence, and that of modern object-like buildings isolated in space, a distinction made earlier by Peter Collins. Dennis argued that we are the inheritors of both traditions and that architects must acknowledge both although, agreeing with Collins, that priority must be given to defining urban space. Terragni might serve as an example of how the language of the Modern Movement can be re-deployed to this end.

Later in *The Other Tradition*, Wilson touches upon his own views, which reflects a conception of space markedly different from that of the Modern Movement. Drawing upon the psychoanalytical writings of Melanie Klein, he alludes to archetypal spatial elements that he believed constitutes fundamental components of a meaningful architecture stemming from different degrees of enclosure. Making for a complete spectrum from maximum protection to complete openness, he identifies these as: totally enclosed room; room without a ceiling (courtyard); room with a wall removed (portico or loggia); and threshold or between space. With this conception of architecture we are jumping ahead of our story, for his theory is informed by the history of post-World War II architecture, to which we must now turn.

Chapter 10: Late modernism and critical histories

REVISIONIST AND CRITICAL HISTORIES

Tournikiotis divides post World War II historians into two groups, 'revisionists' and 'critical', both accepting the narrative of the early operative 'pioneer historians' but their work 'reflects the questioning attitude of a disillusioned generation'.[1] Bruno Zevi (1918–2000) and Leonardo Benevolo (b. 1923) were revisionists who acknowledged the importance of history to architectural design. His second group was critical, but held a range of views: Reyner Banham (1922–88) called for an intensification of technology against history, Peter Collins (1920–81) argued for an accommodation of contemporary architecture with the historically given built environment, whereas Manfredo Tafuri (1935–94) held a position on history more properly termed critical. This is how Tournikiotis saw the groups. A brief review of these historians followed by an outline of architecture after 1945 will help show why history made a comeback in the 1960s

Forced to emigrate from Italy to the United States in 1940, Zevi enrolled at the Harvard Graduate School of Design, where Gropius was the director. This encounter proved to be crucial to his stance on history. He criticised Gropius for removing history from the syllabus and found his design teaching based upon 'a grindingly pragmatic brief' where 'economy appears to be the sole value'.[2] Zevi reacted against this and the International Style, which he regarded as 'reactionary academicism' and as a 'classicisation of functionalism'.[3] (Philip Johnson was a fellow mature student whom Zevi described as 'more Miesian than Mies').[4] Zevi was equally scathing about Giedion's vision of modernism as a 'strengthening of the mechanistic International Style'. When he translated Giedion's *Space, Time and Architecture*, Zevi transposed the chapters on Wright and Le Corbusier for, he wrote, 'it is inconceivable that he considers Wright merely a predecessor of Le Corbusier and Gropius'.[5]

Zevi proposed instead a reappraisal of modern architecture, arguing that it should be organic, based upon 'a reliance on nature' and 'the use of warm and frequently local materials', after the example of Wright.[6] 'Organic architecture', he wrote '[is] for the human being, shaped to the human scale, and following the spiritual, psychological and contemporary needs of man as part of society.'[7]

He returned to Italy in 1945, where he founded the Association for Organic Architecture, and was appointed to a Chair in Venice in 1948, where he stayed until transferring to the University of Rome in 1960 [10.1]. In his *Storia dell'Architettura Moderna* (1950), he demonstrated that the history of architecture and good contemporary design are inextricably linked: 'history, if viewed as a process is the only scientific method for teaching design in the studio.'[8] His Rome professorial lecture of 1963 was entitled *History as a Method of Teaching Architecture*. 'All great architects delve in to the past', he wrote in the later *Il linguaggio moderno dell'architettura* (1973), 'and modern architecture cannot be understood without knowledge of its precedents.'[9] His conception of history was influenced by Benedetto Croce (1866–1952), who had rehabilitated Vico earlier in the century.[10] In opposition to the teleological view of the 'pioneer' historians, Zevi followed Croce in seeing that 'over the centuries every significant advance has been followed by regression'.[11] He interpreted the recent history of architecture as reflecting a crisis 'as our illusions about the future of a technological society ebb away'.[12] He hoped this would be followed by a return to an organic modern architecture.

10.1 Carlo Scarpa, entrance to the Venice School of Architecture

Zevi sees history through contemporary eyes, seeking in the past for elements of inspiration and confirmation for the architecture of our time. He is opposed to the rejection of history expressed by many of the avant-gardes of the interwar period.

Paynayotis Tournikiotis, *The Historiography of Modern Architecture*

Benevolo shared Zevi's commitment to consolidating the modern movement, but differed sharply in emphasising its rational basis.[13] He followed Pevsner in giving a primary role to Morris whom he quotes approvingly. 'Architecture ... means a moulding and altering to human needs of the very face of the earth.'[14] But where Pevsner focused on form, Benevolo stresses the social, economic and cultural factors that underlay the shift from Style Revivalism to the Modern Movement.

He identified the Bauhaus as initiating 'an objective method' that characterised the Modern Movement. The break in the 'stable, recognised relationship between society and architecture' had become most manifest in the city,' he said, hence he supported the planning principles adopted in the Athens Charter.[15] He approved of buildings

10.2 Le Corbusier,
Cité de Refuge, Paris

such as Le Corbusier's Cité de Refuge that ignored the existing fabric as they laid down a partial blueprint for a new type of city[16] [10.2]. Benevolo considered it 'preferable to concentrate on functional advantages, which could be demonstrated rationally, rather than on matters of taste'.[17] His belief in the primacy of rationality was fundamentally at odds with Zevi's condemnation of modernism's mechanistic model. Benevolo's optimistic slant on rationality echoes Theodor Adorno's view that reason and rationality are positive values inherited from the Enlightenment. In contrast, Zevi shared a concern raised by two others of the Frankfurt School, Habermas and Max Horkheimer, about the meaning of rational, rationality and rationalisation to our contemporary cultural situation, which will be considered in the epilogue.

A significant shift in the historiography of modern architecture took place in the 1960s.[18] In contrast to Zevi and Benvolo's broad support for the findings of the 'pioneer historians', Banham's *Theory and Design in the First Machine Age* (1960) criticises early moderns for 'drawing nearer to the Academic tradition' and failing to express a machine age character. His book comprises what Tournikiotis calls a 'narrative of failure'.[19] Pioneer modernists failed, according to Banham, because they 'cut themselves off … from their foothold in the world of technology'.[20] Only the Futurists did he exempt. He praised the 'Futurist tone' of Le Corbusier's city planning projects, but was critical of the Villa Stein and the Villa Savoye for privileging formal qualities over functional criteria of planning and light.[21]

No family can live in one room, not even two if they have children. But any family can live in an equivalent area if it is divided up … A dwelling is an area which should offer protected areas for meals, sleep, work and play.

Alvar Aalto,
The Dwelling as a Problem

Banham's 'narrative of success' reaches its climax in the work of Richard Buckminster Fuller (1895–1953). He praises Fuller's 'Dymaxion House' (1927) project for being 'light, expendable, [and] exploiting every benefit of science and technology'.[22] Its concept 'was entirely radical, a hexagonal ring of dwelling space, walled in double skins of plastic … and hung by wires from the apex of a duralumin mast, which also housed all the services'.[23] This central core of services impressed Banham most, for it spelled the end of 'time-honoured functional differentiations' and heralded the kind of 'Living Pod', or 'Enlightenment Bubble' (1965) – simply a membrane with services – he later designed with Francois Dellagret; very 1960s!

Banham's history was predicated on the combination of teleology and *zeitgeist*; we live in a machine age and architecture should express this. Moreover, the first machine age was giving way to a second, he said, where cars, ships and aeroplanes had been succeeded by domestic 'machines' – 'shavers, clippers and hair-dryers; radio, telephone and gramophone, tape recorder and television'.[24] In his vision, out would go not only any vestige of 'academic tradition' and 'time-honoured functional differentiations', but also any consideration of a building belonging to a particular place, or being grounded at all. Banham later wrote an essay entitled 'The History of the Immediate Future' (1961) where he made explicit his teleological view of history as expressed in Archigrams futuristic visions epitomised by Peter Cook's 'Plug in City' (1964) and Ron Herron's 'Walking City' (1963).[25]

The 1960s was an optimistic period when British politicians spoke of the 'white heat of technology' leading to a better future, an optimism hard to credit now when we are familiar with the potential dangers of unbridled faith in technology. Colquhoun criticised Banham for his naïve belief that the 'evolution of architectonic forms is a constant flow'.[26] He argues instead that meaning is grounded on our tendency 'to see the world in the form of recognisable and nameable wholes'.[27] He opposed Banham's view of architects as simply antennae picking up the waves of the *zeitgeist* by his own view that 'we are historical animals, in the sense that we carry history in our mental attitudes as well as in our accomplishments'.[28] His inference is clear; that architecture should not reject, but respond to received traditions.

This is the thrust of Collins' *Changing Ideals in Modern Architecture* (1965). As the title of the book indicates, Collins focuses on ideals, or ideas, rather than his predecessors' concentration on forms.[29] Collins' riposte to Banham was that 'forms do not beget more forms by a mechanical evolutionary process'.[30] He begins his story at 1750, for he argues that a number of significant intellectual events took place at that time, as we have seen, and 'these, rather than "technological innovations" … first produced the theory of modern architecture'.[31] He concludes his study at around 1950 for he believed it possible then to recognise a 'stability and orthodoxy' in modern architecture which we typically 'associate with classicism'.[32] He connects the rise of modern architecture with changes in society, philosophy and culture, the emergence of the social sciences, and singles out historiography for special mention.[33] He points out, however, that the 'revolutionary'

Universal problem of architecture is to compass space (space being mathematically convertible to time via the abstraction of angularity). Problem is, subsequently, to control the spave compressed; and subsequently to develop selective control of compassed space, which control will allow ever variable complementary harmonic awareness of any and all sense-oeganizations to be sheltered within the compassed space.

R. Buckminster Fuller,
Universal architecture

For Mr Banham, however, determinism of form according to an abstract line of development seems to take the place of a concept of history.

Ernesto Rogers

ideas of the modern era could not be realised until the arrival of steel and reinforced concrete structures in the late nineteenth century.[34]

In his discussion of the pioneers, Collins criticises the historiography of the historians as well as the particular form taken by the Modern Movement. The focus of his criticism is the influence of avant-garde art on early modern architecture. New art-historical concepts led art critics to talk about 'significant form', a notion transferred to architecture as 'pure form', which 'inevitably suggested that the Vitruvian qualities of usefulness and stability were artistically of little importance'.[35] Collins criticised 'pioneer' housing for forcing 'people to adopt new social habits'.[36] Architects should have attended more to sociological research, he says, rather than considering 'that the easiest way to create a new architecture was to change the public's way of life' as had avant-garde theorists after 1919.[37] Under the influence of the avant-garde, modern architecture conflated formalism with technological developments, hence says Colquhoun, it 'was a continuation of the positivistic traits of nineteenth century thought'.[38] Collins had worked for Perret so it is perhaps not surprising that he gave broad support to structural rationalism. But rationalism for him meant no more than that a building's design 'logically followed from the nature of the structural components'.[39] He opposed the doctrinaire aims of the pioneers with his own contention that nothing is as important as 'creating a humane environment'.[40]

Collins is particularly scathing of Giedion – Wölfflin's student – for coining the term 'Space-Time' to characterise modernism with its reference to Einstein's Theory of Relativity. Collins accepts Giedion's claim that the 'sensation of spatial relationships resulting from successive viewpoints … became the principal aesthetic experience sought' in the new architecture. But he points out that this is because the observer moves – as in Le Corbusier's architectural promenade – not the object – the building – hence Giedion falsely uses Einstein's theory. The simple fact of transparency – made by frame structures and extensive glazing – allows the observer to see inside and outside simultaneously.[41] Collins produces an interesting source for Giedion's 'Space-Time'; not Einstein but Spengler. For Spengler wrote of 1920s and 1930s architecture that it 'craves for a style which drives through walls into the limitless universe of space … the Faustian building has a *visage*, and not merely a façade'.[42]

' Oh, our concepts: space, home, style!' Ugh, how these concepts stink! Destroy them, put an end to them! Let nothing remain! Chase away their schools, let the professional wigs fly, we'll play catch with them. Blast blast!

Bruno Taut,
Down with seriousism!

Through the baneful effects of academic teaching, opinion has strayed into an erroneous conception of the dwelling. The true problems of the dwelling have been pushed back behind entirely sentimental conceptions. The problem of the house is not posed.

CIAM,
La Sarraz Declaration

the new house is a prefabricated building for site assembly; as such it is an industrial product and the work of a variety of specialists: economists, statisticians, hygienists, climatologists, industrial engineers, standardization experts, heating engineers … and the architect? … he was an artist and now becomes a specialist in organization!

Hannes Meyer,
Building

Collins cites a passage of Einstein that contrasts with the extravagant cosmic claims made by Giedion: 'as to the concept of space, it seems that this was preceded by the psychologically simpler concept of place. Place is first of all a small portion of the earth's surface identifiable by a name … Now this is precisely the kind of space involved in architectural design, and one might contend that a place (*plaza, piazza*) is the largest space an architect can deal with as a unified work of art.'[43] Collins was not against modernism, but saw the nefarious influence of abstract art leading architects to see 'a building simply as an object in space, instead of as part of a space'.[44]

Collins makes it clear that 'stylistic imitation is as reprehensible as ever' and that he remains committed to 'the principles of the modern age' and 'the ethical problems of architectural design'.[45] He broaches how architects might make use of architectural history by considering the meaning of 'archaic'. Archaism can mean that a form is 'technologically obsolete', he argues, or 'artistically superseded', or simply 'unfashionable'. In making this distinction, he sees a legitimate use of precedent. For he concludes: 'Thus architects should feel no shame at adopting archaic forms and techniques in order to harmonize new buildings with an existing architectural environment, *providing that they do not betray the contemporary principles of stylistic unity*'.[46] Architecture should respond to the spirit or history of a place and to human needs, using technology appropriately rather than giving it rhetorical expression.

Tournikiotis describes Collins' book as being 'of catalytic importance' for the course taken by architecture in the 1970s and 80s when urbanism and careful study of traditional city plans informed building design. Anticipating Aldo Rossi (1931–97), Collins called for continuity in cities: 'It may well be … that future generations will consider the relationship of a building to its environment as more important than the way it expresses its function when considered in isolation.'[47] This would require a return to traditional or pre-modern conceptions of cities when 'an urban building was almost always considered as part of a street; … Thus urban architectural form was thought of in terms of *enclosures* of space.'[48] This insight proved to be of profound significance for research into meaning in architecture.

The most radical 'critical history' was produced by Tafuri. He pitched his work polemically against all other histories by claiming them to

To consider the context means to consider history. To be modern means simply to see contemporary history within the order of all history.

Ernesto Rogers,
Casabella-Continuita

be 'operative', coining the term adopted by Tournikiotis. 'It could be said', he wrote, 'that operative criticism designs past history in order to project it into the future.'[49] Published in the revolutionary year 1968, his *Teorie et storia dell'architettura* adapted the Hegelian conception of history to characterise the history of architecture as an 'ideology' bound up with the production of building in such a way as to prop up a capitalist economic system. From this position Tafuri argues that it is not the role of the architect-critic to propose solutions, but to point out the contradictions in the 'material production of cities and buildings'.[50] Influenced in particular by Adorno's Critical Theory, Tafuri identifies architecture as an 'institution', or in Foucault's terms as a 'discipline', that 'takes its place', says Anthony Vidler, ' like law, religion, and rest as the mystification of material practice'.[51] This led Tafuri to insist that 'the only possible way is the exasperation of the contradictions'.[52] This kind of critical position makes it difficult to draw architectural lessons, for the inference is that these would emerge 'naturally' after a social revolution. However, his critique of the role played by the avant-garde helps understand the rise of what he calls an 'anti-historical modernism.'

In *The Sphere and the Labyrinth; Avant Gardes and Architecture from Piranesi to the 1970s*, Tafuri establishes a lineage to the avant-garde highlighting Piranesi for demonstrating 'the capacity of the imagination to create models valid in the future'.[53] He links the avant-garde's 'stimulus to constant and permanent innovation' with Max Weber's notion of 'estrangement' felt by modern man, a feeling bound up with, says Tafuri, 'the technological universe from which it springs'.[54] He refers to Adorno citing Benjamin to the effect that the 'aura' of art in the age of mechanical reproduction had been substituted by its 'exhibition value', which 'is the "imago" of the exchange process'.[55] This original insight into how capitalism absorbs challenges to it through seductive advertising and glamour has an uncanny parallel to the rise of a sleek corporate architecture after 1945.

Tafuri's radical refusal to propose any specific role for architecture led critics to view him heralding the 'death of architecture'; 'every analysis is therefore provisional', he wrote in *The Sphere and the Labyrinth*. But he did give support to Rossi's early work, which he described as a 'litmus paper' for assessing 'the entire course of contemporary art'. Rossi's reliance upon prismatic forms, he said, 'excludes all justification from outside'. Tafuri argues that by employing 'a syntax

Mass culture is unadorned make-up' It assimilates itself to the realm of ends more than to anything else with a sober look that knows no nonsense. The new objectivity which it apes was developed in architecture. It has made standardization and mass production into a matter of art, where its opposite scorns every law of form that is derived from without.

Theodor Adorno,
The Schema of Mass Culture

of empty signs' Rossi shows a refusal to participate in the market place of post-modernism that rose to dominate the 1970s and 1980s.[56] But we are getting ahead of our story and Tafuri's critical history leaves us with as many questions as answers. We will return to Rossi in the next chapter, but first we must see how these histories were informed by architectural developments through the post-war period.

ARCHITECTURE 1945–66

In *Architecture Culture 1943–1968*, Joan Ockman describes this period as an 'interregnum between modernism and what is now called postmodernism'.[57] Appending 'culture' to architecture in her title indicates the impact of cultural studies on architectural discourse and the negligible part history played during this period. My review differs from Ockman by ending at 1966, for in that year was published both Robert Venturi's *Complexity and Contradiction in Architecture* and Rossi's *Architecture of the City*, books that set out a new theoretical basis for practice, both predicated on history or tradition.

Ockman summarises the period as one when 'modern architecture became dominant while being subjected to increasingly intense questioning'.[58] She identifies significant themes: the integration of more humanistic concerns with the functionalist legacy; a reassessment of some pre- or anti-modernist concerns, such as monumentality; and that functionalism lost its dominant position to the new intellectual currents of structuralism, semiology and sociology.[59]

As her book is more concerned with the cultural discourse around architecture than with buildings themselves, Joedicke's book *Architecture since 1945* is a useful complement. Although completed in 1968, Joedicke seems oblivious to Venturi and Rossi and their book's epoch-defining impact. With its innocence of the upheaval that was to come, it makes for a good source, his late modernist predilections countering any prejudices we may project back from the present.

Joedicke calls the post-war era 'The Third period of Modern Architecture' and divides this into two phases. The first from 1949 to 1958 he characterises under the heading 'Technical Excellence'; 'the trend towards technical excellence and precision as an aesthetic ideal assumes a dominant role of a new kind. It owed much to Mies van der Rohe.'[60] Mies, Gropius, Moholy-Nagy and Breuer, Gropius' former pupil, had all become established in US schools of architecture or design immediately after the war, and played a part in a younger generation of architects enthusiastically adopting the Miesian idiom. Most American examples are commercial buildings reflecting optimism at the expansion of their capitalist economy.

In Europe the response was more pragmatic as the war-shattered countries and their economies set about rebuilding.[61] Swedish modern architecture, a less doctrinaire idiom, became popular in Britain and was dubbed 'The New Empiricism' by the *Architectural Review* in 1947.[62] Influenced by Asplund's Stockholm Exhibition, this more light-hearted, informal approach became adopted for the Festival of Britain in 1951, complemented by the Constructivist-influenced Skylon and Dome of Discovery and the picturesque 'Townscape' of Gordon Cullen.

The modernism as we find it at present, being based on functionalism, can express little except utilitarian ideas.

Henry-Russell Hitchcock, 'In Search of a New Monumentality'. *Architectural Review*, September 1948

Unease began to be voiced about functionalism immediately after the war. Lewis Mumford complained in 1947 about a 'one-sided interpretation of function … The rigorists placed the mechanical functions of a building above human functions.'[63] But the meaning of functionalism was shifting from 'exactitude' to 'flexibility', which led to opposing calls for a 'new monumentality' and initiated new comparisons with history.[64] In an essay entitled 'Monumentality' (1944), Louis Kahn (1901–74) wrote: 'Monumentality in architecture may be defined as a quality, a spiritual quality inherent in a structure which conveys the feeling of its eternity, that it cannot be added to or changed.'[65] Ockman describes Kahn's approach to monumentality as 'reinterpreting historical concepts of construction in light of contemporary technical possibilities'.[66] A 1948 symposium in London entitled 'The need for a New Monumentality' included Giedion, Gropius and Hitchcock among the speakers.[67] There was broad agreement that functionalism had won the argument for a modern architecture and what was required now was an expansion of the modernist vocabulary to 'form a link between the past and the future'.[68]

10.3 David du R. Aberdeen, TUC Building, London

The tension between advancing modernism and monumentality is well-illustrated by the TUC Building (1947–57) in London. The design began as a 12-storey heroic object in space modelled on Le Corbusier's Centrosoyus project for Soviet Russia. The young architect David du R. Aberdeen (1934–89) had trained at the Bartlett School of Architecture pursuing a Beaux-Arts programme. His first design failed to meet light angle requirements, as did his second. Forced to abandon his modernist dream, his third, competition-winning design is arranged around a symmetrical courtyard, one of those traditional, smelly enclosed spaces – streets, alleys, courts – vilified by Le Corbusier [10.3]. But Aberdeen magically transforms the courtyard from its traditional role of circulation to become a theatrical setting for Jacob Epstein's memorial statue to trade union members killed in World War II, the floor of the court covered with rooflights to the conference hall below [10.4]. Aberdeen may have been disappointed at not realising his modernist vision, but the combination of a modernist vocabulary disciplined by traditions of formal planning produced an exemplary work that combines modernism's 'Swedish grace' with a sensitive response to the site [10.5].

10.4 Courtyard

In the year of the TUC competition, the *Architectural Review* published Colin Rowe's seminal essay on the Villa Stein, 'The Mathematics of the Ideal Villa; Palladio and Le Corbusier compared'.[69] Rowe had been taught by Rudolf Wittkower (1901–71), who was working at this time on his *Architectural Principles in the Age of Humanism* (1949). With its title suggesting humanistic principles applicable beyond the Renaissance, the book's central message of a meaning in the use of geometry and proportions made a big impact on young British architects (whose work became dubbed the 'New Humanism' by the *Architectural Review*).

Ernesto Rogers (1909–69) assumed the editorship of the Italian journal *Casabella* in 1955 and promptly changed the title to *Casabella-Continuità* to reflect his conviction that 'to be modern means simply to sense contemporary history within the order of all history'.[70] His journal promoted a modern architecture opposed to a ubiquitous global modernism, insisting instead upon aspects of 'national cultures' and 'rooted in the profound strata of tradition'.[71] In place of an unbridgeable divide between history and modern architecture, Rogers argued for history to be re-interpreted to challenge the notion 'that the new and the old are opposed'. Rather, he said, 'they represent the dialectical continuity of the historical process'.[72] As with Collins, this criticism of the teleological view of history helped shape a new, more reflective approach to modern architecture.

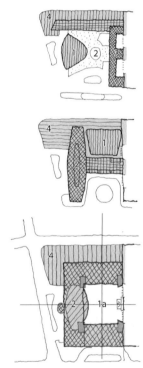

10.5 Sketch diagrams of plan proposals (redrawn from Aberdeen's competition report)
1 Conference Hall
1a (beneath courtyard)
2 Memorial Hall
3 12-story offices
4 College

In what he called the 'Second Phase 1958–66', Joedicke identifies two approaches running in parallel: 'Brutalism and Formalism'. Brutalism clearly had its source in Le Corbusier describing the character of concrete at the Unite d'Habitation as *beton brut*.[73] The young James Stirling (1926–92) visited the Maison Jaoul as it neared completion, and the article he wrote for *Architectural Review* reveals his shock at Le Corbusier's departure from the 'machine aesthetic' of the Villa Stein to arrive at a building site that showed, he wrote, 'no advance on medieval building'.[74] Despite this criticism, Stirling and Gowan's Ham Common Flats (1955–8) are one of the first Brutalist buildings that Joedicke illustrates[75] [10.6]. Joedicke reviews the disputed origin of the designation Brutalism, between Banham's contention that Hans Asplund (no relation) coined the word and the Smithsons' protest that Alison Smithson independently hit upon the phrase 'New Brutalism' as 'a word play countering "The New Empiricism"'.[76]

10.6 Stirling and Gowan, Ham Common flats

For the Smithsons, Brutalism 'implied an ethic not an aesthetic'.[77] Dismayed at what they saw as a drift away from the ideals of early modernism, the Smithsons promoted 'ideas like responsibility, truth, objectivity, material and structural honesty and visibility'.[78] In their first built project, superficially a Miesian school at Hunstanton (1952–4), Norfolk, they not only exposed the steel structure but also service ducts, pipe runs, etc. Because they did not dispute the original achievements of the modern movement, Joedicke considers the Smithson's Brutalism evolutionary rather than revolutionary.

Later in this 'Third Period of modern Architecture', Joedicke describes 'the uncertainty of the frontier between Brutalism and Formalism'.[79] A cursory view of his section on 'International Brutalism' illustrates this, with most buildings confirming Farmer's description of Brutalist buildings as 'battered bunkers', quite hideous piles of over-structured concrete forms with defensive slit windows unrelieved by Corbusian poetry[80] [10.7]. Even such a committed modernist as Joedicke is led by these examples to write: 'Present society stands for the most part in uncomprehending opposition to the aims of avant-garde architects.'[81]

10.7 LCC/GLC Architects Department, Hayward Gallery, London

Formalism was largely an American phenomenon, which Joedicke ascribes to where the received certainties of the modern movement – the rational relationship of form to structure, form to content, form to programme, the whole ideology of form follows function – gave way to a more individual and sculptural expression of form. Philip

Johnson looms large in this for, at the end of the 1950s, as Joedicke says, he 'began to grow out of his Miesian clothes'. Amongst several of Johnson's buildings illustrated are the Museum of Western Art (1961), Fort Worth with its arched arcade and the Sheldon Memorial Art Gallery (1960–3), Nebraska with its vaulted ceiling. Joedicke distinguishes between what he calls the 'Formalism-Neo-Historicism' of buildings such as those by Johnson and others that use arches or other overt historical references, and 'Formalism-Brutalism', such as Paul Rudolph's Art and Architecture Building (1959–63) for Yale.[82] Appraising this 'neo-historicism', Joedicke questions 'whether tradition in general may or may not have meaning in modern work'. Or is it merely 'an exploitable reservoir of forms?'[83] He remains sceptical, seeing in this Formalism of the 1950s and early 1960s a Mannerism which he interprets in the older art-historical sense of the term as an unprincipled decline and departure from an established canon. But the time was fast approaching when the meaning of historical and traditional forms were to be taken seriously in relation to contemporary design.

> No work is truly modern which is not genuinely rooted in tradition, while no ancient work has significance today unless it can resonate through our voice.
>
> Ernesto Rogers,
> *Casabella-Continuita*

TEAM 10

A younger generation of architects formed Team 10 in the 1950s in protest at the dominating rationalism of the pioneer 'masters' who remained in control of CIAM. Critical voices emerged in 1947 at CIAM 6, with a call 'to work for the creation of a physical environment that will satisfy man's emotional and material needs'.[84] The challenge to the Athens Charter took place at CIAM 9 (1953) and initiated the decisive break. Led by the Smithsons and Aldo van Eyck (1918–99), the young challengers were invited to set the agenda for the following congress, hence the name Team 10. The Smithsons voiced the concern that 'the problem of human relations fell through the net of the "four functions"'.[85] Team 10 (which remained a loose affiliation) opposed the abstract zoning of the 'four functions' concrete and familiar expressions, proposing instead 'house', 'community', 'habitat'. Their emphasis on the word 'habitat' pointed to the direction Team 10 was to follow, for 'habitat' defines the natural home of an animal, or plant, a concept expanded in anthropology to include groups of people.

> The time has come to gather the old into the new; to rediscover the archaic qualities of human nature, I mean the timeless ones.
> To discover anew implies discovering something new. Translate this into architecture and you'll get new architecture – real contemporary architecture.
>
> *Team 10 Primer*

The Smithsons had described their Golden Lane housing project at CIAM 9, where they elaborated upon 'the problem of identity'. Their design, they wrote, 'proposes that a community should be built up

The street wears us out. And
when all is said and done we
have to admit it disgusts us.

Le Corbusier

Alignment on the streets and
enclosed courts and light wells,
two forms entirely contrary
to human well-being.

Le Corbusier,
Concerning Town Planning

And the street only knew your name.

Van Morrison

Today, when one is searching
desperately for some sense
of continuity and hoping for
development and not destruction,
some knowledge of our position
in time, as well as space is essential.
Therefore I consider that the
learning of history in an academic
or systematic way is necessary.

John Voelcker,
Team 10 Primer

from a hierarchy of associational elements and tries to express these various levels of association (THE HOUSE, THE STREET, THE DISTRICT, THE CITY)'.[86] These concrete and familiar terms, linked to the concept of 'identity', were geographical concepts drawn from traditional cities, which they contrasted with the abstract categories of the Athens Charter.

The inspiration for this reading of the city came from the Smithsons' association with the photographer Nigel Henderson (1917–85). He introduced the Smithsons to the working-class community of Bethnal Green, East London, where he lived. Henderson's wife, Judith, was an anthropologist who had begun working on a sociological research project called 'Discover your Neighbour' in Bethnal Green in 1945.[87] Through their connection with the Hendersons, the Smithsons may have been familiar with the researches of the sociologists Michael Young and Peter Willmott, whose seminal book *Family and Kinship in East London* was published in 1957. Young and Willmott used the anthropological concept of 'kinship networks' to characterise the close bond between families inhabiting streets in close proximity to one another. In working class areas, the street, almost empty of cars, became the basis of an extended community. Forty or fifty houses make a good street, said the Smithsons, and 'streets with many small local and some larger local facilities in the interstices and round about make up a fairly recognisable district ... Much of the social pattern as observed by the sociologist in the Bye-Law street is a survival – modified by the particular built environment – of even earlier patterns.'[88]

From research into the 'simple relationship between house and street' sprang the Smithsons' concept of 'the street-in-the-air'. A bold, innovative attempt to deal with new problems of mass-housing while accommodating traditional concepts of identity and association, the idea when translated into building proved unsuccessful. As Frampton commented: 'the street itself, now divorced from the ground could no longer accommodate community life. Above all, its one-sided nature had only the capacity to stress the linearity of a route rather than engender a sense of place.'[89]

In their rejection of the placeless, rationalism of CIAM, the Smithsons explored the ordinary and the everyday under the rubric of 'As Found'. Their thinking about this received its clearest expression in the installation 'Patio and Pavilion' that they made with Henderson and Eduardo Paolozzi (1924–2005) at the 'This is Tomorrow' exhibition in 1956. The 'patio' was enclosed by standard fence panels and the 'pavilion' was a simple wooden shed with corrugated polyester roofing. Peter Smithson described it as 'a kind of symbolic habitat in which are found responses to basic human needs'.[90] The patio was filled with symbols, such as wheels to represent movement and machines. Smithson explained that 'we were taking a position on the acquisitive society ... by offering ... a reminder of other values, other pleasures'.[91]

The Smithsons' interest in anthropology would have been reinforced by their association with van Eyck, for he had undertaken fieldwork research into the Dogon peoples from Mali. He described how the Dogon embody meaning at every level of their culture, from artefacts such as the basket, the buildings, and to the village compound.[92] At each of these levels the combination of form and material symbolise the Dogon peoples' place in the cosmos.

The cosmos that one inhabits – body, house, tribal territory, the whole world – communicates above with a different place that is transcendent to it.

Mircea Eliade,
The Sacred and Profane

Young men and women in the 1950s were fired by the philosophy of Existentialism to plumb deeper meanings to life, prompted no doubt by the horrors of the war just ended. The existentialist search for deeper meaning in architecture is particularly prevalent in van Eyck's writings, shaped not only by anthropology but also by the widespread influence of Structuralism, which he would have known from the writings of the anthropologist Claude Levi-Strauss (1908–2009). From this heady mix of disciplines, van Eyck believed it was possible to re-orientate architecture in a more humanised direction, not unrelated to the significance that it had for the Dogon, as he explained:

> The time has come to gather the old into the new; to rediscover the archaic qualities of human nature, I mean the timeless ones ... Architecture implies a constant rediscovery of constant human qualities translated into space. Man is always and everywhere essentially the same.[93]

The most well-known building where van Eyck attempts to implement this idea that indicates the tension between 'cosmic rhythms' and modern technology is the Children's Home in Amsterdam (1946–50). The accommodation is broken down into a series of small, domed spaces gathered together as 'family' units around courtyards reflecting its origins in the Dogon's organic patterns of settlement [10.8]. A key concept for van Eyck is what he called the 'in-between'. He developed this to reconcile what he described as the 'split polarities'

10.8 (Right) Aldo van Eyck,
Children's Home, Amsterdam
10.9 (Above) Children's Home,
'in-between' space,

of CIAM thinking where thinking about the house was separated from thinking about the city. The 'in-between' also expressed his distaste for 'the tendency to erase every articulation between spaces, i.e. between outside and inside ... Instead the transition must be articulated by means of defined in-between places which induce simultaneous awareness of what is significant on either side'[94] [10.9].

Van Eyck had developed this concept after hearing the Smithsons talking about the domestic 'doorstep'. From this most everyday phenomenon he could take off into lyrical passages of almost metaphysical beauty at the same time as attacking Giedion's conception of modern architecture.

> Whatever Space and Time mean, place and
> Occasion mean more
> For space in the image of man is place, and time in
> the image of man is occasion ...
> Provide that space, articulate the inbetween ...
> Whoever attempts to solve the riddle of space in the
> abstract will construct the outline of emptiness and
> call it space[95]

LOUIS KAHN

In her book, *Louis Kahn's Situated Modernism*, Sarah Goldhagen argues that Kahn's Trenton Bathhouse project of 1955 occupies a 'fundamental place' in 'the history of postwar modern architecture'.[96] Kahn was then 54 years old and, dissatisfied with functionalism and the 'open plan', he revisited the lessons taught him by the French émigré Paul Cret, who had introduced him to *Beaux-Arts* precepts. Cret combined his commitment to classicism with a keen interest in the French tradition of structural rationalism – Viollet le Duc, Baudoyer and Labrouste in particular. Anticipating Kahn's mature vision of design, Cret wrote: 'What is fruitful is the conception of form.'[97]

Frampton has suggested that Cret's interest in structural rationalism had a lasting impact on Kahn's career, which, in the mid-1950s took a significant turn from what Goldhagen calls his 'techno-organicism' 'to explore a different symbolic language loosely drawn from history'.[98] Combining his interest in tectonic form with a predisposition to seek the essence or origin of things, Kahn developed an architecture that was not so much 'loosely drawn from history' as in fact a very particular reading of its restored relevance to design. As Scully says, 'Kahn was trained in the Beaux-Arts manner to regard buildings of the past as friends rather than enemies, friends from whom one was expected … to borrow'.[99] Kahn came to reject modernism's associations with mass production and imagery inspired by industrial technology, although he remained committed to modernism's social agenda. He came to disapprove of transparency and the open plan 'in favour of more heavily bounded, anchoring spaces'.[100]

A number of experiences in the early 1950s led him to the revisionary position first explored in the Trenton Bathhouse. In 1951 he was a Fellow of the American Academy in Rome, where he was struck by the powerful presence of Roman ruins, with their massive brick walls and strong geometric form, now stripped of their ornament and marble facing.[101] Kaufmann's *Three Revolutionary Architects; Boullée, Ledoux and Lequeu* was published in Philadelphia in 1952, and the striking geometric forms of Ledoux clearly interested Kahn.[102] Although he may already have been familiar with Wittkower's *Architectural Principles in the Age of Humanism*, the potential for this to inform design may have been reinforced by a 'prolonged conversation' with Rowe, one of Wittkower's most brilliant students, in the same year Kahn designed the Trenton Bathhouse.[103]

Kahn acknowledged that this project marked the turning point in his approach to architecture: 'I discovered myself after designing that little concrete block bathhouse in Trenton.'[104] The 'Palladian' plan led him to the use of precedent and which formed the template for the bathhouse design, a Greek cross with rooms in three of the four arms of the cross around a central square courtyard. He discovered 'that a bay system is a room system. A room is a defined space – defined by the way it is made … [This] is strictly Palladian in spirit, highly ordered for today's space needs'.[105] Goldhagen has suggested that the centralised cruciform plan, an ideal of the early Renaissance church 'bore iconographic associations with humanism', and she proposes Geoffrey Scott's *The Architecture of Humanism* as the source, although Wittkower seems more likely.[106] With its pyramid roofs, no visible windows and curious blocky form, the building does resemble the severe geometrical forms favoured by Ledoux in his 'revolutionary' projects, but equally it resembles semi-ruined Roman remains covered with a modern protective roof, such as the Temple of Vesta in Rome.

The Trenton Bathhouse is the first example of Kahn's conviction that the elements enclosing a space, the structure and building's surfaces, should be immediately apprehensible: 'A room should be a constructed entity – or an ordered segment of a constructed system'.[107] 'Kahn challenged Siegfried Giedion's definition of modern architecture as … "space-time"', says Goldhagen.[108] This marks an important step in Kahn's pursuit of 'authenticity', an existential notion that has become increasingly significant as a counter to our media-driven virtual world. In contrast to the dynamic and fluid spaces of the modern movement, Kahn's buildings appear as solid, monumental masses containing tectonically defined spaces.

> I think of a plan as a society of rooms. A real plan is one in which rooms have spoken to each other. When you see a plan, you can say that it is the structure of the spaces in their light.
>
> Louis Kahn

Kahn began to teach full-time at the University of Pennsylvania in 1955, where he found the faculty intensively engaged with the problem of deteriorating city centres, as people flocked to the suburbs. A consensus emerged that this could be counteracted by rebuilding the public realm in city centres.[109] Kahn made 'Civic Centre' projects for Philadelphia where he demonstrated his belief that only 'buildings of overwhelming monumentality' could preserve the city centre and its traditional public role from the destructive impact of commercialisation and the automobile.[110] From the debates at Penn, Kahn came to believe that 'modern buildings that echoed historical ones bound a viewer to a greater community of past users' and could 'reinforce the social bonds that make a community cohere'.[111]

> The city is the place of availabilities. It is the place where a small boy, as he walks through it, may see something that will tell him what he wants to do his whole life.
>
> Kahn

When commissioned in 1959 to design the First Unitarian Church of Rochester, New York, he saw the opportunity to explore how monumentality might strengthen a sense of community, albeit in a modestly sized building. His first sketches propose a circular or polyhedral form inside a square, a concept influenced by Wittkower's illustrations of Renaissance centrally planned churches. The design went through many modifications before construction began in 1961, although the idea of a central prayer hall surrounded by an ambulatory encased in ancillary accommodation remained.[112]

By setting the windows back in deep faceted reveals, Kahn emphasised the mass of the building. Suppressing the elements that indicate scale – doors and windows – Kahn achieved a sense of monumental mass that belies the fact that the church is a relatively small two-storey building. Corner towers over the prayer hall admit light and add to the four-square monumentality. Rather than directly emulate historical forms, he engenders a sense of historic monumentality by exaggerating the scale and producing 'imageable' massive forms. During this same period, construction was underway on his Tribune Review Publishing Company Building (1958–62) where unusual-shaped window openings evoke a more specific historical association. Concerned to obtain plenty of light without glare, Kahn designed large, square openings just beneath the roof with a narrow slot cut into the wall below. Dubbed 'keyhole' windows by commentators, these unusual-shaped windows recall those in Roman Ostia that Kahn had seen.[113] Opening up the brick enclosing wall in this way can be read as a 'ruined' masonry wall.

Kahn's buildings are the antithesis of the Miesian 'high modernism' described by Joedicke as the chosen idiom of corporate America. Colleagues at Penn were preoccupied with what they saw as the disturbing effects of an emergent consumer culture fast being promoted in the 1950s. Kahn believed that a building with abstracted but recognisable historical allusions might help thwart this; evoking historical forms might act as reminders of other or higher cultural practices antithetical to a consumer culture.[114]

With this in mind he began to choose materials such as his favoured brick that showed the presence of the human hand at work [10.10]. Although much reduced from Ruskin's high aspiration at the Oxford Museum, the idea of authenticity developed through material to tradition was enhanced by showing that the act of building comprises a series of human decisions. By the time Kahn came to design the First Unitarian Church he specifically rejected steel because of its association with high technology. The reinforced concrete roof structure spanning the prayer hall was the first of a series of imaginative responses in the major spaces of his subsequent buildings [10.11].

It is important that you honor the material you use. You don't bandy it about as though to say, 'Well, we have a lot of material, we can do it one way, we can do it another way.' It's not true. You must glorify and honor the brick instead of short-changing it and giving it an inferior job to do in which it loses its character.

Kahn

10.10 Kahn, Exeter Library,
detail of façade

Kahn's rejection of the modernist-functionalist belief that a building's form should be derived from analysis of the programme led to his idea of the 'form-concept'. 'The program is nothing', he wrote, the 'program is a hindrance'. From this position he developed, if not a theory of architecture, a set of firm convictions expressed in somewhat gnomic terms. He would begin by asking, 'What does this building want to be?'[115] With echoes of the philosophers Schopenhauer, Nietzsche and Heidegger, Kahn considered 'Form' to mean an 'existence-will'. Everything in the natural world has an inherent self-actualisation – 'A rose wants to be a rose', he said – and, by analogy, a building's essence, should be similarly divined and drawn out.

Kahn pursued this notion of form-concept or simply 'Form', by reflecting upon the original impulse that gave birth to human institutions. 'Of all things, I honour beginnings', he wrote. 'I believe, though, that what was has always been, and what will be has always been.'[116] What he meant by institution was very different from its more general bureaucratic association: 'Institution stems from the inspiration to live.' Kahn may have been influenced in this by Emile Durkheim, who said that a society knows itself

10.11 First Unitarian Church,
Rochester, New York, interior

through its institutions – religion, government, culture, etc. – and that alienation comes from the erosion of these from the collective unconscious. 'This inspiration remains meekly expressed in our institutions today', said Kahn. 'The three great inspirations are the inspiration to learn, the inspiration to meet, and the inspiration for well-being' [10.12].[117]

Norburg-Schulz has shown striking similarities between Kahn's expressed design intentions and Heidegger's philosophy – which centred on the notion of being-in-the-world.[118] There is not space to explore this here, although we will return to Heidegger in the epilogue. Very briefly, the deep-seated idea of 'institution' gave Kahn the basis for working out the form-concept: 'I am trying to find new expressions of old institutions.'[119] He used the term 'Order' for the typological configuration of the institution, and 'Design' for the mediating principle between them.[120]

Clearly, the study of historical precedents would be helpful, if not essential in pursuing such an approach to design. But this did not involve explicit borrowings from history.[121] Rather Kahn's buildings evoke a sense of historical forms by their massive presence and the suggestion that they may have been present from a time before or beyond their own time. It has been suggested that Kahn's conception of Form has similarities with Jung's theory of the collective unconscious, a realm that transcends, or lies beneath the personal unconscious, a realm that manifests itself in archetypes, patterns or forms that embody universal themes of human experience.[122] Kahn is a pivotal figure in showing how history can be viewed as a meaningful aspect of architectural design, where memory of past cultural forms, deep-seated archetypal memories, can be evoked without the literal and overt display of historical forms that would raise them from the subconscious level to overly conscious appearance. John Lobell describes Kahn's approach to history and historical form as one 'which disregards actual and legitimate temporal sequences and is always ready for slips of the memory and that mysterious selection of form, which is all the more mysterious in that the forms rise out of a submerged world'.[123]

10.12 Exeter Library, detail of reading carrels

Kahn's journey to this position began in earnest when he was offered a teaching post at Yale in 1947. The chair of architecture re-established history into design discourse by inviting members of the art history faculty to be visiting critics, Scully being the most notable.[124] History became increasingly significant in the US as Kahn discovered in 1950 whilst a visiting critic at Princeton.[125] For he sat on Robert Venturi's thesis jury and was highly impressed by the student's careful use of precedents, although their ideals were to diverge fundamentally in the years that followed. Norberg-Schulz came to draw a sharp distinction between Venturi's semiological approach to architecture and Kahn's archetypal historical forms. In his essay 'Kahn, Heidegger and the Language of Architecture', written in 1979 at what was perhaps the nadir of post-modernism, he stated: 'Language … does not primarily serve communication, but discloses the basic existential structures.'[126]

Like so many thinkers – Zevi, Collins, van Eyck, the Smithsons – during this post-war period, Kahn identified a crisis in modernism's ideological focus on the *zeitgeist* and its technological expression. With functionalism, the machine and abstraction rejected, architects turned again to history for suggestions about how to translate new human-centred theories into the material facts of building.

Chapter 11: From post-modernism to meaning in architecture

ROBERT VENTURI AND POST-MODERNISM

The publication in 1966 of Robert Venturi's *Complexity and Contradiction in Architecture* signalled the re-entry of history into the architectural mainstream. In his introduction to the book, Scully described it as the most important since Le Corbusier's *Vers une architecture.*[1] It was given status by being the MoMA's first in a series of occasional papers on the background to modern architecture. Scully considered it to make a paradigm shift equivalent, but opposite, to that of Le Corbusier's. Where his 'purism' opposed the historicist eclecticism of the nineteenth century, Venturi's book opposed the 'simplistic and diagrammatic forms' of the Modern Movement.[2] Viewed in retrospect, the book has the hallmark of presenting a very personal, idiosyncratic approach to architectural design. But Venturi introduced it as a 'gentle manifesto', which could have played no little part in it being seized upon by architects grown weary of the banal, if elegant, Miesian-inspired modernism, or baffled by the 'originality' of late-modern structural expressionism.[3] The book proved highly controversial and marked, if not the death of modernism, then the birth of post-modernism. Post-modernism came to shape a wide range of cultural forms, but it was most easily recognised in buildings by their colourful, decorative character that contrasted with the functional forms of the Modern Movement.

Architecture publications are at present dominated by studies on topics taken from sociology and psychology, economy and ecology, mathematics and communication theory. The only subject which, paradoxically, is missing, is architecture.

A review of *Complexity and Contradiction in Architecture*, Norberg-Schulz, *Architectural Review*, March 1968

Complexity and Contradiction not only reads as a manifesto, but also looked like one. Small, postage-stamp size illustrations fill the margins of every page of what is a pocket-size book of only 140 pages, the last 30 of which illustrate Venturi's projects and buildings. On the opening page he writes that he is 'guided not by habit but by a conscious sense of the past – by precedent thoughtfully considered'.[4] Like Kahn (for whom he worked in the 1950s) he considers analysis of the programme an inadequate basis for generating architectural form. Opposite in almost every way from received modernism, he states that the 'historical comparisons' he refers to in his own work 'are part of a continuous tradition relevant to my concern'.[5]

On the one hand he writes 'frankly about what I like in architecture', his taste extensively influenced by Italian Mannerist architecture, which he studied when Architect in Residence at the American Academy in Rome. On the other hand, he broke with the narrowly rational, technocratic definition of modernism peculiar to architecture by referring to the literary criticism of the early modern poet T.S. Eliot. Eliot refuted the avant-garde's pejorative labelling of tradition, arguing that tradition involves 'the historical sense, which we may call nearly indispensable to anyone who would be a poet beyond his twenty-fifth year; and the historical sense involves perception, not only of the pastness of the past, but of its presence'.[6] It was this digested historical sense, embracing awareness of 'the whole of the literature of Europe' that Eliot meant by tradition. This had to be combined with the poet's 'own contemporaneity' to make a modern literature. Venturi took the same line, for as well as architectural history, 'the richness and ambiguity of modern experience' was also to be embraced in his architecture of *Complexity and Contradiction*.

He reminds his reader of the growing complexity of modern building programmes. Even the domestic programme requires more than fits conveniently in a glass box pavilion, such as Johnson's Miesian derived 'Glass House', Venturi's second illustration. 'Blatant simplification means bland architecture', he wrote. Perhaps Venturi's most well-known remark is his riposte to Mies van der Rohe's 'Less is More'; 'Less is a bore', he retorted.[7] Over and against the pure form of the Modern Movement, Venturi set out an agenda for an architecture that used historical precedent at the same time as it responded to contemporary cultural conditions and everyday needs.

The thrust of Venturi's critique is that modernism ultimately failed because it allied itself with the rational and technical conditions of modern life. His counter argument is best summarised by Colquhoun as that the 'language of architecture rests on a dialectic between memory of past cultural forms and the experiences of the present'.[8] Venturi's method is to draw upon a multitude of historical precedents which he analyses under categories he devised, categories that suggest their applicability to modern conditions. His chapter headings give a flavour of his approach: 'Non-straightforward Architecture'; 'Ambiguity'; 'Contradictory Levels: The Phenomenon of "Both-And" in Architecture' (among many illustrations to make this point he uses the 'contradiction' between the façade and the plan of the Karlskirke);

'Contradictory Levels Continued: The Double-Functioning Element'; and 'The Inside and the Outside'. This last, a challenge to modernism's flowing inside/outside space, had a major impact on subsequent architecture, effectively reviving the façade as a significant form of expression. Modernism's functional-organic conception of a building denied the façade's significance, for the form was all, the rounded resultant of internal forces generated by the programme. 'Architecture occurs at the meeting of interior and exterior forces of use and space, general and particular, generic and circumstantial', wrote Venturi. 'Architecture as the wall between the inside and the outside becomes the spatial record of this resolution and its drama.'[9]

More than 50 percent of the 253 illustrations (excluding those of his projects) are classical buildings. Unlike a treatise on classical architecture, which would have constructed a well-defined reading of the Vitruvian canon, Venturi scours every Mannerist – and other buildings – for 'traditions' of design decisions that support his own agenda. It is not a book to read (or re-read) at a single sitting, for the reader is left dizzy by the myriad examples illustrated and dissected in unfamiliar ways. It was perhaps inevitable that the sheer number of classical buildings illustrated and combined with his emphasis on the façade would lead to the mock-classical 'facadism' that came to characterise post-modernism. The exuberant way Venturi wrote about his examples perhaps contributed to a sense that 'anything goes' in post-modernism.

Whilst this is a reasonably fair assessment of the book's influence, it would be an unfair criticism of Venturi's architecture, although some raise difficult questions. His most well-known and successful is the house he designed in 1962 for his mother in Chestnut Hill, Pennsylvania. This best illustrates his argument for *Complexity and Contradiction* and became the first icon of post-modernism [11.1]. At one level the front façade reads as a small classical villa with Mannerist split-pediment – the 'rear pavilion at the Villa Maser', he says, was his source.[10] At another it looks like the archetypal house a child might draw for his or her mother. But the overall symmetry is broken by the irregular shape and disposition of the windows, whose size, shape and location are determined by the plan and specific functions: a

11.1 Robert Venturi, 'Mother's House', Chestnut Hill, Pennsylvania.
Venturi, Scott Brown. Collection, The Architectural Archives, University of Pennsylvania, photo by Rollin LaFrance

strip window over the kitchen counter on the right; a small square window for the WC adjacent to the entrance; and on the left a large square window with cill at floor level for a bedroom. A shallow arch over the entrance and a dado are simply tacked-on sections of timber, undercutting any classical pretensions. This is no stone or stucco villa but an 'ordinary' American balloon-frame suburban house; 'Both-And'.

Venturi criticised the 'diagrammatic planning' of modern functionalist buildings and this little house is anything but. The inside spaces, he writes, 'are complex and distorted', responding to the complexities inherent in the domestic programme.[11] But he exaggerates this for particular effect. Accepting the idea of symmetry suggested by the façade, he has two elements – stair and hearth/chimney – competing for the central position. This produces the most extraordinary stair, open to the living room, whose width expands and contracts as it rises and wraps around the chimney. Furthermore, he also seems to have drawn a line in the plan parallel with the façade and established by the face of the chimney breast, then arranged all movement between spaces to the front of this, a tactic that increases the complexity of the plan [11.2]. Locating kitchen, WC and spare bedroom at the front of the plan prompted the disparate, but functionally fitting, windows that undercut the symmetry of the façade.

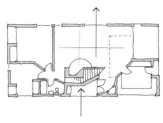

11.2 'Mother's House', ground-floor plan

Much more could be – and has been – said about this little building. But here it is sufficient to say that his desire to enrich architecture by reference to history, at the same time as accommodating contemporary experience, is very apparent and successful. His Guild House (1960–3), however, does raise the criticism of 'facadism' that can be aimed at post-modernism.

Venturi closes the main body of his text by suggesting that 'Main Street is almost alright'.[12] On the one hand he designs the Guild House – 91 apartments for the elderly – to be quite ordinary. 'The dark brown brick walls with double-hung windows recall traditional Philadelphia row houses', he wrote.[13] But on the other hand he gives the building a rhetorical façade onto the street, the composition of which alludes to classical precedent: a tripartite vertical articulation; a 'giant order'; and a segmental arch at top centre [11.3]. Venturi overlays

11.3 Guild House, Philadelphia Venturi, Scott Brown Collection, The Architectural Archives, University of Pennsylvania, photo by Skomark Associates

11.4 Las Vegas

this ambiguous mixture of ordinariness and high culture with references to contemporary Pop Art: the over-scaled granite column at the centre of the entrance; bold commercial lettering; and a gilded television aerial (in fact a non-functioning 'sculpture') caps the façade. He presents this as both a 'functional' reference to the common room immediately below, where the elderly 'spent so much time looking at TV', and an ironic response to the classical tradition of sculpture-lined pediments.

In a reassessment written in 1989, Scully continued to support what he called 'Robert Venturi's Gentle Architecture'. He situates Venturi's buildings 'halfway between modernism and historicist postmodernism'.[14] He described his buildings as contextual, 'prepared to get along' with their neighbours and, with a nod to Brutalism, playing 'their role in a gentle comedy of citizenship rather than in a melodrama of pseudoheroic aggression'.[15]

11.5 Venturi, Sainsbury Wing
    extension to the
    National Gallery, London
11.6 Side elevation

Colquhoun, in contrast is more critical. He focuses on 'the shift of viewpoint' that took place between *Complexity and Contradiction* and Venturi's subsequent book, *Learning from Las Vegas* (1972), which he wrote with Denise Scott-Brown (and Steven Izenour). As the title indicates, the lessons for architecture here were to be taken from the 'billboard' buildings that line the most commercial strip in the US [11.4]. The populism of 'Main Street is almost alright' became now the 'main theme', but was rejected by Colquhoun for not representing 'the shared and positive view of the value system of the user/client'.[16] He challenged what Venturi now called the 'Decorated Shed', a notion that struck a blow against all previous conceptions of architecture for it asserted 'that architectural meaning has become irretrievably separated from its substance'.[17] Venturi combined his interest in Pop Art with an awareness of the new interest in semiology (the theory of signs, derived from Ferdinand de Saussure's analysis of language, of which more later). The 'Decorated Shed' became for Venturi 'a vehicle for ornament in architecture',[18] said Colquhoun, where the decoration was a two-dimensional image – Andy Warhol-like flowers for the 'Best' supermarket; cut-out Doric columns for a house in Delaware; a concatenation of Corinthian capitals at the Sainsbury Wing extension to the National Gallery in London – applied to simply-planned, box-like buildings [11.5 and 11.6]. Colquhoun concludes by arguing that in proposing an architecture split into two distinct and separate parts – shed plus sign – 'Venturi is proposing a reduction just as simplistic as that of the kind of modern architecture which he effectively attacked in *Complexity and Contradiction*.'[19]

Frampton was even more scathing about this aspect of Venturi's work and its nefarious influence on the ascent of post-modernist architecture. He described it as 'scenographic', which he contrasted with his own understanding of architecture, over-and-above issues of style, as essentially 'tectonic'. Having praised *Complexity and Contradiction* for its sensitive and sane assessment of the cultural realities confronting everyday practice', he lambasts *Learning from Las Vegas* for degenerating 'into total acquiescence'. Here 'the cult of the "ugly and the ordinary" becomes indistinguishable from the environmental consequences of the market economy'.[20] Where Venturi presents Las Vegas as OK populist expression – which irony and Pop Art tactics would elevate to architecture – Frampton sees it as representing 'a society that is exclusively motivated by ruthless economic drives'.[21] With a brief review of the post-modernism it spawned, Frampton concludes:

> By scenographically simulating the profiles of classical and vernacular and thereby reducing the architectonics of construction to pure parody, Populism tends to undermine society's capacity for continuing with a significant culture of built form.[22]

Such a damning indictment suggests that we need not linger over post-modernism, except to illustrate a few of the abuses of history that characterised the movement and need no comment [11.7 and 11.8]. But it would be unfair to leave the impression that Venturi's legacy was wholly negative. The charge that he confused commercialisation for a popular culture sticks, and the Decorated Shed – banal box with applied sign – only added to this; such a reductive architecture can only be considered an abuse of history. On the other hand, he enriched architecture by insisting upon it being culturally responsive and using history to expand architecture's vocabulary. In particular Venturi made a major contribution to restoring the art of planning to its historically significant place in architecture.

11.7–11.8 Ricardo Bofill, social housing, Marne-le-Vallée, Paris

Figures of past architecture are put in inverted commas and distorted.

Alan Colquhoun

* * *

If Tournikiotis had continued his study beyond the 1960s he would almost certainly have led with Charles Jencks as the 'operative' historian of post-modern architecture. Having written about semiology and architecture, Jencks was quick to see the importance of Venturi and his immediate followers. In 1977 he wrote, *The Language of Post-Modern Architecture,* which was followed shortly afterwards by *Late-Modern Architecture* (1980), his attempt to distinguish how one morphed into, or differed from, the other. In this same year he was part of the advisory panel to the First International Exhibition of Architecture at the Venice Biennale. Post-modernism had spread and now held the field in architecture. For the exhibition catalogue Jencks wrote an essay 'Towards radical eclecticism' where he welcomed the diversity on view: 'one that seeks to enhance a pluralist society'.[23] Later that year, however, he guest-edited an edition of *Architectural Design* where he coined the term 'Post-Modern Classicism' and now noted 'that a loosely shared approach has emerged', which he supported, asserting that 'some ... consensus must develop in order for architects to communicate with an audience'.[24]

Colquhoun's opinion that the 'term "postmodern" seems, by turns, empty or tendentious' is borne out by Jencks' frantic search for ever new names for the style.[25] Colquhoun considers that an acceptable definition can say no more than post-modernism was a movement in art and architecture that replaced 'an exhausted high modernism', adding 'that the unifying concepts of modernism have been replaced by a plurality of tendencies'.[26] Jencks' repeated invention of new names for the style reinforces Habermas' view that 'with the prefix *post*, the protagonists wish to dismiss the past, unable as yet to give the present a *new* name'.[27] Although post-modernism is difficult to define, its challenges to the certainties of modernism had a singular affect on the humanities, as the historian Thompson explains: 'in all intellectual disciplines it relates to questions of the possibility and the status of knowledge and interpretation.'[28]

Nevertheless, certain characteristics can be enumerated as is implied by the title of Jean-Francois Lyotard's *The Postmodern Condition* (1984). Post-modernism set itself against the seeming certainties of modernism, the earnest belief in progress, and against the idea that the objective truths of science could be applied to cultural fields.

Language, for Saussure, is a social contract, an agreement implicit between people as a whole that each word should have a particular meaning.

Charles Jencks,
Meaning in Architecture

The phenomenon of modern man has become wholly appearance; he is not visible in what he represents but rather concealed by it ... Whatever 'form' is nowadays demanded ... what is involuntarily understood by it is a pleasing appearance, the antithesis of the true concept of form as shape necessitated by content.

Nietzsche,
Untimely Meditations

To acknowledge ... that no foundation of absolute and undeniable truth exists is not the same thing as saying that ... truth is meaningless.

Willie Thompson,
What Happened to History?

Lyotard uses the term 'meta-narrative' to describe the over-arching ambition of disciplines such as science to construct unassailable truths and hence occupy positions of power. He argues that the rise of information and communication technology has irreversibly changed the way society functions and that the past can no longer be seen as providing absolute models.

Words are generally considered as 'signs' that represent a thing or concepts, but this innocent understanding became elaborated in semiology, the science of signs founded by Saussure. He divided the sign into two parts, the signifier – the sound of the word or visual image – and the signified. But the sound of the spoken word and its appearance in written form – the signifier – are different from one language to another, whereas the meaning – the signified – is the same. From this Saussure demonstrated that the relationship between the signifier and the signified is arbitrary, a point latched onto by post-modernists. A new emphasis on the surface and sign can be traced to the way Saussure's analysis of language came to be applied to art, architecture and culture. A significant role in promoting this extension of semiology from language to cultural forms was played by Roland Barthes' immensely popular *Mythologies* (1957). This became the central concern of the book *Meaning in Architecture* (1969), where Jencks wrote that because semiology is a science of communication, 'it is naturally central ... to ... meaning in architecture.'[29] Heterogeneity, parody, quotation and pastiche became characteristic of post-modernism as tactics to challenge the authority of modernist discourse. Hence, as Colquhoun says, 'Lyotard's emphasis on the indeterminate, the mixed, the pluralistic, and the fragmentary seems to echo the thesis of Venturi's *Complexity and Contradiction* and much of his architecture.'[30]

On the one hand post-modernism is a catch-all term and describes the intellectual and visible changes that accompanied the frantic expansion of communication media in the period after 1960. On the other it refers more specifically to the new intellectual challenges; post-structuralism, deconstruction, critical theory, or simply 'theory'. These lines of thought were taken up by architect-critics in schools of architecture and had a major impact. Jorge Ortero-Pailos describes how this generation, influenced by French intellectuals, came to challenge what he calls 'architectural phenomenology', a philosophical position held by an older generation who, he says,

Buildings are appropriated in a twofold manner: by use and by perception – or rather by touch and sight. Such appropriation cannot be understood in terms of the attentive concentration of a tourist before a famous building.

Walter Benjamin,
The Work of Art in the Age of Mechanical Reproduction

I do not think of it [architecture] primarily as either a message or a symbol, but as an envelope and background for life which goes on in and around it, a sensitive container for the rhythm of footsteps on the floor, for the concentration of work, for the silence of sleep.

Peter Zumthor

Postmodernist concerns with surface, for example, can be traced to the necessary format of television images.

David Harvey,
The Condition of Postmodernity

Blithely we exchange our already tenuous hold on the public sphere for the electronic distractions of a private future.

Kenneth Frampton

dominated discourse in American schools. The most well-known exponent was Charles Moore, who was the first to introduce Bachelard to architectural circles, and whose book *Body, Memory, Architecture* (1977) proved to be a popular introduction to the topic; Ortero-Pailos describes architectural phenomenology as 'a turn towards history' and against the Miesian notion of universal abstract space. Followers of theory, however, accused it of being an anti-intellectual and intuitive position. Developing Tafuri's initiatives, they focused on interrogating the 'institutions' that supported traditional practice. Challenging phenomenologists' search for a fundamental ground for architecture, Mark Wigley's 'emphasis on a non-foundational architectural theory' 'was code for the autonomy of theory from traditional "foundation" in practice'. Ortero-Pailos' book captures well how 'architect-theorists' attempted to subvert the link between theory and building practice, by expanding the definition of practice to encompass collage, graphic design, installation and photography. It became not uncommon to hear the refrain 'We don't make buildings in schools; we make drawings.' As a critical tool this seemed reasonable enough, but for an architectural proposition itself drawing could only be a means to an end.

A typical post-structuralist response viewed everything, including architecture, as text, a view opposed by phenomenologists who insisted upon the texture of the world. Ortero-Pailos paints a picture of architectural phenomenology as a superseded intellectual fashion in American discourse. But he does acknowledge that architectural phenomenology differs from the philosophy of phenomenology itself, which in Britain and Europe has been considered as a more fundamental examination and explanation of how humans are situated in the world, and how a primary role of architecture is to engage with this given that architecture constructs the world in which we live. Phenomenology underpinned the search for deeper meaning in architecture which rejected an increasingly superficial post-modernism. At stake in the condition of post-modernity is whether architecture embraces what has been called a 'spectre present', a virtual, media-shaped 'simulacrum', or if it can bolster what is seen as an increasingly fugitive and elusive 'reality'.

ALDO ROSSI AND THE ARCHITECTURE OF THE CITY

Aldo Rossi's *The Architecture of the City* was published in the same year as Venturi's *Complexity and Contradiction* and likewise, it advanced a polemical critique of modernism, but was unlike it in every other way. Rossi's target was the functional zoning of the city proposed by CIAM and enshrined in the Athens Charter. In opposition to this abstract conception of the city, Rossi defined the city in concrete terms as a 'collective artefact' constructed over time. The book grew out of notes he prepared for students while teaching in Venice and consequently is somewhat disjointed.[31] Although the book did not have the immediate impact of Venturi's, in the long run its influence was more extensive, lasting and profound.

Three principal themes emerge from the book. Firstly, a critique of what Rossi calls 'naïve functionalism', which he applies both to CIAM's vision of the city and individual buildings. Secondly, the idea of the city as an artefact, which he interprets as constituted by 'primary elements' – monuments and other persistent features – and residential districts. And, thirdly, the notion of 'typology'. As can be seen, implied in these three areas of investigation is an idea of history very different from Venturi's. Where Venturi cast his net wide across the whole history of architecture, Rossi focuses narrowly on particular aspects of architecture's relation to a city and prefers to cite geographers and historians rather than architects.[32]

His early involvement with *Casabella-Continuata* proved decisive in directing him to the idea of continuity in architecture and the city. Rossi wrote thirty-one articles for the journal between 1955 and 1965. The editorial line during this period was much influenced by the writings of the Frankfurt School, in particular Adorno's critique of the consumer society, which in turn influenced Rossi.[33]

In place of the functional analysis of the city into separate zones pursued by CIAM, Rossi proposes instead that the city should be understood as a fundamental given, the permanent and enduring record of mankind's collective response to dwelling, in the widest sense. He opens chapter 1 with the proposition:

> By architecture of the city we mean two different things: first, the city seen as a gigantic man-made object, a work of engineering and architecture that is large and complex and growing over time; second, … urban artefacts, which like the city itself are characterized by their own history and thus by their own form.[34]

11.9 Piazza del Signori with statue of Dante, Verona

To speak of evocation in the particular world of architectural representation is to speak of forms. The notion of fitness must therefore always include that which interconnects the forms themselves in history.

Giorgio Grassi

11.10 Palladio, Basilica, Vicenza

This is the territory he sets out to explore and explain and from where comes his conception of architecture. Thus the city *is* its architecture and consequently architecture is *of* the city. Architectural form should respond to the city's history and how it has grown over time [11.9].

The term he prefers for his study is 'urban artefact'. He is particularly interested in how urban artifacts contribute to the character of the city and he identifies two key aspects: 'their collective character', and that they are 'permanences' stabilising the urban dynamic. Because both aspects refer to traces of the past, he finds that 'urban history seems more useful than any other form of research on the city'.[35] Nevertheless, he refers to the geographers Pierre Lavedan and Marcel Poète for a theory of permanences. Summarising Poète's hypothesis, Rossi states that permanences are 'the form of the past that we are still experiencing'.[36]

A building he uses to illustrate this is the Palazzo della Ragione in Padua.[37] Built in the fourteenth century and extended in 1425, it was at first the city's guild hall but today is shops and market. Rossi is 'struck by the multiplicity of functions that a building of this type can contain over time and how these functions are entirely independent of the form that impresses us; we live it and experience it and it in turn structures the city.'[38] This is how he arrives at his critique of naïve functionalism. He points to the changing uses that have occupied the Palazzo della Ragione as evidence against the biological analogy used by functionalists, the belief that functions constitute form. If this were the case then a building's form would change just as an organism does with a change of function. If functionalism were a true hypothesis, he says, urban artefacts renewing themselves by establishing new functions would logically change form. If urban artefacts are considered only as functioning then they have 'neither continuity nor individuality'.[39] Moreover, if they were able to constantly renew themselves – form following function – then 'the permanence of buildings would have no significance'.[40] Rossi is not against the concept of function as such, only that it does not satisfactorily explain the existence or meaning of a building, and ultimately he is dismissive of it as a compositional tool for architecture. It impedes us from studying forms, he says, and hence from understanding architecture from its own laws. One might think of Rossi's as a 'hermit crab' view of buildings. The Basilica at Vicenza (originally called the Palazzo della Ragione) modified by Palladio in 1546–9 is a similar example [11.10].

In support of Rossi's thesis, Rowe illustrated how the Uffizi changed from being Florence's sixteenth century offices to become one of the world's best-known art galleries with no change of form.[41]

A 'permanence' might be a building with significant form such as these, a lesser building whose presence persists and structures an area of the city, or a monument such as the Karlskirche that marks a significant moment in the city's history – it commemorates the end of the Turkish siege of Vienna in 1683. 'Primary elements have an absolute clarity', asserts Rossi, 'and it is a quality and destiny which distinguish monuments … from primary elements.'[42] Primary elements can be vital and 'propelling' in that they become a nucleus around which urban development takes place, such as Parisian 'faubourgs' or Italian 'borghi', distinct areas of cities, that grew up around markets or monasteries. Or they can be 'pathological' like the Alhambra that no longer constitute an element of the city's experience (it no longer houses kings or sultans) but around which grew the city of Granada.[43] The way that a specific character of 'residential district' develops around a 'primary element', into a particular pattern of dwelling and streets can itself become a primary element in stabilising the growth of a city.

The basis of the city and its continuity, therefore, is the city plan. Consequently Rossi considers 'the plan to be a primary element'.[44] An example he mentions is the Cerda grid of Barcelona, which established the pattern of the city's expansion in the late nineteenth century. Cerda took his cue from the city's Roman wall, setting out the grid by running a road parallel to it from the harbour to the hinterland where subsequent development took place. In Vienna the informed citizen can walk along the Graben towards the eighteenth century Plague Column and medieval cathedral, knowing that the Roman city wall forms the foundations to the buildings on his or her left [11.11].

In his introduction to the American edition of *The Architecture of the City*, Rossi explains that in the original Italian edition he 'spoke of *la fabbrica della citta* and not "urban architecture", pointing out that *fabbrica* means "building" in the old Latin and Renaissance sense of man's construction as it continues over time.'[45] He makes the point firmly that this is not the same as urban design; urban artefacts arise from 'a city's actual historical condition', not as in planning from 'a general projection of how things should be'.[46] Against this implied criticism of CIAM's functional planning, he argues that the conception

11.11 The Graben, Vienna. The Roman city wall forms the foundations of buildings to the left.
1. The Graben
2. Ringstrasse

'of a city as founded on primary elements is … the only rational principle possible' that can 'explain its continuation'.[47]

The way that Rossi turns this reading of the city into a strategy for architectural design is through the notion of typology. 'The typology of buildings and their relationship to the city', he wrote, constituted 'a basic hypothesis' of *The Architecture of the City*. He argues that types developed in response to the particular needs of a people and their aspirations to beauty. Hence a particular type of building would become associated with a particular way of life in a particular place. Referring to Quatremere de Quincy's distinction between type and model, Rossi defines 'the concept of type as something that is permanent and complex, a logical principle that is prior to form and constitutes it'.[48] Within established urban districts, considered as 'permanent elements in the city', sociological and other factors cohere to produce buildings with local or regional typological character.[49] In this way, the type links the past to the present and helps construct a shared cultural context without which, says Rossi, 'art would have no meaning'.[50]

In a section of the book entitled 'The Locus', he writes of how certain Renaissance paintings of piazzas fix the image of a 'place' so central to Italian culture, which he links to the significance of history, tradition and memory.[51] In a later section called 'The City as History', he expands upon this to 'say that the city itself is the collective memory of its people' and thus 'the union between past and future exists in the very idea of the city that it flows through, in the same way that memory flows through the life of a person'.[52]

The importance of collective memory Rossi elaborated in the notion of 'analogous' architecture. Using the example of a 'capprichio' by Canaletto, which depicts an ostensible view of Venice but is in fact composed of two buildings by Palladio from Vicenza plus his unrealised project for a bridge over the Grand Canal, Rossi describes a 'compositional procedure', or design method, whereby 'certain fundamental artefacts', or types can be transposed to form a new reality.[53] In a later essay entitled *An Analogical Architecture* he cites Jung defining the concept of analogy in a letter to Freud: 'Analogical thought is sensed yet unreal, imagined yet silent; it is not a discourse but rather a meditation on themes of the past, an interior monologue. Logical thought is "thinking in words". Analogical thought is archaic, unexpressed, and practically inexpressible in words.' [54] Rossi was clearly familiar with Jung's notion of 'collective memory', for he described 'Barns, stables, sheds, workshops etc.' in Jungian terms as 'Archetypal objects whose common emotional appeal reveals timeless concerns'.[55]

In a postscript to Rossi's *A Scientific Autobiography*, Scully emphasises the importance of memory to Rossi's work and points out how his drawings, strangely 'primitive, or child-like', 'explore the mysteries of remembrance'.[56] Rossi repeatedly draws the same objects, 'recording the basic structural types of a vernacular both peasant and industrial and reflecting always the pervasive classical past'.[57] In this way Rossi attempts to condense and confirm the essence of typical forms peculiar to the culture of his own region. This is also his approach to architectural design, an approach best illustrated in his residential block known as the Gallaratese (1969–73) in Milan. Rossi writes of how he pursued:

> an analogical relationship with certain engineering works that mix freely with both the corridor typology and a related feeling I have always experienced in the architecture of the traditional Milanese tenements, where the corridor signifies a life-style bathed in everyday occurrences, domestic intimacy, and varied personal relationships.[58]

Located on the outskirts of Milan surrounded by an urban wasteland of tower blocks and 'open space' – the utopian turned dystopian vision of CIAM planning made real – Rossi's Gallaratese slides in unobtrusively beside Carlo Aynomino's neighbouring project to make a distinct street [11.12]. This traditional scaled space is often shown in photographs hosting a street market. A long, three-storey block, its proportions are not so dissimilar to the surrounding tower blocks, but horizontal as opposed to vertical [11.13]. The conception of the project, as Rossi states, is of a long gallery or arcade onto which all circulation

11.12 (Left) Aldo Rossi, The Gallaratese, Milan. Seen in the context of typical urban blight

11.13 (Above) View from the street

11.14 Gallery access

is gathered [11.14]. On the opposite side to the street and contrasting with it, the gallery opens on one side to a large open space, which the rhythmic march of thin rectangular columns helps to articulate a garden edge as in a traditional loggia.

In his introduction to a Portuguese edition of *The Architecture of the City* (1977), Rossi describes the book's aim as an architectural project which:

> subsequently became elements of a design theory: urban topography, the study of typology, the history of architecture as the material of architecture … In these elements time and space are continually intermixed. Topography, typology, and history come to be measures of the mutations of reality, together defining a system of architecture wherein gratuitous invention is impossible. Thus they are opposed theoretically to the disorder of contemporary architecture.[59]

Written eleven years after *Complexity and Contradiction*, this is clearly a criticism of post-modernism. Rossi is known for the importance he placed on typology which, because it 'is shaped only through a long process of time', runs counter to the 'gratuitous invention' characteristic of post-modernism.[60] But even when writing before post-modern architecture became known, he stated that 'a discourse about images is fruitless if it is not concretised in the architecture that forms these images'.[61] In concentrating on the abstract character of Rossi's forms, Tafuri overlooked this aim of his work.

In elaborating upon the notion of type as an idea prior to form but taking shape as archetypal form, Rossi states that it operates through an interactive process involving 'its functions, its constructional techniques, the collective users'.[62] Despite this seemingly well-rounded account of what the type embraces, the notion of typology has been criticised for being reductive. Vesely explains that type 'is always the result of abstraction-eidetic imagination and thus only a secondary expression of historical reality'.[63] Once the type is isolated from the depth and fullness of lived experience it becomes an empty form. He contrasts this with what he calls the 'typicality of experience … which cannot be understood by reference to form alone'.[64] Veseley explains 'typicality of experience' by the example of a library, where a typical form used as the basis of design would fall short of the actual phenomenal experience of reading a book.

Rossi's conception of typology is certainly important, but remains sterile as long as the local circumstances are left out.

Christian Norberg-Schulz,
Genius Loci

Rossi's early buildings such as the Gallaratese and the school at Fagnano Olona (1972–6) invite criticism of this kind, for the austere vocabulary of the Gallaratese in particular feels as if it is the skeleton or ghostly reminder of a typical form without the full fleshly reality of lived experience. Perhaps only time can add this. But Rossi's allegiance to rationalism played a part in his choice of form and expression. Rossi founded the movement called *Tendenza*, which burst upon the scene at the Milan Triennale of 1974 and which later became known as the Neo-rationalists. Reviewing the exhibition, Rykwert was scathing about the severe architecture exhibited which purported to be independent of functional considerations.[65] He specifically criticised the idea of types as portrayed, stating that types 'are not void forms, repeated in and out of different contexts. They are living forms, elaborated over centuries of use … they shelter a pre-existing behaviour, and can condition the behaviour that comes after, and the ways of thinking.'[66] Nevertheless, by re-introducing the idea of type into architectural discourse, Rossi made a significant contribution to how architects could reflect more deeply upon issues of meaning. It was perhaps his desire to link his severe architectural vocabulary with the Italian Rationalist movement of Terragni, Cattaneo, etc. and thereby demonstrate his intention to renew and redirect modernism rather than reject it, that led to such criticism.

Despite these criticisms, *The Architecture of the City* caught the imaginations of serious young architects across Europe and much good work ensued. The book became known early in Spain, where the conditions were ripe for its reception following the death of Franco. In Spain architects tend to study and then work in the city where they grew up, a circumstance that helps with the idea of identifying and transforming the typical forms of a region, and incidentally, provided early inspiration for Frampton's project for a 'Critical Regionalism'. In the space available here it is impossible to give more than two or three examples. Two housing projects by Cruz and Ortiz are good examples, for they translate the typical courtyard form of Spanish dwelling into a modern idiom. The project on Dona Maria Coronel Street in Seville (1974–6) has a kidney-shaped courtyard adjusting the accommodation to an awkward-shaped site [11.15]. The courtyard walls are in brick, a typical Spanish advance in materiality on Rossi's austere forms. A later project on Hombre de Piedra Street (1983–5) has a linked pair of courtyards penetrating deep into an urban block. Blinds on wire runners over the court reduce solar gain [11.16]. Rafael

11.15–11.16 Cruz and Ortiz, apartment buildings, Seville
11.17 Cabrero and Perea, Collegio, Seville

Moneo describes the work of Cruz and Ortiz here as 're-establish[ing] contact with the old tradition of neighbourhood houses with a courtyard, the well-known Sevillian *corrales*'.[67] Another example from Seville is the *Collegio* (the College of Architects) by Cabrero and Perea. Here, a brick screen wall adjusts a tall corner block to the height of its neighbour and forms a courtyard to the fully glazed wall of the *Collegio's* foyer [11.17]. The brick wall provides a sense of protection to this fragile material, and blinds over the courtyard form a canopy to provide shade.

Under the banner of 'Rational Architecture', the most radical, yet paradoxically conservative, offshoot of Rossi's influence was a loose affiliation led by the Belgian Maurice Culot and Leon Krier from Luxembourg. They came to propose what they called 'The Reconstruction of the European City'.[68] Like Rossi, they were dismayed at the 'physical and social destruction of the city' caused by the emphasis given to efficient movement by the car.[69] When his home city of Luxembourg was threatened by such a development, the very young Krier produced a counter-project. This became a regular feature of European Rationalists, whose projects typically took the form of dramatic aerial perspectives illustrating a part of the city repaired, reorganised or extended in a traditional pattern of streets and houses. Krier's brilliant drawings became influential and the example to follow [11.18].[70]

11.18 Kreis and Schaad, project for the new station square in Lucerne

The Internationale Bauaustellung (IBA) featured an extensive application of ideas for the reconstruction of war-ravaged Berlin along traditional lines. The Neubau department of the IBA organised more than 20 architectural competitions where many of the leading Rationalists were invited to contribute to ideas for the regeneration of the Southern Friedrichstadt area of the city. The overall aim was to make a modern interpretation of the original Baroque layout. The majority of projects feature perimeter blocks that explore how the traditional urban block structure can be re-configured. A typical example is the Victoria block where the 'urban villa' typology is used for apartment buildings, the whole block contained by Kreis, Schaad and Schaad's apartment building on Lindenstrasse [11.19].

11.19 Kreis, Schaad and Schaad, apartment building, Berlin

'*Zeitgeist* is no concern of Architecture', wrote Krier, setting himself resolutely against the forces of progress. Greatly influenced by his early reading of Adorno, whom he considered had 'made the most radical criticism of industrial society so far', Krier was at this time a curious mixture of Marxism and conservatism.[71] He saw no contradiction in this, however, as in his view it was 'the whole structure of industrial society that was responsible for the decay of the city'.[72]

The basis for such urban-orientated projects was usually the 'figure-ground' plan, a city or site plan that blocked out all built form in black to emphasise the spatial configuration shown in white. The use of this technique sparked a renewed interest in Camillo Sitte's book, *City Planning According to Artistic Principles*, originally published in 1889, where this technique is used to analyse the spatial configuration of European cities [11.20]. Against the charge that Sitte was a romantic concerned only with the picturesque, Krier retorted that he was 'totally misunderstood … he was a thinker. He conceptualised the idea of urban space.'[73] This emphasis on space over form differentiates this group from Rossi. It also led to other old mappings of the city being revisited for inspiration, in particular the Nolli plan of Rome (1748) – where interiors of public buildings are show in the same manner as streets, squares and courts – and Letarouilly's *Edifice de Rome Moderne* (1858) where a building's inflection to the urban matrix is emphasised [11.21]. Rowe proposed an eclectic collage of historically informed architecture in his book *Collage City* (1978, written with Fred Koetter), but based securely on the figure-ground technique, which formed the basis of his studio teaching at Cornell in the 1970s and 1980s. He coined the phrases 'object fixation' and 'physics envy' to characterise the Modern Movement and illustrated the destructive impact of this on the city's matrix by comparing Le Corbusier's object-like Unité d'Habitation with Vasari's design for the Uffizi in Renaissance Florence, where a long colonnaded space between the Piazza Signoria and River Arno was the primary design decision.[74]

Krier introduced to the English-speaking world ideas inherited from Rossi when he came as a teenager to work for Stirling. His influence can be seen in the way Stirling's work changed radically at this time, from the object-like History Faculty Building (1964) at Cambridge to the competition entry for the Derby Civic Centre (1973), jointly designed with Krier, where the figure-ground is the main design tool and delineation of urban space the primary design objective. Of his time with Stirling, Krier wrote: 'Stirling is not the kind of artist who has a grand vision of life and the world. Rather he sees what is going on and allows himself to be influenced.'[75]

11.20 Camillo Sitte, project for 're-urbanising' the Ringstrasse, Vienna. *City Planning According to Artistic Principles*

11.21 The Nolli Plan of Rome, detail

In this way, traditional city form, capable of combining many different uses within its continuous, densely woven fabric, has found itself superceded by an economically optimizing 'motopia'.

Frampton, *On the Predicament of Architecture at the Turn of the Century*

11.22 Abbotstown Laboratory.
John Tuomey, Project
Architect, Office of Public
Works. Photo courtesy of OPW

A few years later, in the late 1970s, a trio of young Irish architects – John Tuomey, Paul Keogh and Sheila O'Donnell – worked in Stirling's London office and came under the influence of Krier and Frampton, who was teaching at the Royal College of Art where Keogh, O'Donnell and Rachel Chidlow studied.[76] In the early 1980s this group returned to Ireland with the specific objective of implementing a Rossian programme. In his preface to the catalogue of Rossi's Dublin exhibition (organised by the group) in 1983, Keogh wrote that although Rossi's 'built work is universal yet intrinsically linked to his native Lombardy', it nevertheless afforded lessons 'particularly relevant to Irish architecture'.[77] The early un-built projects of this group exhibited at the Architectural Association as 'Figurative Architecture' demonstrate Rossi's influence, particularly Keogh's Regional Administration Offices, Tralee, Tuomey's Laboratory at Abbotstown (built in 1985) and O'Donnell and Tuomey's Kew Garden's competition entry [11.22].

The influence of Rossi's ideas on Stirling can be seen most clearly in his series of competitions for museums and galleries that culminated in the Neues Staatsgalerie (1977–84) in Stuttgart. In an essay written at the time of the building's opening, Stirling said that he 'likes it all'. I could have illustrated it as a work of post-modernism, for the building appears, with echoes of Fischer von Erlach, as a collage of historical fragments from an Egyptian cornice through to a Constructivist entrance canopy and hi-tech glazed wall [11.23]. The plan composition, centred on a rotunda, is based on Schinkel's Altes Museum, although the rotunda is designed as a creeper-clad ruin [11.24]. Nevertheless, the design defers to the existing city matrix at the same time as it presents a collage of past and contemporary architectures. All the lines on the ground that establish the forms respond to adjacent buildings [11.25]. As it is an extension to the existing gallery, its own new front – the terrace above the car-park – is set by aligning with the back of the forecourt towers of the old building. The new galleries have their face set back and aligned with the entrance façade of the original gallery within the forecourt. The rear of the new gallery aligns with the rear of the existing gallery, and the library projects to pick up the neighbouring buildings on the other side.

11.23 James Stirling,
Staatsgalerie, Stuttgart
11.24 Courtyard as 'ruin'

In the way that he drew upon the history of architecture, breaking it apart to re-assemble a new whole, Stirling's design for the Neues Staatsgalerie is another paradigmatic example of the argument presented here. The building's appearance is very much of its time and of the man himself, but in its careful adjustment to the existing city plan, in this case both historic and modern highway, the composition reflects Rossi's thesis that the city, particularly its plan, constitutes the ground for cultural continuity.

11.25 Staatsgalerie, model.
Photo: With kind permission of John Donat/RIBA Library Photographs collection

MEANING IN ARCHITECTURE

In the work of Venturi and Rossi we witnessed the return of history to the centre of architectural discourse. There is a curious symmetry between their responses to the declining authority of the modern movement and the events that followed the challenge to Vitruvius in the eighteenth century. Venturi's *Complexity and Contradiction* shares certain features with the iconographical approach of Fischer von Erlach. Over and against this, Rossi's Neo-rationalism carries an echo of Laugier's insistence on reason; the type as exemplar on the one hand, the primitive hut on the other. Despite the extreme differences between Venturi and Rossi, they shared and articulated a widespread belief that the modern movement's functionalism and reductive vocabulary had led to an impoverishment of the built environment, with late modernism's flamboyance serving only as a distraction. This sense of shortcomings in modern architecture stimulated the search for something more meaningful. We saw this clearly in Venturi and Rossi's theories, but also emerging immediately before this in the built work and words of Kahn, van Eyck, the Smithsons, Team 10 and the Brutalists. It was perhaps inevitable that these scattered researches would lead to a more considered theoretical investigation into meaning in architecture.

The traditional museum as represented by Schinkel's Altes Museum was fragmented into a combination of elemental volumes connected to circulation routes, embedded in the urban context.

Anthony Vidler,
James Frazer Stirling; Notes from the Archive

But what has meaning to do with history, it might be asked in this context? Its emergence as a significant concern in the aftermath of World War II reflects the uncertainties attached to human existence in the fallout from the atomic bomb and the ongoing threat of the Cold War. Existentialism became a popular philosophy that seemed to articulate these concerns. So in some respects the search for meaning

Meaning can only exist within an already existing cultural context.

Ernst Cassirer

in architecture reflects the spirit of the age. But unlike the teleological idea of history, this search did not presume progress. It was an idea that responded to mankind's search to understand his or her existence over and beyond any particular time. Instead, the horrors of two world wars urged reflection upon the spirit of man and a resistance to the spirit of the age. Underlying history's record of our collective past, and tradition's hold on cultural memories, is a more primordial sense of time which we grasp sub-consciously in the way our lives correspond to the rhythms of the Earth. Meaning in architecture was essentially a search to find how the built environment might contribute to the broader and deeper existential needs of humanity, dwelling on the Earth, dwelling in building.

A first attempt to tackle this directly came in Rykwert's essay 'Meaning in Building' published in 1957.[78] Commenting on recent and current 'movements' he concludes that these 'suggest that there is a feeling that rationalism is not enough'.[79] He identifies the 'less credible followers of Mies' as enabling speculators to dictate an increasingly commercial and corporate language because architectural discourse had 'abdicated responsibility' for framing man's environment. In Rykwert's impassioned words, 'it is the attitude of the technocrats and administrators of architecture, of zoners and curtain-wallers that has brought this about'.[80]

His argument is that architecture does not 'command public support or consent because it has lost the power of touching emotion'.[81] By this he did not hope for more 'expressive' buildings – such as the Sydney Opera House (1957–73), of which he was scathing – but that architects needed to investigate 'content'. Whilst against the expression of rationalism, Rykwert was not against 'rational working methods'.[82] Nevertheless, he considered that 'the age demands that we should acknowledge the unconscious element in man'. Rather surprisingly at this point he urges architects to look at the advertising industry to see how this is pursued. Not to follow its lead, but rather to oppose it, he insists. Nor to assuage desire by promoting superficial luxury but instead, he concludes, 'to make every building an integrating, reconciling and cleansing form'.[83] Rykwert was extremely suspicious of advertising and the emerging electronic media. He refers to G.K. Chesterton who, on seeing the lights of Times Square, New York, said that, 'if he couldn't read he'd think he was in paradise'.[84]

Advertising becomes information when there is no longer anything to choose from, when the recognition of brand names has taken the place of choice, when at the same time the totality forces everyone who wishes to survive into consciously going along with the process. This is what happens under monopolistic mass culture.

Theodor Adorno,
The Schema of Mass Culture

In an introductory note to a reprint of 'Meaning in Building', Rykwert remarks upon a reference he made to a 'semantic study of environment' at the end of the essay.[85] He says at the time of writing he did not know that semiology could be applied to architecture. Despite this disavowal, he must have encountered the early stages of semiology being applied to design, because this had become introduced at the *Hochschule fur Gestaltung* in Ulm during the time he taught there. The essay was developed, he says, from a course of lectures he had given at Ulm.[86] The 'Ulm experiment' as it became known, applied Charles W. Moore's *Foundations of the Theory of Signs* (1938) to design theory. Tomas Maldonado was the driving force, arguing that meaning in design must embrace the study of 'the representatives of modern semiotics'.[87] Rykwert sensed that the extension of semiological analysis to the world of design was based on the model of the physical sciences and hence to be treated with suspicion. He considered that 'technological advance is now so rapid that it demands a critical and discerning stand against the flood, not surrender'.[88] Instead of semiology's quasi-scientific methodology, he argued that architects should 'look to the scattered material which psychologists and anthropologists have been gathering'.[89] This became the approach he was to follow in trying to identify meaning in architecture, an approach shared by Norberg-Schulz, who was teaching at Ulm with Rykwert at this time.

Norberg-Schulz's essay 'Meaning in Architecture' became chosen as the title of the book that disseminated these researches more widely. Edited by George Baird and Jencks, the book was a collection of essays by a range of thinkers, each of whom was invited to make marginal comments on other essays to facilitate the sense of a debate, 'Because the issues are current and by no means settled.'[90] Although the book does contain a range of essays and opinions, the potential application of semiology to architecture dominates. Jencks and Baird had devoted a whole issue of the journal *Arena* to semiology in 1966 and their essays were expanded to form the basis of the book *Meaning in Architecture*.[91] They may not have been aware of Venturi at the earlier stage, but by 1969 they almost certainly were and no doubt saw the tide of opinion going with them.

The central proposition of the book was set out by Jencks: 'Semiology, literally the theory of signs, has been postulated as the fundamental science of human communication, so it is naturally central or at least relevant to all the following disputes over meaning in architecture.'[92]

The book did not begin auspiciously for those like Norberg-Schulz and Rykwert who were concerned with the emphasis given to semiology. For the book opens with the sentence, 'A book is a machine to think with.' In contrast to Jencks and Baird linking semiology with post-modern design, Colquhoun saw it valid only for criticism. Where Jencks was taken up in the enthusiasm of discovery, Colquhoun subjected semiology's application to architecture to the searching scrutiny of logic. He examined the validity of applying Saussurian semiology, which was based on 'structural linguistics', to aesthetic systems. He identified a number of points that called this into question.[93] Two points seem particularly noteworthy. Firstly, change takes place in only one part of the system in language, whereas in aesthetic systems the whole can change: 'e.g. the change from Gothic to classical architecture or from eclecticism to modernism'.[94] Secondly, in economic systems (which Saussure treated as analogous to language) the value of the metal in money does not have value in itself, whereas in aesthetic systems, 'it is precisely the intrinsic quality of the metal that is important'.[95] In semiotic terms, the signifier is arbitrary and conventional, whereas in this example the signifier, or 'sensible form is interesting in itself'.[96] Another way of considering this difference is that in language, according to Saussure, the structure is a closed system where the 'value' of the signifier is taken for granted – i.e. the green of traffic lights for 'go' – whereas in aesthetic systems the signifier has an intrinsic and culturally determined value which affects the meaning of things for us.[97] Colquhoun's concluding statement is perhaps sufficient here to explain why semiology had a relatively short-lived impact on architecture and meaning.

> We tend to forget that in analyzing language we do not attempt to change it. Structural linguistics is a descriptive, perhaps explanatory, method. It is concerned with the formal structures underlying language, not with its meaning or value system.[98]

Colquhoun did not explain beyond why semiology might be useful for criticism but not design, although perhaps there is no need. Whilst Saussurian analysis of a thing into signifier and signified enriches our understanding of perception, nevertheless the thing itself remains as an entity and not simply the sum of this or that particular analysis. While semiology might explain how we see a cat, for example, the cat itself remains. This form of analysis helps us understand how we perceive a building, but not the way a building has to be designed and made for occupation. With Venturi's decorated shed in mind, adding a sign to the shed may communicate an idea, but the actuality of the shed/building, all of its inner workings, structure and skin need to be designed and made, just as all the inner workings of a cat, its physiognomy and fur, have evolved to shape its characteristic form. The pursuit of meaning in architecture, as understood by Rykwert and Norberg-Schulz, implies that architects should investigate how the built environment could be made more meaningful to fundamental human needs, not simply how we perceive things.

Jencks goes on to argue that we can either use semiology to understand 'how meaning works in a technical sense, or we can remain content with our intuition'.[99] This, of course, would have been contested by Rykwert, who argued that using psychology and anthropology would help recover meaning in architecture rather than the quasi-scientific methodology of semiotics. Norberg-Schulz's essay explicitly criticises 'self-expression' (which is not so far from mere intuition).[100] The whole tenor of his essay is against natural science as the description of reality. He describes the 'space conception' of functionalist modernism as symbolising 'a logico-scientific view of the world'.[101] 'Open' and 'dynamic' will remain as an aspect of modern architecture, he says, but, with echoes of van Eyck, 'differentiation' and 'humanization' will re-emerge and prevail. Expanding upon this, Norberg-Schulz hints at an early awareness of a phenomenological approach, perhaps growing from fascination with structuralism or early twentieth century art-critical theory. He defines our experience of space in concrete terms with structural oppositions or polarities, such as a vertical axis and a horizontal plane. 'Meaning consists of relations', he argues. 'All objects are experienced as part of situations; they are connected with other subjects.'[102] He considers it essential to shift thinking from abstract conception of 'space' to the more concrete 'place'. 'It is the task of the architect to give to places such a form that they may receive the necessary content.'[103] He develops these ideas that ran counter to semiology in his book *Existence, Space and Architecture* (1971), the most philosophical contribution to the debates at this time.

As the title *Existence, Space and Architecture* suggests, Norberg-Schulz broached the problem of a deeper, existential meaning head-on. Central to this was his elaboration of the concept of what he called 'existential space'. In the foreword he briefly reviews recent or

Language … does not primarily serve communication, but discloses the basic existential structures.

Norberg-Schulz,
Kahn, Heidegger and the Language of Architecture

contemporary approaches – semiological/structuralist; Christopher Alexander's 'building task analysis'; and Venturi's 'renewal of the theory of architectural form' – before adding that he is to examine 'the basic problem of space as a dimension of human existence'.[104] Later on in the book he discusses how space is considered in architecture and concludes that there are basically two conceptions; Euclidian, where a 'grammar' of geometry informs design; and one based on 'perception psychology'.[105] The work of Jean Piaget in this field is central to Norberg-Schulz's conception of existential space. In particular he refers to two of Piaget's studies on child development, *The Child's Construction of Reality* (1955) and *The Child's Conception of Space* (1956). Piaget states that 'It is quite obvious that the perception of space involves a gradual construction and does not exist ready-made at the outset of development.'[106] Picking up on this, Norberg-Schulz says that we have an immediate 'perceptual space' but also more stable 'space schemata'. These combine universal elementary structures (or archetypes) and socio-cultural conditioned structures. Piaget's researches revealed that this stable schemata develops as a child learns to grasp that objects, which are perceived in particular places, are still there when he or she returns his or her look. Piaget interprets this as that objects once experienced are 'conserved' and that the child gradually 'situates them in a more comprehensive totality, a space'.[107] From this, fixed points form a frame of reference into which all things are located, at first ordered topologically – 'proximity, separation, succession, closure (inside–outside) and continuity'. From this an elementary organisational schema develops which Norberg-Schulz summarises as consisting 'in the establishment of centres or places (proximity), directions or paths (continuity) and areas or domains (enclosure)'.[108]

It is beyond the scope of this book to expand further upon this, except to reiterate the principle components of Norberg-Schulz's conception of existential space, which adapt Piaget's psychological researches: 'Centre and place'; 'Direction and path'; 'Area and Domain'. In his later book, *Genius Loci; Towards a Phenomenology of Architecture* (1980), he summarises his work in overtly existential terminology. Man 'dwells', he says, 'when he can orientate himself within, and identify himself with, an environment, in short, when he experiences the environment as meaningful.'[109] In this later book he explains that his phrase 'existential foothold' is a synonym for what Heidegger describes as 'dwelling'. Heidegger's philosophy underpins the direction taken by

We have said that space is existential; we might just as well have said that 'existence is spatial'.

Maurice Merlau-Ponty

The constructed city, the arrangements of the rural landscape, and in general everything that tells of man's domination of the natural elements express collective meanings. Architecture is to a great extent the mirror of such meanings, and it is in this way that its forms acquire stable meanings.

Georgio Grassi

Norberg-Schulz in *Existence, Space and Architecture*. It was Heidegger's profound analysis of the human condition in *Being and Time* that directed Norberg-Schulz to explore the part the built environment might play in enabling what Heidegger and other existentialists called an 'authentic existence'.

Norberg-Schulz identified the functionalism of the modern movement and the unsatisfactory environment it had produced with 'scientific understanding'.[110] He argued that mankind cannot gain an 'existential foothold' through this, but needs '*symbols, that is works of art which represent life-situations*'.[111] Meaning in architecture thus sets itself against quasi-scientific semiology and its manifestation in post-modernism. In response to the superficialities of post-modern architecture, for Norberg-Schulz the idea of meaning took a deep hold. He illustrates aspects of how a meaningful environment presents itself with examples from landscape, traditional (or vernacular) buildings, historical and modern buildings. Implied in his examples is the significance of time and memory. Just as a child develops a sense of orientation as he or she grows and remembers, so a culture forms layers of remembered forms that cohere as meaningful places. 'An ever-changing world would not allow for the establishment of schemata', comments Norberg-Schulz on Piaget's researches, 'and would therefore make human development impossible.'[112] As Rykwert indicated, the rapid growth of technology and the speed of change argue for a 'critical and discerning stand against the flood'. This became the impetus for the pursuit of meaning in architecture. Inspired by an increasing awareness of the significance of Heidegger's philosophy and its contribution to thinking about architecture, the existential concept of authenticity became a many-pronged resistance to the overwhelming forces of a rationalised society. Norberg-Schulz's later *Meaning in Western Architecture* (1974) explored how his conception of existential space could be found in the great epochs of Western architecture. For he says, the 'existential dimension … becomes manifest in history, but its meanings transcend the historical situation'.[113]

The concern for a deeper existential meaning to architecture was a product of its particular moment in history, reflecting the worries people felt with the war a close memory and the shadow of the atomic bomb hanging over them. The global environmental crisis that has emerged in the past few decades presents another deep-seated

The temporal structure of our existence is the foundation of memory in the same way that spatiality is the foundation of space.

Dalibor Veseley,
Architecture in the Age of Divided Representation

What, then, is time? I know well enough what it is, provided that nobody asks me; but if I am asked what it is and try to explain, I am baffled.

St. Augustine

A sense of personal identity depends essentially on memory, but a sense of the past could only have arisen when man consciously reflected on his memories … Man must have been conscious of memories and purpose long before he made any explicit distinctions between past, present, and future.

G. J. Whitrow,
Time in History

We never keep to the present. We anticipate the future as if we found it too slow in coming and were trying to hurry it up, or we recall the past as if to stay its too rapid flight.

Blaise Pascal,
Pensées

Arbitrariness has to do with a generation which has been brought up on shopping for ideas.

Zaha Hadid

We must resolve the possibilities of a shapeless future with the significance and meaning of established forms and experience. That which has been with that which could be, memory and imagination.

David Chipperfield,
Tradition and Invention

problem that we face on planet Earth. This situation is exacerbated by the fact that increasingly sophisticated advertising, and a media in thrall to glamour, divert us from this while at the same time induces us to consume more, such that the problem becomes greater. We should heed Rykwert's warning and oppose the 'paradise' of signs with buildings that are 'integrating, reconciling, cleansing forms'. The main message from meaning in architecture is that our existential needs can be satisfied only by buildings that embody an authentic relationship between human beings and the earth that sustains us. History, tradition and memory would appear to be the areas of experience and understanding that give shape to this, as will be expanded upon in the epilogue.

* * *

So we find ourselves in a position not so dissimilar to where we began. I have ended the historical part of this survey in the period following *Complexity and Contradiction* and *The Architecture of the City* because these two books made perhaps the last coherent attempts to articulate a consensus as to what might constitute meaning in architecture. In a similar way to how Fischer von Erlach, Laugier, Piranesi, Ledoux, Boullée, et al proposed new theoretical bases for architecture after history and science dethroned Vitruvius, so Venturi and Rossi put forward programmes for re-grounding architecture following disenchantment with the Modern Movement. But in a pluralist, individualistic society, such as developed in the second half of the twentieth century, it has proved to be impossible to establish any widespread consensus. Nevertheless, the search for meaning in architecture will not go away as architecture contributes so much to the built environment, which increasingly makes up the background to our lives. Architecture differs from other arts, not only in this responsibility, but also because buildings last for a long time. This suggests that we should take note of Piaget's work on child development and turn architecture to making the stable background to our lives in this fast-changing, media-dominated world; let's search for a fundamental ground for architecture rather than individualistically express the spirit of a fragmented, fast-changing technology.

Epilogue: History, tradition, memory

Post-modernism soon fell from fashion and ideas about the architecture of the city became absorbed into the mainstream, although increasingly ignored as fashion followed fashion. Writing at the nadir of post-modernism in 1988, Colquhoun described this phase as an 'exhausted high modernism' spawning a 'plurality of tendencies'. But serious concerns for architecture raised by questions of meaning and memory did not and will not go away. We began by discussing how a new sense of history became a significant aspect of self-understanding in the period we have looked at, coinciding as it did with the rise of modernity. I would like to reflect upon this situation by drawing out the principal themes that emerged in the preceding survey. History, tradition and memory are the interrelated measures or modes of our understanding of time, and their implications for architecture cannot be ignored.

As Moneo says, the 1990s and the first years of the new millennium have been 'dominated by fragmentation', with deconstruction 'a new aesthetic ideology'.[1] This led more recently to a 'formlessness', he continues, reflecting the overwhelming impact of 'electronic communication, global information and virtual imagery'.[2] In addition there has been an explosion of purely sculptural forms of building based on technical prowess. Fragmentation has become a commonplace description of the cultural condition of modernity, but whether architecture should express this spirit of the age is a critical question, given the built environment's role in providing shelter, stability and well-being.

Deconstruction began as a critical literary project aimed at overthrowing institutionalised meanings in established traditions of discourse. Jacques Derrida's method of looking for contradictions forced upon an argument by the differing claims of rhetoric and logic was all too easily transposed to architecture, where rhetorical form came to rule over logic of construction and a building's context and content. The word deconstruction itself almost demanded that the language of building be dismantled. Revolutionary Russian Constructivism provided a ready-made language to deconstruct.

In his *Technology as Symptom and Dream* (1989), Robert Romanyshyn worries about the extension of the scientific microscopic world-view into all walks of life and argues that a fundamental aspect of human lived experience is that gravity binds us to the earth.[3] He interprets 'technology as a cultural dream' and as a 'dream of distancing ourselves from the body and of departing the earth'.[4] With this provocative image in mind and its implied challenge to deconstruction's vision of the *zeitgeist*, we might distinguish between the purely subjective form-making of, for example, Frank Gehry's Guggenheim Museum (1997) in Bilbao, a free-standing aesthetic object aimed at the tourist market, and the more intellectual work of Bernhard Tschumi's Parc de la Villette (1984–7) in Paris, which stemmed from engagement with Derrida's ideas [12.1 and 12.2]. It speaks volumes that in his *Postmodern Culture* (1985), Hal Foster writes that 'media reproduction … is indeed a primary "site" of this architecture'.[5] Despite deconstruction's critical aims, these kinds of buildings – and contemporary icon architecture – glamourise technologically driven progress. The infinite potential for computers to generate Bilbao-type forms increase these concerns not only about the relationship between form and content, but also about the role of human imagination; a twenty-first century echo of Ruskin's concerns. In this future-forward focus we see, to use Romanyshyn's terminology, the shadow of Hegel's teleological conception of history.

12.1 Frank Gehry, Guggenheim Gallery, Bilbao

12.2 Bernard Tschumi, Parc de la Villette, Paris

HISTORY

History is the tale of the victors, it is said. In 'Technology and Science as "Ideology"', Habermas argues that science is not simply the neutral pursuit of objective knowledge but, driven by capitalism, is complicit with technology in what he calls a 'tyranny' over 'the social life-world'.[6] Unlike earlier forms of tyranny made visible by castle, cathedral, or palace, the tyranny of what he calls 'instrumental rationality' is concealed: 'this repression can disappear from the consciousness of the population because the legitimation of domination has assumed a new character: it refers to the "constantly increasing productivity and domination of nature which keeps individuals living … in increased comfort."'[7] Because humans have always been involved in making material improvements to their socio-economic world, technological progress appears but a successful extension of this seemingly neutral aim. Progress seems 'natural' and beneficial. But progress in the past was not driven primarily by technological aims. The soaring height and shimmering light of a Gothic cathedral, for example, was not shaped by what could be done with stone but rather to give expression to humans' image of heaven.

Like most thinkers, Habermas identifies the specific character of modernity arising from the Enlightenment with its aspiration for progress through an all-embracing application of reason. He sees the combination of science and technology having its own internal dynamic, which is what he calls 'instrumental or strategic rationality'.[8] The threshold of the modern period came when the process of rationalisation undermined traditional forms of activity, such that working practices 'could now be criticised against the standards of rationality of means-ends relations'.[9] Not until the emergence of capitalist economics, for example, were yearly increases in production demanded: production for profit, not people's needs; exchange value, not use value. Henceforth forms of production came 'to assume the form of technical control of objectified processes', a modus operandi we saw implicated in the ideology of *Neue Sachlichkeit* that shaped the rationalised character of the Modern Movement in architecture.[10]

The proposition I have explored in this study is that Hegel's view of history, which he put forward as advancing a consciousness of freedom, became transmuted to a materialist idea of progress driven by technology, capitalism and a consumer culture. Hegel's linear philosophy of history, was in fact, concerned with free individuals operating rationally within the context of society. This has become conflated with a spurious idea of freedom linked with free market ideology, which elides all-too-easily to a belief in architectural free expression. We have seen how a conception of history arose in opposition to this future-forward view predicated on the undeniable fact that the present moment contains both past and future, memory and anticipation. Heidegger characterises this as an 'authentic' relationship to time and the world. This is very much in contrast to the rise and expansion of a 'me-now' consumer culture , with its focus on novelty and glamour, the ever-new promising a more desirable life-style in the immediate future, just as novel forms of building are acquired to 're-brand' a city.

In *The Question Concerning Technology,* Heidegger explains that it is not technology in itself that is the problem; rather it is its modern 'challenging' character.[11] Heidegger distinguishes between the essence of technology where it emerged to serve humankind and its modern, means-to-an-end, challenging practice. In exploring what should be our proper relationship to technology, and through it our relationship to the Earth, he traces its root meaning to the archaic Greek word *technē,* which means bringing forth, and is connected to *poiēsis.* Through this chain of words we get closer to the essence of technology, for *poiēsis* is closely related to *physis,* he says, the Greek word which meant the bursting forth in and of itself as in plants and other natural forms.[12] The essence of technology, then, lies in poetically bringing forth man-made things such that they share in the character of natural life-forms, with the overriding aim that the world we make becomes reconciled with the natural world. Technology therefore entails revealing the poetic nature of things rather than being a means–end rational calculation, a view that Heidegger calls 'enframing' and 'standing reserve', a predominant world-view, which sees the world as merely a stockpile of resources to exploit.

All art is essentially 'poetic' according to Heidegger, and draws upon the traditions and customs of a people to articulate their understanding of reality.[13] He hoped that his redefinition of technology would bring about a new focus on human needs rather than rational means-to-an-end, and with it a re-alignment of art and technology. Heidegger's elevated view of art developed in opposition to Hegel. Hegel dismissed the idea of mankind's 'immediate unity with nature', arguing instead that 'art lifts him out of and above imprisonment in nature'.[14] Religion was superior to art, in his schema, because 'our consciousness makes God' – 'spirit's mirror image' – 'its object in itself', i.e. without the assistance of material. He set out a hierarchy of the arts which were, in ascending order: architecture, the lowest because it is most bound up with material; sculpture, because in classical Greece inner undivided spirit was presented 'in bodily shape'; and painting, music, and poetry the higher, because least material arts, with poetry the highest because 'it unites the infinite space of ideas with the *time* of sound'.[15] Nevertheless, in his *Lectures on Aesthetics* delivered in the 1820s, Hegel described architecture as building a 'temple', metaphorically to foster humans' relation to the World Spirit, i.e. as 'a place for the inner composure of the spirit … against the threat of storm … [and] tempest'.[16] The role of art was 'the sensuous presentation of the Absolute itself'.[17]

Hegel had a pessimistic view of art, seeing it as no longer satisfying spiritual needs; the 'beautiful days of Greek art, like the golden of the later Middle Ages are gone'.[18] Art and religion had both been surpassed by philosophy. Art was no longer involved in the search for truth because philosophy grasped the World Spirit conceptually in contrast to the sensuous medium of art. This idealisation of the spirit became taken up and opposed by Heidegger, whose own view was that art provides deep insights into humanity's relationship to the life in and of the Earth. More specifically, he interpreted art as an expression of our situation between earth and sky. As was his way, he found this understanding supported in early Greece. Bearing in mind that for Heidegger all art was poetic, he stated that 'memory is the source of poetry' and recounted the mythical connection between memory, art, earth and sky. The Greek goddess Mnemosyne, whose name means 'Memory', was born of the earth goddess Gaia and the sky god Ouranous. Mnemosyne was the mother of the muses – her daughters who 'were addicted to song'[19] – and was married to Zeus, another sky god. So original inspiration for the arts was saturated with the memory of earth and sky, which Heidegger believed should continue to be embodied in art.

Heidegger's late writings concentrated on art, for in this realm the modern conception of technology could best be countered. Of all the arts, architecture is most involved with technology, which places on architects a special obligation to consider its proper role in responding to human needs. In 'Building Dwelling Thinking', Heidegger shows by a similar etymological method that the German verb 'to build' (*bauen*) is linked with 'to dwell' (*baun*) and has its root in 'to be' (*bis*). In the light of this, he reverses the means–end commonplace understanding that we can dwell thanks only to building, saying instead that to build we must first properly dwell. Building in this sense means 'preserving and nurturing'.[20] (Our word 'bower' hints at such a sheltering environment.)

This reading of buildings is best understood in relation to Heidegger's expression *Dasein,* usually translated as being-in-the-world, which encapsulates the way human existence is inseparable from the reality of the natural world; we are totally involved in the world as we might be in love or in pain. Opposite in every way to the Cartesian separation of subject and object, there is no breaking the continuum of our minds in our body in the world, a phenomenological notion that indicates the importance of an experiential understanding of architecture. John Maquarrie expands upon this to develop an existentialist idea of what he calls 'being-with-others', the fact that the human environment is not simply a world of things but involves 'constant interaction with other existents.'[21] This serves to remind us that cultural developments are not like mutations stemming from evolution's blind drive for life, but adaptations made by minds reflecting upon what is and what might be, as Vico first noted. This returns us to the role history plays in our understanding of the built environment.

12.3–12.4 Enric Miralles, Scottish Parliament, Edinburgh

I highlighted Schinkel's reinterpretation of the Greek *stoa* as a good example of the way an architect uses history to effect such a cultural adaptation, re-using the *stoa* as an element to express the openness of the new nineteenth century building type, the public museum. Lining one side of the agora at Athens, the *stoa* symbolised the space of public discourse. With this deep cultural history, Enric Miralles chose the long, open colonnaded form of the *stoa* as a primary element of his competition-winning Scottish Parliament Building (1998–2000), which he adapted to a modern idiom. Stretching from where Edinburgh's Royal Mile meets the Palace of Holyrood out into the Scottish landscape, the stoa-colonnade is elaborated to mark the entrance to the Parliament building and gives emphasis to the accessibility demanded of modern democracy [12.3 and 12.4]. Another more directly recognizable use of history is Moneo's Roman Museum (1980–5) at Merida, where the structure evokes the scale and material construction of Roman monuments [12.5]. Long, thin Roman bricks act as permanent shuttering to a modern concrete construction, and semi-circular arches contrast with a modern repeated bay system to lend a rich ambiguity to the central museum space. The bare brick walls stand ready to receive Roman fragments unearthed in the archaeological excavations that surround and, indeed, underlie the new museum itself; the scale and material provide an appropriate setting for the fragments, resonant with their original context.

12.5 Rafael Moneo, Roman Museum, Merida, Photo: Michael Moran

In *History and Truth* (2007), Paul Ricouer acknowledges that finding objective truth in history may be impossible, but argues that by 'successive approximations' historians can get closer to understanding past events. This way of making sense of the past – the historian's craft – for the present – the community of historians and readers – parallels the way Schinkel, Miralles and Moneo made use of architectural history. While Miralles and Moneo brought forward the historical element for use today, they transmuted it such as to establish 'a consciousness of remoteness and temporal depth', an essential attribute of the use of history.[22]

TRADITION

Tradition, in contrast, is the tale of the vanquished. The Enlightenment's subjection of traditional practices to the scrutiny of reason led to their demise. Although reason played a key role in political emancipation, improved health and human betterment, nevertheless traditional skills and meaning in work were diminished. (Ruskin and the Arts and Crafts movement recognised this and tried to resist. Loos wore brogues.) Hannah Arendt says that 'only twice in our history' have people become 'conscious and over-conscious of the facts of tradition'.[23] The first time was when the Romans adopted Greek thought, culture, arts and architecture. And the second was when the Romantic Movement defended tradition as a bulwark against the upheaval wrought by the Enlightenment.[24] 'Romanticism conceives of tradition as an antithesis to the freedom of reason and regards it as something historically given, like nature.'[25] Arendt makes a distinction between tradition as a burden and the past as a force. Retrieving fragments of the past frees us to make a new and meaningful beginning, which liberates us from the burden of tradition.

The philosopher Hans-Georg Gadamer has more recently pointed out that our relationship to the past cannot be grasped by simply 'distancing and freeing ourselves from tradition'. Rather, he says, 'we are always situated within traditions' and tradition 'is always part of us, a model or exemplar'.[26] Tradition for Gadamer is not simply something that lies behind us and that we take over automatically, but is a task that confronts us. Central to his conception of tradition is the notion of 'understanding', which involves an 'interplay' or dialogue between what we inherit from the past and our self-understanding in the present. The way we grasp 'truths' in art directly or through a process of interpretation based on our embedded cultural experience became a particular concern of his major work *Truth and Method* (1975), for as he says, 'past and present are brought together in art'.[27] He highlights how a building in particular preserves and 'points back' to its original 'context of purpose and life'. Up to the time of the twentieth century avant-garde, art made evident the continuity of culture yet open to ongoing reinterpretation. This points to the profound consequences that follow from the avant-garde's determination to break with tradition in architecture for, Gadamer continues, 'a building is never only a work of art. Its purpose, through which it belongs in the context of life, cannot be separated from it without losing some of its reality.'[28] It is difficult not to agree with Gadamer that such an understanding of tradition as a dialogue with the past is predicated on the fact that 'history does not belong to us; we belong to it'.[29]

Frampton's 'Critical Regionalism' made an important contribution to the part tradition might play in architecture. He formulated this notion as a form of resistance to what he calls the 'optimized technology' in modern buildings that marked 'the victory of universal civilisation over locally inflected culture'.[30] His essay 'Critical Regionalism' begins with a quotation from Ricoeur, who describes the 'phenomenon of universalization' spreading 'a mediocre civilisation [and a] basic consumer culture'.[31] Frampton sees late modern architecture polarised between 'a so-called "high-tech" approach predicated exclusively upon production' and buildings with what he calls a 'compensatory façade', a legacy of post-modernism's 'decorated shed'.[32]

His use of 'culture' shows the influence of Romanticism's conception of culture in opposition to civilisation, although his direct inspirations were Arendt, Habermas and the Frankfurt School's critique of the rationalisation of society. From reading Arendt's *The Human Condition* (1958), Frampton noted the distinction she made between labour and work, which he transposed to distinguish between building as an active process and architecture as stasis [12.6 & 12.7]. He came to see how Arendt's linking labour to 'the life process' supported his belief that a focus on regional building techniques using local materials could emancipate architecture from its ties to modernism's universal vocabulary and technological domination. Critical Regionalism is 'not intended to denote the vernacular'. Rather, he advocates a synthesis of local building cultures with the universal steel or concrete frame; framework, he says, 'tends towards the denial and dematerialisation of mass', whereas traditional load-bearing construction is 'telluric, embedding itself ever deeper in the earth'.[33]

In its first iteration as 'Prospects for a Critical Regionalism' Frampton illustrates his hopes with several buildings, but his optimism is missing from later versions where only two buildings are illustrated; Jørn Utzon's Bagsvaerd Church (1973–6), Copenhagen and Aalto's

12.6 Arneberg and Poulsson
City Hall, Oslo
12.7 Statue of building workers

Säynätsalo Town Hall.[34] In his 'Prospects' he illustrated Critical Regionalism with buildings by Aalto, Alvaro Siza, Luis Barragan, Sverre Fehn and Tadao Ando, amongst others. '"Cultivating" the site', he says, in his later reworked, 'Towards a Critical Regionalism; Six Points for an Architecture of Resistance', resists modern developer's preference for bulldozing a site into 'absolute *placelessness*'.[35] Interestingly, Frampton refers to Heidegger's 'Building Dwelling Thinking' in calling for 'the absolute precondition of a bounded domain ... to create an architecture of resistance' and backs this up by Ando describing 'Enclosed Modern Architecture' as his way of expressing 'the sensibilities, customs, aesthetic awareness, distinctive culture, and social traditions' of Japan that he found impossible to do 'by means of an open, internationalist vocabulary of Modernism'.[36]

Frampton posits 'tectonic form' in architecture to resist the sleek packaging of increasingly homogeneous global buildings. An attack at first on post-modernism's scenographic approach, he elaborated it to make the case for 'stable references' against 'dissolution' in the late modern digital and virtual world.[37] He describes how Carlo Scarpa drew upon a Venetian tradition of craftsmanship to forge a modern regional architecture specifically at odds with the machine-smooth Milanese approach to modern design, which Frampton reads more generally as 'a critical commentary on the economic expediency of our utilitarian age'.[38] Scarpa brought the traditions of a craftsman's thinking to his designs, which are characterised by a rich sense of materiality and a montage of disparate elements [12.8 & 12.9].

Frampton here develops a similar point about architecture to that which Semper made about the way traditional artefacts contribute to cultural continuity by their time-worn adaptation to use and familiar material. The significance of a shared world of language, culture and artefacts with significance for us has come to be called the *lebenswelt*, the lived world of everyday experience by which we grasp meaning in contrast to the methods of what Frampton calls 'advanced-techno science', which has an existence independent of architecture. Critical Regionalism implies a reinterpretation of the traditional languages of building and giving clear expression to this: how a building is constructed; how it resists gravity; how details resist weathering; how its bounded character needs careful consideration of thresholds and apertures; how it responds to conditions of light; all this while accommodating, but not prioritising, modern technology [12.10].

12.8–12.9 Carlo Scarpa, Castell Vechio Museum, Verona, detail

12.10 Peter Zumthor,
Art Museum, Bregenz

Frampton argues that the architectural avant-garde, and the post-modern avant-garde in particular, has proved ineffective in resisting the combination of corporate capitalism and instrumental reason, and proposes in its place what he calls 'an *arrière-garde* position'. Only this, he says, has 'the capacity to cultivate a resistance'.[39] Frampton held only limited hope for this, albeit one to be grasped: 'Beyond the aporias of history and progress and outside the reactionary closure of historicism and the neo-avant-garde lies the potential for a *marginal* counter-history'.[40] To occupy this marginal position, architecture must not 'regress into nostalgic historicism or the glibly decorative', nor must it associate itself with 'the optimization of advanced technology', although contemporary building techniques must play a part.[41] Advancing traditions, not advanced technology.

MEMORY

In her book *The Art of Memory,* Frances Yates explains how important were architecture and city spaces to classical memory training and to the preservation of knowledge and culture itself. The character of city spaces was integral to the development of memory and these were bounded spaces. She reviews Cicero's account of the art of memory where he describes its objective as being to 'imprint on the memory a series of *loci*, or places'.[42] Students were bidden to walk through a city and memorise a series of striking features. Order and sequence were vital as the aim, when preparing a speech, was to locate a particular series of points on the memorised sequence of *loci;* the phenomenological nature of spatial memory being stronger than ephemeral thoughts held in the mind. From our point of view with easy access to paper and printed material, says Yates, it is not easy to grasp the significance of 'what the artificial memory of Cicero may have been like, as it moved among the buildings of ancient Rome, *seeing* the places, *seeing* the images stored on the places, with a piercing inner vision which immediately brought to life the thoughts and words of his speech'.[43] The art of memory did not completely disappear with the advent of printing, for she recounts how the late Renaissance magus Giordano Bruno (1548–1600) added the streets and squares of Paris and London to his memory system.[44]

Sitte pursued the relation between cities and memory, and it is interesting to note that he described the Roman forum as 'like a well-appointed and richly furnished main hall' where 'frequently hundreds or thousands of statues and busts, etc. were brought together'.[45] Writing of the Greek Acropolis, although he could be referring to any number of major city public spaces, he says that the 'most elevated poetry and thought has found spatial embodiment here', where a 'people's philosophy of life becomes tangible'.[46] Just as our rooms are filled with things that display our values and hold memories, so did city spaces. All the city spaces illustrated in Sitte's book are bounded spaces. In 'Building Dwelling Thinking', Heidegger explains how the German word for space, *Raum* (from which derives our word 'room') originally meant 'a place cleared or freed for settlement'.[47] Similarly, he says that for the ancient Greeks this notion applied also to things; i.e. a boundary is where a thing 'begins its prescencing'. Things, in this formulation, are not simply the pure objects of measurement. He insists upon the use of *Raum,* or place, instead of space in dealing with buildings, for space means 'now no more than extension', a reduction to 'purely mathematical' manipulation. The bounded character of Roman and traditional city spaces not only made possible the art of memory, but also indicate the significance of memory to what it is to be human. It is hard to imagine the art of memory possible, yet orientation, in Le Corbusier's Cartesian city plans.

Just how specific aspects of memory can be embodied in the design of a city's built fabric is illustrated by the Parc del Clot (1988–91) in Barcelona by Freixas and Miranda. Part of Barcelona's redevelopment that accompanied the 1992 Olympics, the park was formed out of the site of a disused railway depot. Some of the existing warehouse walls were retained and integrated into the new design, juxtaposed with new functional elements, such as a concrete bridge and lighting pylons [12.11 & 12.12]. In one corner the walls form a backdrop to a stepped, sunken play area that evokes the setting of a football stadium, complete with floodlights. Boys might dream here of playing for Barca, while their mothers might remember their fathers and grandfathers who worked here on the railways. Adding to the poetry of time recollected, a copper trough attached to the old walls commences to pour a sheet of water into a pool at the break of school [12.13].

A more direct drawing upon memory in the city is illustrated by Peter Zumthor's Kolumba Museum (2003–7) in Cologne. The museum is built over the ruins of the bombed church of St. Kolumba and incorporates fragments of the old building. A large grey box of a building, it was designed by the carpenter-architect Zumthor as the

12.11–12.13 Freixas and Miranda, Parc del Clot, Barcelona

antithesis of what he described as 'the Bilbao effect'.[48] For Zumthor, the aim of architecture is not formal invention, but to develop an appropriate setting – in this case for the art collection. (Siza said that 'architects don't invent, they transform reality'.) The Kolumba Museum combines the modern 'vernacular' of steel or concrete frame with the enclosing presence of traditional masonry walls [12.14 & 12.15].

12.14 (Above) Zumthor, Kolumba Museum, Cologne
12.15 (Right) Interior

The innovation here comes in the honeycombed brick walls that filter light through such that it seems to be held in the wall itself, a modern reinterpretation of the Gothic cathedral's glass wall of embodied light.

* * *

In contrast to these poetic uses of history, tradition and memory, aspects of time separated in analysis although bound together in experience, is the abuse of history that originated in Hegel's view of history being conflated with evolution to underpin progress, and with it material gain. In this way advancing technology in itself became seen as the be-all and end-all, as 'natural', and as an expression of the spirit of the age, rather than a means to be considered in relation to human life goals. Any search for a fundamental ground for architecture must take note of the presence of the past in the present as a fundamental fact of human experience. For architecture, this means acknowledging the significance of history, tradition and memory. The role of historically developed cultural typical forms as expounded by Rossi played a positive role in countering the gratuitous invention of post-modernism. Modified by the understanding of the significance of the spatial configuration of the historically given city in stabilising a relationship to traditions embodied in the city plan, this combination provides a philosophically secure basis for continuity in architecture consistent with Piaget's description of human development. The city has provided psychic as well as physical shelter since cities arose 4,000 years ago and, until the past hundred years or so, architecture submitted itself to the greater good in playing its part.

In the course of this study we have seen how Soane, Schinkel and Stirling made use of history, which gave clues to the way architects might use it to respond to the circumstances we find today. Soane tried to reconcile Enlightenment reason with imagination, the classical tradition with experiential concepts raised by Romanticism, the Sublime and Picturesque. Schinkel was able to lose a good deal of his individuality in the lingering consensus that classicism remained relevant as he re-assembled elements, *stoa* and Pantheon, in an original way to make a new meaningful whole. Following on from Schinkel, Stirling took the Altes Museum as the point of departure for his competition entry for the Nordrhein Westfalen Museum (1975) in Düsseldorf. The way that Stirling took elements from history and re-assembled them into a new meaningful whole can serve as a paradigm for the thesis I have advanced on the critical use of history [12.16].

12.16 Stirling Nordrhein-Westfalen Museum, Düsseldorf, model. Photo: With kind permission of John Donat/RIBA Library Photographs collection

Having chosen the title for this book, I was interested to discover that an archaic Greek word *legein,* which translates as 'to assemble' has as its root meaning 'to enfold in meaningful shape'.[49] This seemed to me to encapsulate Stirling's strategic thinking about design at this time, selecting forms that resonate through architecture's history, taking elements stripped of historical detail, and composing a new whole in such a way as to repair the city's archetypal bounded character ravaged by modern planning. We noted how his Neues Staatsgalerie responded to the context of the city, a primary objective reflecting the change in his work from the object-like Cambridge History Faculty Library, for example.

Stirling said that he 'likes it all', but Vidler argues that Stirling's use of history differed from post-modernism's parody by being based in an 'extension of the modernist preoccupations'. A continuous revision of modernism underlies each phase of his work. In his study, *James Frazer Stirling; Notes from the Archive,* Vidler explains how the Düsseldorf project draws together 'two dominant themes of modernism: that of *typicality,* the rational construction of buildings for collective and individual social tasks, and that of *tradition,* or history, and the need to respond to existing contexts and ideas of the past.'[50]

The Düsseldorf project took Schinkel's Pantheon-like circular central space as its focal point linked by a sinuous circulation route to a free-standing cube, which formed an entrance 'portico'. Vidler suggests Stirling here recapitulates Le Corbusier's entrance sequence at the Cité de Refuge with its combination of box-like porch, curving reception desk, and cylindrical foyer. These older and more recent historical elements, Stirling re-assembles to make a new whole that embeds itself into the existing and broken city fabric. The free-standing primary form of the portico is used to give the building civic presence by being located in the centre of the re-instated Grabbeplatz and being orientated to make a formal connection to the old town. Stirling's optimistic and particular use of history in the Düsseldorf project makes clear the more general use and meaning of history; that architecture can embrace both continuity and innovation in the built environment. However, I would not like it to be inferred that Stirling be upheld uncritically as the model, for more recent thinking has added to our understanding of materiality and the contingencies of everyday life, aspects of architectural meaning not at the forefront of his thinking. The Düsseldorf project most of all might serve as the paradigm because, remaining as seen here in model form, Stirling's idiosyncratic use of colour and material do not deflect from the success of his broader architectural strategy of reinterpretation and repair as a contribution to cultural continuity.

So we come back to where we began with Nietzsche saying that a critical history is essential for the 'life' of a culture. His own life was spent as a solitary wanderer finding his thoughts in nature and agitating for the return of something akin to Dionysian rituals to revitalise culture. Humans increasingly spend their lives immersed in the city, however, and how architecture should respond to this by creating conditions for a meaningful life raises profound new questions. One way forward is to recognise the part a city's spatial morphology plays in stabilising the relationship between present activity and past cultural traditions, and architects might begin from there.

Architecture perhaps could be studied along similar lines to that of philosophy, where philosophers critically evaluate the tradition or history of their subject, so as to advance understanding. The often dry-as-dust tradition of philosophy is leavened for us architects by turning to Heidegger, whose early impulse came from sharing Nietzsche's mistrust in reason alone to shape our world. He followed Nietzsche down to the history before history, giving philosophic expression to the roots of the Western tradition of thought in the pre-Socratic thinkers, contemporaries of the Dionysian rites. Heidegger posits being-in-the-world, our relationship to the Earth, as the fundamental ground of human existence. We live on time's line but are surrounded by time's cycle; the intersection of these two aspects of time forms the pre-reflective background to our lives, shaped on the one hand by our personal 'history' of everyday repetitive tasks, and on the other hand by the hardly comprehensible fast-forward flight to the future. But all within the eternal return of the seasons.

This is one aspect of the alienation that characterises the experience of modernity. Architecture might play a marginal, albeit important, part in redressing this experience. As Romanyshyn says, at 'the most primitive and emotionally powerful levels, the very rhythms of the earth – the tides of the sea, the cycles of the seasons, the rising and setting of the sun – have been a kind of guarantee of our own continuity.'[51] Architects might build a stable world by attending to those experiential qualities that foreground our relationship to the earth and sky, the meanings inherent in materials drawn from the earth, and the spectrum of natural light as it reflects the passage of the day and the seasons. This would provide a stable counterpoint to the fragmentation and flux of the digital world. In taking up this task, architects might also follow historians, in Ricoeur's formulation, by making successive approximations to understand and reinterpret the past from the perspective of today. The history of architecture itself provides a body of work, strategies for responding to the city, and architectural elements with existential characteristics, that can be critically taken apart and re-assembled to form new meanings appropriate for today, related to yesterday, and ready for the future.

Notes

Introduction

1 F. Nietzsche, *The Use and Abuse of History*, p. 3.

2 Ibid., p. 28

3 Nietzsche, op. cit.

4 F. Nietzsche, *Ecco Home*, p. 121

5 J. Tosh, *The Pursuit of History*, p. 1

6 D. Watkin, *The Rise of Architectural History*, p. vii

7 R.G. Collingwood, *The Idea of History*, p. 105

8 A. Forty, *Words and Buildings*, p. 203

9 W. Thompson, *What Happened to History*, p. 102

10 The first edition was very small and its readership limited to the Hapsburg court. The more widely available second edition was published in 1725, the same year as Vico's *Scienza nuova*.

11 A.R. Caponigri, *Time & Idea; The Theory of History in Giambattista Vico*, p. x

12 G.J. Whitrow, *Time in History*, p.5

13 J. L. Gaddis, *The Landscape of History*, p. 6

14 Ibid.

15 Forty, op. cit., p. 213

16 Ibid., p. 219

17 Francis Fukoyama wrote provocatively of *The End of History* (1998)

18 K. Harries, *The Ethical Function of Architecture*, pp. 3–4

Chapter 1: Vico and the 'New Science' of history

1 Whitrow, op. cit., p. 30

2 Herodotus, *The Histories*, p. xiv

3 T. Garnham, *Lines on the Landscape, Circles from the Sky*, pp. 141–77

4 M. Frisch (ed.), *The Autobiography of Giambattista Vico*, p. 46

5 R. Wittkower, *Architectural Principle in the Age of Humanism*, pp. 101–42

6 J. Summerson, *The Classical Language of Architecture*, pp. 11–12

7 Vico, *New Science*, pp. xxvii–xxviii

8 H. Mallgrave, *Modern Architectural Theory*, p. 3

9 Perrault, cited, J. Rykwert, *The First Moderns*, p. 33

10 Rykwert, ibid., p. 37

11 A. Leach, *What is Architectural History?*, p. 28

12 Ibid., p. 8

13 W. Hermann, *The Theory of Claude Perrault*, p. 39

14 E. Cassirer, *The Philosophy of the Enlightenment*, p. 42.
'The true essence of nature is not to be sought in the realm of the created (*natura naturata*) but in that of the creative process (*natura naturans*).'

15 Ibid., pp. 40–1

16 Hermann, op. cit., p. 23

17 A. Braham, *The Architecture of the French Enlightenment*, p. 17

18 Hermann, op. cit., p. 32

19 J-F Blondel's second volume of his *Cours d'architecture* (1683)

20 Whitrow, op. cit., p. 138. Descartes 'dismissed history as mere opinion and arbitrary subjectivity.'

21 Ibid., p. 138

22 Vico, op. cit., p. 46

23 Ibid., p. 114

24 *Times Literary Supplement*, 10.12.99., p. 30

25 Vico, cited, *Autobiography*, op. cit., p. 38

26 Ibid. p. 129. The title of his book paid homage to Bacon's *Novum Organum* and Galileo's *Dialoghi delle Nuove Scienze*.

27 Ibid., p. 76

28 Ibid., pp. 45–6

29 Ibid., pp. 22–3

30 Vico, *New Science*, p. 56

31 Ibid., p. 120

32 Vitruvius, *The Ten Books on Architecture*, 2.1.2

33 Ibid.

34 Vico, op. cit., p. 98

35 Ibid., pp. 44–5

36 Ibid., pp. 68, 115, 152

37 Ibid., p. 461

38 Ibid., p. 129

39 Vico, *Autobiography*, op. cit., p. 169

40 Vico, *New Science*, p. 130

41 L. Marsak, *The Nature of Historical Enquiry*, pp. 83–4

Chapter 2: After Vitruvius: The search for a new fundamental ground

1 The English translation is titled, *A PLAN of CIVIL and HISTORICAL ARCHITECTURE, in the Presentation of the Most noted Buildings of Foreign Nations, Both ANCIENT and MODERN*

2 H. Aurenhammer, *J. B. Fischer von Erlach*, p. 154

3 M. Beard, *The Work of Christopher Wren*, p. 48

4 Aurenhammer, op.cit., p. 158

5 J. B. Fischer von Erlach, *A Plan of Civil and Historical Architecture*, p. A2

6 Aurenhammer, op. cit., p. 157

7 It was influenced by Kircher's treatise on a universal symbol language in his *Oedipus Aegyptians (1652)*.

8 H. Rosenau, *Visions of the Temple*, see pp. 101–2, 116–17, 146–7

9 Aurenhammer, op. cit., p. 132

10 Fischer illustrates this in his book.

11 Aurenhammer, op. cit.

12 V. Hart, *Nicholas Hawksmoor; Rebuilding Ancient Wonders*. Hawksmoor had illustrated Wren's reconstruction of this.
K. Downes, *Hawksmoor*, p.138

13 Shaftesbury, *Characteristics of Men, Manners, Opinions, Times*, pp. 222–3

14 Ibid.

15 Shaftesbury was befriended by Vico's friends, *The Autobiography of Giambattista Vico*, op. cit., p. 81

16 J. Harris, *The Palladian Revival*, pp. 36–7

17 Shaftesbury, *A Letter concerning the Art or Science of Design*

18 Ibid.

19 R. Wittkower, 'English Palladianism', in *Palladio and Palladianism*, p. 181

20 Rykwert, op. cit., p. 156

21 J. Dixon Hunt, *Garden and Grove*, p. 184

22 J. Lees–Milne, *The Earls of Creation*, pp. 114–15

23 J. Harris, *The Palladian Revival*, p. 66

24 Ibid., pp 108–13

25 D. Coffin, *The Villa in the Life of Renaissance Rome*, pp. 241–8, 327

26 Shaftesbury, op. cit.

27 D. Leatherbarrow, 'Character, Geometry and Perspective: the Third Earl of Shaftesbury's 'Principles of Garden Design', in *Journal of Garden History*, Vol. 4, No. 4. p. 344

28 J. Rykwert, *On Adam's House in Paradise*, p. 46

29 W. Hermann, *Laugier and eighteenth century French Theory*, pp. 37–8

30 M. Laugier, *An Essay on Architecture*, p. 11

31 Hermann, op. cit., pp. 46–7, 215–16

32 Laugier, op. cit. p. 12

33 Vitruvius, op. cit, pp. 38–40

34 Hermann, op. cit., p. 46

35 Laugier, op. cit.

36 J. Wilton–Ely, *Piranesi, Arts Council of Great Britain Exhibition catalogue*, 1978, p. 57

37 Vico, op. cit., p. 149

38   A. Braham, *The Architecture of the French Enlightenment,* pp. 174 –5

39   A. Vidler, *Claude-Nicholas Ledoux*, p. 25

40   W. Kaufmann, *Three Revolutionary Architects*

41   A. Perez–Gomez, *Architecture and the Crisis of Modern Science*, p. 137

42   Ibid., p. 300

43   Ibid.

44   R. Sennett, *The Conscience of the Eye*, p. 40

45   D. Veseley, *Architecture in the Age of Divided Representation*, p. 24

Chapter 3: Aesthetics and questions of style

1   J. Summerson, *The Architecture of the Eighteenth Century*, p. 75

2   Forty, op. cit., p. 211

3   J. D. Le Roy's *Ruins of the Most beautiful Monuments of Greece* (1758), Stuart and Revett's *Antiquities of Athens* (1762)

4   J. Winckelmann, *Thoughts on the Imitation of Greek Works in Painting and Sculpture,* cited in L. Eitner, *Neoclassicism and Romanticism, 1750–1850; Sources and Documents*, p. 6

5   Ibid., p. 10

6   Winckelmann, *Thoughts,* cited Eitner, op. cit., p. 9

7   Eitner, op. cit., p. 4

8   Ibid., p. 74.

9   Ibid., p.13. See also Rykwert, *First Moderns*, op. cit., p. 269

10   A. Vidler, *The Writing of the Walls*, p. 129

11   Winckelmann, *Observations on the Architecture of the Ancients,* cited Vidler, ibid., p. 131

12   Rykwert, op. cit., p. 352

13   Vitruvius, op. cit., Book 4, chapter 1.7

14   Winckelmann, *Thoughts,* cited Eitner, op. cit., p. 9. and Rykwert, op. cit., pp. 348–52

15   Winckelmann, *The History of Ancient Art*, cited Eitner, op. cit., p.16

16   Harries, op. cit., pp. 16–26

17   Summerson, op. cit., p. 77

18   K. Clark, *The Gothic Revival*, pp. 28–31

19   Cited, C. Hussey, *The Picturesque*, p. 196

20   Ibid., pp., 43–5

21   H. Walpole, A chapter in his *Anecdotes of Painting* (1762)

22   Walpole, cited, Clark, op. cit., p. 42

23   R. Middleton and D. Watkin, *Neo–classical and Nineteenth Century Architecture*, p. 39

24   Burke, cited Hussey, op. cit., pp. 57–8

25   Hussey, ibid., p. 73

26   Ibid., p. 66

27   F. Coppleston, *A History of Philosophy*, vol. 5. pp. 161–2

28   Ibid., p. 162

29   J. Herder, *Fragments concerning Recent German Literature* (1783), in ibid., p. 161

30   J. Herder, *Ideas for the Philosophy of the History of Mankind* (1784–91), in ibid.,

31   Vico, *Autobiography*, op. cit., p. 67 Walpole op. cit.

32   J-B Herder, *Another Philosophy of History* (1774)

33   I. Berlin, *The Crooked Timber of Humanity*, p. 39

34   Johann Gottlieb Fichte (1762–1814) in, Coppleston, op. cit., p. 27

35   Coppleston summarises this as 'the Universe knows itself in and through the mind of men.' Ibid. p. 25

36   W. Vaughan, *German Romantic Painting*, p. 9

37   Ibid., p. 32.

38   The books are in the Drawing Room front bay window.

39   Soane; Royal Academy Lecture X, in D. Watkin, *Sir John Soane; Enlightenment Thought and the Royal Academy Lectures*, p. 347

40   D. Stroud, *Sir John Soane, Architect*, p. 32

41   J. Summerson, 'Soane: the Man and the Style', in *Architectural Monograph; Soane*, p.13

42   Ibid., p.14

43   Watkin, op. cit., p. 626

44   Ibid.

45   Stroud, op. cit.

46   Watkin, op. cit., p. 19

47   Stroud, op. cit., p. 80

48   Watkin, op. cit., p. 1. Soane possessed this in 33 volumes.

49   R. Middleton, and D. Watkin, *Neoclassical and 19th Century Architecture*, p. 30

50   Uvedale Price, cited Middleton, ibid.

51   In his unpublished M.Phil thesis on Soane's manipulation of light, Nigel Craddock counts nine different sources for the 'Museum' space alone.

52   Soane, *Description of the Museum*

53   Summerson, op. cit., pp. 15–16

Chapter 4: In What Style should we Build?

1   Coppleston op. cit., p. 185

2   F. Hegel, cited T. Rockmore, 'Introduction' to Hegel's *Introductory Lectures on Art, Religion, and the History of Philosophy*, p. 8

3   Coppleston, op. cit., pp. 207–9

4   TV interview with Bill Moyers.

5   Hegel, *On the History of Philosophy*, p. 217

6   Rockmore, op. cit., p. 9

7   Ibid., p. 11

8   Copplestone, op. cit, p. 207

9   A. Colquhoun, 'Three Kinds of Historicism', in *Modernity and the Classical Tradition*, p. 13

10   Copplestone, op. cit., p. 285

11   Ibid., pp. 252–5

12   Hegel, cited ibid., p. 257

13   Ibid., p. 263

14   Watkin, op. cit., pp. 3–4

15   Ibid., p. 70

16   Germann, *The Gothic Revival* , pp. 70–1

17   Ibid., p. 72

18   A. Colquhoun, 'Three Kinds of Historicism', op. cit., p. 3

19   Meinecke, cited Colquhoun, ibid., p. 12

20   W. Hermann (ed.), *In What Style Should We Build?*, pp. 2–3

21   Hübsch, cited ibid., p. 3

22   Germann, op. cit., p.12

23   Blondel, cited ibid.

24   Ibid., p. 65 In Aubin–Louis Millin's *Dictionnaire des Beaux–Arts*, 1806.

25   A. Vidler, op. cit., p. 128

26   Hermann, op. cit., p. 2

27   Ibid., p.4

28   Hübsch, cited ibid., p. 68

29   Hübsch, cited ibid., p. 93

30   Ibid.

31   Kugler, cited, Hermann, op. cit., p. 6

32   Ibid., p. 8

33   Romberg, cited ibid.

34   Hermann, op. cit., p. 42

35   Bötticher, cited Hermann, op. cit., p. 10

36   Schinkel, cited, A. Dobbs, 'Schinkel's Architectural Theory', in M. Snodin, *Karl Friedrich Schinkel; Universal Man*, p. 49.

37   Ibid., p. 48

38   Ibid., p. 51

39   Ibid., pp. 50–1

40   Ibid., p. 45

41   Ibid., p. 149

42   Hugo, *Notre Dame*, cited N. Levine, 'The book and the building', in R. Middleton (ed.) *The Beaux–Arts*, p. 160

43 Ibid., p. 153

44 Ibid.

45 Ibid., p. 156

46 P. Davey, *Arts and Crafts Architecture*, pp. 14, 73

47 J. Ruskin, *Lectures in Architecture*, pp. 87–8

48 J. Ruskin, *Modern Painters*, Vol. 2, p. 306

49 J. Michelet, *The People*, pp. 6–8

50 Ibid., p. 45

51 Burrow, op. cit., p. 391

52 Vico, *Autobiography*, op. cit., p.75 quote p. 76

53 Ibid., p. 76

54 Ruskin, *Seven Lamps*, op. cit., p. 8

55 J. Ruskin, *The Stones of Venice*, Vol. 2, p. 165

56 This phrase, which aptly captures Ruskin's aim, was coined later by Oswald Spengler in his *Man and Technics*, p 41

57 J. Ruskin, *Lectures on Architecture*, pp. 139–40

58 H. Acland and J. Ruskin, *The Oxford Museum*, pp. 107–9

59 See T. Garnham, *The Oxford Museum*, for a detailed account of the Museum.

60 Minutes of the Oxford Museum Delegates, 23rd April, 1858

61 J. Ruskin, 'On Iron and Polity', in *The Complete Works, Vol. 16*, p. 386

62 Minutes, op. cit., 23rd February 1858

63 *The Builder*, 21 July 1855, p. 319

64 *The Builder*, 19 March 1853, p. 185

65 Mallgrave, op. cit., p.4

66 Semper clearly had Winckelmann in mind when he later wrote of the 'dreary impoverishment of the art form helped on …by so–called connoisseurs and art patrons'. Cited W. Hermann, *Gottfied Semper; In Search of Architecture* p. 153

67 W. Ungless, 'Semper in Suffolk', *Architecture Today 123*, Nov. 2001, pp. 43–8

68 Hermann, p. xii

69 Ibid.

70 N. Pevsner, *Some Writers of the Nineteenth Century*, p. 257. Semper's competition entry for St. Nicholas Cathedral, Hamburg (1844).

71 Mallgrave, op. cit., p. 120

72 Hermann, op. cit., p. 84

73 Mallgrave, op. cit., p. 197

74 Ibid., p. 198

75 He initially proposed to call the book a *Theory of Artistic Forms* but following a dispute with his original

publisher, the first volume appeared in 1863 with the full title *Style in the Technical and Tectonic Arts a Practical Aesthetics: a handbook for Technicians, Artists and Patrons of Art.*

76 M. Hvattum, *Gottfried Semper and the Problem of Historicism*, p. 1

77 Cited ibid., p. xii'

78 Semper, cited Hermann, op. cit., p. 157

79 Semper, *Vergleichende Baulehre* (Comparative Building Theory, 1849–50), ms. Cited by Hermann, op. cit., p. 169

80 T. Garnham, *Lines on the Landscape, Circles from the Sky*, pp. 91–2

81 Hermann, op. cit., p. xiv

82 J. Rykwert, 'Semper', in *The Necessity of Artifice*, p. 123

83 Rykwert, op. cit., p. 128. His organisation of material artefacts by the 'four elements' had been inspired by Cuvier's arrangement at the Jardin des Plantes in Paris, which Semper had visited, and contrasted with the confusion at the Great Exhibition.

84 Ibid., p. 129

85 Semper, Wintergarten (1849), 'Report on the Jardin d'Hiver, Paris', cited Hermann, p. 175

86 Ibid., p. 179

87 Mallgrave, op. cit., p. 299

88 Semper, *The Four Elements*, cited ibid., p. 305

89 Mallgrave, op. cit., pp. 345–6. Semper rejected Darwinian survival of the fittest, often if mistakenly linked with Nietzsche.

90 Semper, *Über der Bau evangielischer Kirchen* (1845), cited ibid., p. 159,

91 Semper, ms. V&A, London, cited ibid., p. 160

Chapter 5: Nietzsche and the 'history beyond history'

1 J.P. Stern, *Nietzsche*, p. 17

2 The title *The Use and Abuse of History* dates from the English translation of the first edition of Nietzsche's collected works. It was retained in The Library of Liberal arts edition published in 1949, perhaps for its more dramatic effect and has been retained here. The Stanford University Press edition of the complete works (Volume 11) translates it as 'On the Utility and Liability of History for Life', something of a mouthful.

3 R. Small, *Nietzsche and Rée; a Star Friendship*, p. 60

4 R. Hollingdale, *Nietzsche; the Man and his Philosophy*, p. 102

5 F. Nietzsche, *Untimely Meditations*, p. 49

6 Ibid., p. 95

7 Nietzsche, cited in S. Rosen, *The Mask of Enlightenment; Nietzsche's Zarathustra*, p. 34

8 Nietzsche, op. cit., p. 72

9 Ibid., p. 75

10 Ibid., p. 77

11 Ibid.

12 Ibid., p. 75

13 Ibid., p. 24

14 Ibid., p. 67

15 Ibid., pp. 95–6

16 Nietzsche, cited Rosen, op. cit., p.5

17 F. Nietzsche, *The Birth of Tragedy*, p. 5

18 Ibid., p. 72

19 Nietzsche, *Untimely Meditations*, p. 67

20 J. Burrow, op. cit., p. 455

21 Burrows, op. cit., p. 461

22 Thompson, p. 2

23 Nietzsche, op. cit., p. 106

24 Ibid., p. 108

25 Small, op. cit., p. 70–73

26 F. Nietzsche, *Human, All Too Human*, p. 14

27 L. Marsak, *The Nature of Historical Enquiry*, p. 85

28 H. Rickman, Introduction to W. Dilthey, *Pattern and Meaning in History*, p. 15

29 Ibid., p. 32

30 Ibid., p. 39

31 T. Buddenseig, 'Architecture as Empty Form; Nietzsche and the Art of Building', in A. Kostka, and I. Wohlfarth (eds.), *Nietzsche and 'An Architecture of Our Minds'*, p. 260

32 Ibid.

33 Ibid., p. 261

34 Ibid.

35 Nietzsche, *Untimely Meditations*, pp. 242–52

36 H. Mallgrave, *Gottfried Semper; Architect of the Nineteenth Century*, pp. 348–50

37 Nietzsche, *The Birth of Tragedy*, p. 62

38 Nietzsche, cited in Buddenseig, op. cit., p. 272

39 F. Coppleston, *A History of Philosophy*, vol. 7 part 2, p. 171

40 Schopenhauer was a major influence on Nietzsche and subject of the third *Untimely Meditations*

41 Buddenseig, op. cit., p. 270

42 Avoiding 'the merely pretty and pleasing', Nietzsche noted in 1881. Cited ibid., p. 270

43 Kostka and Wohlfarth, op. cit., p. 4
44 Hollingdale, op. cit.
45 Ibid., p. 264
46 See M. Swenarton, 'Site Planning and Rationality in the Modern Movement', *AA Files 4* pp. 48–55.
47 A.C. Danto, *Nietzsche as Philosopher*, p. 222
48 Ibid., p. 215
49 Rosen, op. cit., p. 15
50 F. Nietzsche, *Thus Spoke Zarathustra*, p. 42
51 Rosen, op. cit., p. 21
52 M. Löwy, *Fire Alarm; Reading Walter Benjamin's 'On the Concept of History'*, p. 6
53 Hollingdale, op. cit. p. 59
54 Ibid., p. 116
55 Nietzsche, cited, Danto, op. cit., p. 205
56 Rosen, op. cit., p. 21
57 Nietzsche, op. cit., p. 237
58 Danto, op. cit., p. 196
59 Rosen, op. cit., pp. vii–x
60 Danto, op. cit., p. 212
61 Rosen, op. cit., p. xiv
62 Nietzsche, *Untimely Meditations*, p. 150
63 Rosen, op. cit., p. 5

Chapter 6: Approaches to modernism

1 P. Tournikiotis, *The Historiography of the Modern Movement*, p. 2
2 Ibid., p. 17
3 Ibid., p. 27
4 Ibid., p. 32
5 N. Pevsner, *Pioneers of Modern Design*, pp. 20–7
6 Ibid., p. 39
7 Ibid., p. 39
8 E. Kaufmann, cited Watkin, op. cit., p. 18
9 W. Kaufmann, cited, A Vidler, *Histories of the Immediate Present*, pp. 23, 27
10 Cited Mallgrave, op. cit., p. 197
11 Ibid., p. 434
12 Ibid., p. 201
13 Wölfflin applied this to architecture in his *Prolegomena to a Psychology of Architecture* (1886)
14 Cited ibid., p. 199
15 A. Colquhoun, 'Modern Architecture and Historicity', in his *Essays in Architectural Criticism*, p. 12
16 Ibid.
17 Ibid.
18 Ibid., p. 13

19 H. Mallgrave, Introduction to Otto Wagner's, *Modern Architecture*, p. 1
20 Wagner, ibid., p. 73
21 Cited ibid., p. 3
22 The reviewer was Richard Streiter. Ibid., p. 4
23 Wagner, ibid., p. 30
24 Pevsner, op. cit., p. 30
25 Wagner, op. cit., p. 92
26 Ibid., p. 94
27 Ibid., p. 91
28 Ibid., p. 69
29 Ibid., p. 92
30 Ibid., p. 93
31 Ibid., p. 83
32 Ibid., p. 82
33 Ibid.
34 Ibid., p. 86
35 Ibid., p. 74
36 Ibid., p. 80
37 Ibid., pp. 108–9
38 Ibid.
39 Ibid., p. 65
40 Ibid., p. 122
41 C. Schorske, *Fin de Siecle Vienna; Culture and Politics*, p. 346
42 Wagner, op. cit., p. 41
43 Ibid., p. 221
44 Schorske, op. cit., p. 220
45 Ibid.
46 Ibid., p. 200
47 A. Loos, 'Die potemkinische Stadt' in *Ver Sacrum 1* (1898)
48 A. Loos, 'Cultural Degeneration' (1908), in *The Architecture of Adolf Loos*, Y. Safrom and W. Wang, (eds.), pp. 98–9
49 A. Loos, 'Interiors; the Rotunda', in *Spoken into the Void; Collected Essays* pp. 23–4
50 Pevsner, op. cit., pp. 200–1
51 A. Loos, 'Vernacular Architecture' (1914), in Safrom and Wang (eds)., op. cit., p. 113
52 See ibid. p. 19
53 A. Loos, 'Men's Fashions', in *Spoken into the Void*, op. cit. pp. 11–12
54 Ibid., p. 12
55 A. Loos, 'Ornament and Crime', in Safrom and Wang (eds)., op. cit., p. 100
56 Ibid., p. 102
57 A. Loos, 'Cultural Degeneration (1908), in ibid., p. 98
58 A. Loos, 'Arnold Schoenberg (1924), in ibid., p. 114
59 Loos, 'Architecture', in ibid., p. 106
60 Loos, cited in D. Stener, 'The Strength of the Old Masters: Adolf Loos and Antiquity', in ibid., p. 24

61 A. Gravagnulo, *Adolf Loos; Theory and Works*, pp. 94–5
62 K. Frampton, 'Adolf Loos and the Crisis of Culture', in Safrom and Wang (eds)., op. cit., p. 11
63 Loos, cited ibid., p. 20
64 Loos, cited ibid., p. 22
65 A. Loos, 'Meine Bauschule' (1913), cited in ibid., p. 56
66 A. Loos, 'Josef Veillich' (1929), cited ibid., p. 84
67 Frampton, op. cit., p. 68
68 Wagner, cited Mallgrave, *Modern and Architectural Theory*, p. 204
69 Berlage, cited ibid., p. 219
70 Guimard, cited K. Frampton, *Modern Architecture: A Critical History*, p. 69
71 Berlage, 'Thoughts on Style in Architecture' (1905), cited Mallgrave, op. cit., p. 219
72 Berlage, cited ibid., p. 219
73 T. Garnham, 'Crafts and the Revival of Architecture', in N. Jackson (ed.), *F.W. Troup, Architect 1899–1941*
74 Berlage, 'The Foundation and Development of Architecture' (1908), cited Mallgrave, op. cit., p. 220
75 Berlage, 'Modern Architecture', op. cit., p. 92
76 Pevsner, op. cit., p. 179
77 K. Britton, *Auguste Perret*, p. 23
78 Cited R. Banham, *Theory and Design in the First Machine Age*, p. 17
79 Perret, 'Architecture', lecture 30 May 1933, cited Britton, op. cit., p. 238
80 Britton, op. cit., p. 218
81 S. Giedion, *Space, Time and Architecture*, pp. 328–33
82 Perret, cited Britton, op. cit., p. 143
83 Britton, ibid., p. 10
84 Perret, *Paris Journal*, 1 Dec. 1923, p. 5, cited ibid., p. 136
85 Britton, ibid., pp. 136–7
86 Ibid., pp. 49–51, 59–61
87 Ibid., p. 26
88 Banham, 'The Perret Ascendancy', cited ibid., p. 216
89 Britton, op. cit., p. 92
90 Perret, 'Architecture', cited ibid., p. 238.
91 R. Middleton, 'Auguste Choisy: Historian (1841–1909), in *International Architect; Vol/Issues/1981*, p. 38
92 Ibid., p. 39
93 Perret, cited Britton, op. cit., p. 77
94 Britton, ibid.
95 O. von Simson, *The Gothic Cathedral*, pp. 21–54

96 Britton, op. cit., p. 218

97 Ibid., p. 90

98 Perret, 'Architecture', cited ibid., p. 243

99 J.M. Richards, *An Introduction to Modern Architecture*, p. 76

100 H-R. Hitchcock, and P. Johnson, *The International Style*.

101 J. Joedicke, *A History of Modern Architecture*, p. 61

102 S. Anderson, *Peter Behrens and a New Architecture for the Twentieth Century*, p. 59

103 Ibid., pp. 75–6.

104 Behrens, cited Mallgrave, *Modern Architectural Theory*, op. cit., p. 232

105 Ibid., p. 139

106 Behrens, cited ibid., p. 232

107 Anderson, op. cit., p. 111

108 Mallgrave, op. cit.

109 Frampton, op. cit., p. 112

110 Anderson, op. cit., p. 105

111 Behrens, an article in the *Scientific American Supplement* (1913), cited Mallgrave, op. cit.

112 Anderson, op. cit., p. 161

113 Muthesius, *Stilarkitektur und Baukunst*, p. 67. See also H. Muthesius, *The English House*, p. 162

114 Ibid., p. 67

115 Ruskin, *Lectures on Art and Architecture*, p. 111

116 Reported in *The Builder*, 2nd, 9th, and 16th Nov. 1895, and AA Notes (1895) and AA Notes (1896). See T. Garnham, 'William Lethaby and the Two Ways of Building', *AA Files 10*, Autumn 1985, pp. 27–9

117 Mallgrave, op. cit., p. 229

118 S. Anderson, op. cit., p. 11

119 Muthesius, op. cit., p. 89

120 Muthesius, ibid.

121 Ibid., 90

122 Ibid., p. 91

123 H. van de Velde, 'Werkbund antitheses', in U. Conrads, *Programmes and Manifestoes of 20th Century Architecture*, p. 29

124 H. Muthesius, 'Werkbund Theses', in ibid., p. 28

125 Van de Velde, op. cit.

126 L. Ploegaerts, 'Nietzsche and van de Velde', in A. Kostka and I. Wohlfarth (eds.), *A Nietzsche of our Minds*, pp. 233–4

127 Van de Velde, cited ibid., p. 236

128 Ploegaerts, op. cit.

129 Muthesius, 'Aims of the Werkbund', in Conrads, op. cit., pp. 26–8

130 Anderson, op. cit., p. 38

131 Ibid.

132 Ibid.

133 Pevsner, op. cit., p. 217

134 Anderson, op. cit., p. 35

Chapter 7: Modernism against history

1 M. Tafuri and F. dal Co, *Modern Architecture*, p. 219

2 Cited Frampton, op. cit., p. 269

3 Tafuri and dal Co, op. cit.

4 Frampton, op. cit., p. 270

5 Swenarton, op. cit., p. 54

6 Ibid., p. 56

7 Gropius' address to the Brussels CIAM meeting, cited ibid.

8 Swenarton, ibid., pp. 54–5. May had worked for Raymond Unwin in England on Hampstead Garden Suburb.

9 Gropius, cited ibid., p. 56

10 Swenarton, ibid.

11 Ibid., p. 212

12 Ibid.

13 Forty, op. cit., pp. 87–92

14 Swenarton, op. cit., p. 58

15 W. Pehnt, 'The Bauhaus', in *Encyclopaedia of 20th Century Architecture*, p. 68

16 W. Gropius, *The New Architecture and the Bauhaus*, pp. 38–43

17 Ibid.

18 H–R. Hitchcock and P. Johnson, *The International Style*, p. viii

19 *Architectural Record*, Aug. 1951, cited ibid., p. 241

20 Ibid., p. 28

21 Ibid., p. 30

22 Ibid., p. 31

23 Ibid., p. 28

24 Ibid., p. 44

25 Ibid., p. 45

26 Ibid., p. 64

27 H-R. Hitchcock, *The International Style Revisited*.

28 Hitchcock and Johnson, op. cit., p. ix

29 Tournikiotis, op. cit., p. 130. See Hitchcock and Johnson, op. cit., p. xi

30 K. Frampton, 'On the Predicament of Architecture at the Turn of the Century', in *Labour, Work, and Architecture*, p. 8

31 Ibid., pp. 116 and 127

32 Ibid., p. 133

33 The Futurist manifesto written by Filippo Marinetti (1876–1944) was published in the Paris newspaper *Le Figaro* on 9th February 1909

34 Marinetti, *The Founding and Manifesto of Futurism*, cited in *Encyclopaedia of 20th Century Architecture*, p. 114

35 Ibid.

36 Conrads, op. cit., p.34

37 C. Tisdall and A. Bozzolla, *Futurism*, pp. 124–5

38 Ibid., p. 36

39 Cited Frampton, op. cit., p. 142

40 Ibid.

41 Mallgrave, op. cit., p. 242

42 Frampton, op. cit., p. 142

43 Van Doesburg, '16 Points of a Plastic Architecture', cited Frampton, op. cit., 145

44 Cited Conrads, op. cit., p. 67

45 Malevich, *Suprematist Manifesto*, cited Conrads, op. cit., p. 87

46 Mallgrave, op. cit., p. 238

47 Ibid., p. 88

48 Mallgrave, op. cit., p. 240

49 Frampton, op. cit., p. 174

50 El Lissitzky, cited K. Frampton, 'Constructivism', in Lampugnani, op. cit., p. 73

51 *Encyclopaedia of 20th Century Architecture*, op. cit., p. 71

52 Loader, op. cit., p. 2

53 W. Gropius, in Conrads, op. cit., p. 49

54 T. Benton, *Expressionist Utopias*, p. 8

55 B. Taut, 'Work Council for Art etc', in Conrads, op. cit., p. 44

56 Ibid., p. 14

57 Mallgrave, op. cit., p. 249

58 F. Whitford, *Bauhaus*, pp. 53–4

59 Ibid., p. 53

60 N. M. Schmitz, 'Johannes Itten', in J. Fiedler (ed.), *Bauhaus*, p. 241

61 Whitford, op. cit., p. 138

62 Gropius, *Principles of Bauhaus production*, cited Conrads, op. cit., p. 96

63 M Kieren, 'Walter Gropius; the Architect and Founder of the Bauhaus', in Fiedler, op. cit., 192

64 Ibid., p. 198

65 W. Pehnt, op. cit., p. 37

66 Kieren, op. Cit., p. 215

67 Cited N. Schmitz, 'Mazdaznan at the Bauhaus', in Fiedler, op. cit., p. 121

68 Mallgrave, op. cit., p. 250

69 V. Scully, *Modern Architecture*, p. 17

70 V. Scully, *American Architecture and Urbanism,* pp. 12–13

71 H-R. Hitchcock, 'American Influence Abroad', in E. Kaufmann Jr. (ed.), *The Rise of an American Architecture,* p. 21

72 Ibid., p. 19

73 'Adolf Loos, and the Anglo Saxons', in Drew (ed.), *The Architecture of Adolf Loos,* p. 15

74 Ibid.
75 Ibid., p. 18

76 Loos, cited ibid., p. 15

77 Cited J. Drew, op. cit., p. 14

78 Scully, *Modern Architecture,* p. 20

79 Wright, cited ibid.

80 V. Scully, 'Wright vs the International Style', in *Modern Architecture and Other Essays,* p. 54

81 Wright, cited Scully, op. cit., p. 55

82 Ibid., p. 367

83 F. Wright, *An American Architect,* p. 190

84 Scully, *Modern Architecture,* op. cit., p. 29

85 Wright, cited Lampugnani, op. cit., p. 369

86 Ibid., p. 33
87 Ibid., p. 34
88 Ibid.

Chapter 8: Le Corbusier: for or against history?

1 C.S. Eliel, *L'Espirit Nouveau,* pp. 76, 80

2 C. Green, 'The Architect as Artist', in *Le Corbusier; Architect of the Century,* pp. 112–13

3 Le Corbusier and Ozenfant, 'Purism', in R. Herbert (ed.), *Modern Artists on Art,* p. 63–4

4 Eliel, op. cit., p. 80
5 Ibid., p. 63

6 K. Foster, 'Antiquity and Modernity in the La Roche–Jeanneret Houses of 1923', in *Oppositions 15–16,* p. 131

7 Le Corbusier, *Towards a New Architecture,* p. 176

8 R. Etlin, 'A Paradoxical Avant–garde; Le Corbusier's Villas of the 1920s' in *Architectural Review, Jan. 1987,* pp. 21–31

9 W. Curtis, *Le Corbusier; Ideas and Forms,* pp. 76–7

10 Ibid., pp. 124–5

11 This description is drawn from largely John Farmer's *Green Shift.*

12 C. Rowe, *The Mathematics of the Ideal Villa,* pp. 2–13

13 Ibid., pp. 3–5

14 Le Corbusier, op. cit., p. 92

15 Green, op. cit., p. 124–6

16 T. Benton, 'Urbanism', in *Architect of the Century, op. cit.,* p. 206

17 K. Frampton, *Le Corbusier,* p. 90

18 Green, op. cit., pp. 114–5

19 Curtis, op. cit., p. 126

20 *Beton brut* is the name given to rough-boarded concrete, a term echoed in Brutalism.

21 J. Farmer, 'Battered Bunkers', *Architectural Review,* January 1987 pp. 60–5

22 Scully, op. cit., p. 45

23 Cited, Frampton, op. cit.

24 The interpretation given here is based upon a seminar course taught with Daphne Beckett. Others have followed Daphne in exploring the mythical themes suggested by Le Corbusier's enigmatic lithographs. My role was to explore how the ideas set down in *Le Poème* found a response in his post-War buildings.

25 A. Wogenscky, Introduction to Le Corbusier, *Le Poème de l'Angle Droit.*

26 Le Corbusier, *Le Poème de l'Angle Droit,* p. E4

27 Ibid., p. C1

28 M. Eliade, *The Myth of the Eternal Return; or Cosmos and History*

29 Le Corbusier, op. cit., p. A1

30 Ibid.
31 Ibid.
32 Ibid., p. A5

33 M. Eliade, *The Sacred and the Profane.*

34 Frampton, op. cit., pp. 204–5

35 Le Corbusier, op. cit., p. B2

36 Ibid. p. A2
37 Ibid., p. A3
38 Ibid. p. F3

39 He drew a version of this in his Buenos Aires lecture, 8 October 1929. Le Corbusier, *Precisions,* p. 75

40 Frampton, op. cit., p. 201

41 P. Carl, *AA Files,* No 22, p. 52

42 Le Corbusier, *Towards a New Architecture,* p. 31

43 Le Corbusier, *Poème, op. cit.* p. G3

Chapter 9: Regional resistance to the International Style

1 C. Norberg–Schulz, *Nightlands; Nordic Building,* p. 149

2 Nils Erik Wikberg, cited in S.

Wrede, *The Architecture of Erik Gunnar Asplund,* p. 126

3 Uno Åhren, cited ibid., pp. 125–7

4 Wrede, ibid., p. 129

5 H. Andersson, *Nordic Classicism,* p. 125

6 L.B Jørgensen, ibid., pp. 51–2

7 Wrede, op. cit., pp. 26–32

8 J.C Forsyth, 'The Woodland Crematorium', in D. Cruickshank (ed.), *Erik Gunnar Asplund; Masters of Building,* p. 100

9 Asplund, 'Our Architectonic Concept of Space', in *International Architect,* No. 8: Vol.1/Issue 8/1982, p. 40

10 Ibid.

11 O. Spengler, *The Decline of the West,* see in particular the chapter 'Symbolism and Space', pp. 163–80

12 Ibid., p. 174

13 Asplund, op. cit., p 41

14 Spengler, op. cit., p. 46

15 Ibid., p. 31

16 Ibid., p. 32. The title of his book was perhaps influenced by Edward Gibbon's (1737–94) *The History of the Decline and Fall of the Roman Empire* (1776).

17 Ibid., p. xiv

18 R. Warne, Introduction to W. Goethe, *Faust, part one,* p. 17

19 Spengler, op. cit., p. 22

20 Ibid., p. 21
21 Ibid., p. 21

22 Asplund, cited k. Frampton, 'Stockholm 1930; Aspund and the legacy of the Funkis', in C. Caldenby and O. Hulton, *Asplund,* p. 39

23 P. Blundell–Jones, 'Gothenburg Law Courts', in Cruickshank (ed.), op. cit., pp. 60–75

24 S. Knight, 'Swedish Modern Classicism in Context', in *International Architect,* op. cit., p. 14

25 Ibid., p. 94

26 A. Aalto, *Arkkiteheti No 11–12, 1940,* in G. Schildt (ed.), *Alvar Aalto in his Own Words,* pp. 242–3.

27 Aalto, 'Karelian Architecture', in Schildt, ibid., p. 116

28 Ibid.
29 Ibid., p. 117

30 Aalto, 'Rationalism and Man', ibid., p. 91

31 Aalto, 'Karelian Architecture', ibid., p. 118

32 Aalto cited in R. Weston, *Alvar Aalto,* p. 137

33 Aalto, 'Rationalism and Man' *Own Words,* op. cit., p. 92

34 T. Schumcher, *Terragni; Surface*

and Symbol, p. 38, The Maestri Comancini, legendary medieval master masons, hailed from Como.

35 Cited ibid, p. 75. Terragni's assistant Luigi Zuccoli described it as having: 'timpani under the windows, with pilasters, fascias, cornices, adornments, etc.'

36 E. Shapiro, 'Architecture II: the Foreigners'. Il Gruppo 7', in Oppositions, Fall 1976/77, p. 86

37 Ibid.
38 Ibid.
39 Ibid.
40 Ibid. pp. 89–90
41 Ibid., p. 90
42 Ibid., p. 91
43 Ibid., p. 92
44 Ibid. p. 91

45 B. Zevi, Giuseppi Terragni, p. 70

46 Cited Shapiro, ibid., p. 88

47 Zevi, op. cit.

48 G. Terragni, 'The Construction of the Casa del Fascio in Como', cited in Schumacher, op. cit.,, p. 142

49 Ibid., p. 66
50 Ibid., p. 67
51 Ibid.

52 Terragni, cited ibid., p. 143

53 Ibid., p. 152
54 Ibid., p. 157
55 Ibid., pp. 143, 151

56 Zevi, op. cit., p. 74

57 P. Eisenman, 'From Object to Relationship; Giuseppe Terragni/ Casa Giuliana/Frigerio', in Perspecta, 13/14, 1971, pp. 36–75

58 Cited T. Schumacher, 'From Gruppo 7 to the Danteum', in Oppositions, Summer 1977/9, p. 92

59 Terragni, Relazione sol Danteum, in ibid., p. 102

60 Ibid., p. 94

61 Ibid. 'One is the rectangle, three are the segments that determine the golden ratio'.

62 Ibid.
63 Ibid., p. 96
64 Ibid., p. 96

65 Dante, Divine Comedy; Inferno

66 Terragni, op. cit., pp. 102–3
67 Ibid., p. 103 'Dante imagines Purgatory in the form of a truncated conical mountain of seven terraces'.

68 Schumacher, op. cit., p. 106

69 C. St. John Wilson, The Other Tradition; the uncompleted project., p. 25

70 Ibid., p. 28
71 Ibid., p. 31
72 Ibid., p. 43
73 Ibid., pp. 30, 38

74 Ibid., p. 43
75 Häring, cited ibid., p. 32
76 Wilson, ibid., p. 32
77 Ibid., pp. 34–42
78 Ibid., pp. 131–9
79 Meyer, cited ibid., p. 72
80 Ibid.
81 Wilson, ibid., p. 62
82 Aristotle, cited ibid.
83 Wilson, ibid., p. 63
84 Ibid.
85 Ibid., p. 64
86 Ibid., p. 67
87 Ibid.
88 Ibid., pp. 68–72
89 Ibid., p. 75

Chapter 10: Late modernism and critical histories

1 Tournikiotis, op. cit., p. 15

2 Wilson, op. cit., p. 140

3 A. Dean, Bruno Zevi on Modern Architecture, pp. 13, 23

4 Zevi, cited ibid., p. 22

5 Zevi, cited Dean, op. cit., p. 23

6 Tournikiotis, op. cit., p. 51. B. Zevi, Towards an Organic Architecture, p. 125

7 Ibid., p. 39
8 Ibid., p. 40
9 Ibid., p. 52

10 B. Croce, Aesthetics as the Science of Expression and General Linguistics (1902).

11 Zevi cited Dean, op. cit., pp. 42–3

12 Zevi cited Tournikiotis, op. cit., p. 57

13 Tournikiotis, op. cit., pp. 110–11

14 L. Benevelo, History of Modern Architecture, p. x

15 Tournikiotis, op. cit., p. 88

16 Ibid., p. 107

17 Benevelo. op. cit., p. 494

18 Tournikiotis, op. cit., p. 145

19 Tournikiotis, op. cit., p. 151

20 Banham, op. cit.

21 Ibid., pp., 250, 262
22 Ibid., p. 327
23 Ibid., p. 326
24 Ibid., p. 10

25 R. Banham, 'The History of the Immediate Future', RIBA Journal no. 7 (May 1961), pp. 252–60

26 A. Colquhoun, in op. cit., p. 22

27 Ibid., p. 23
28 Ibid., p. 24

29 P. Collins, Changing Ideals in Modern Architecture, p. 16

30 Ibid.
31 Ibid., p. 15
32 Ibid., p. 295

33 A chapter in the first section is called 'The Influence of Historiography'. Ibid., pp. 29–41

34 Ibid., p. 225
35 Ibid., p. 272
36 Ibid., p. 230
37 Ibid., p. 229

38 A. Colquhoun, 'Modern Architecture and Historicity', in Essays, op. cit., pp. 12–13

39 Collins, op. cit., p. 200
40 Ibid., p. 299
41 Ibid., pp. 287–90

42 Spengler, cited ibid., p. 292

43 Einstein, cited ibid., p. 289

44 Collins, op. cit., p. 284

45 Collins, op. cit., pp. 297, 299

46 Ibid., p. 298
47 Ibid., p. 234
48 Ibid.

49 A. Vidler, Historians of the Immediate Present, p. 157

50 Tafuri, cited ibid., p. 161

51 Vidler, ibid., p. 178

52 Tafuri, cited ibid., p. 199

53 M. Tafuri, The Sphere and the Labyrinth; Avant Gardes from Piranesi to the 1970s, p. 29

54 Ibid., p. 16
55 Ibid., p. 20
56 Ibid., p. 273

57 J. Ockman, Architecture Culture 1943–68, p., 13

58 Ockman, op. cit., p. 13

59 Ibid.

60 J. Joedicke, Architecture since 1945, p. 27

61 Ibid., pp. 100–7. Joedicke illustrates only Miesian buildings in Germany and Switzerland from this 'First Phase 1949–58'

62 Ockman, op. cit., p. 42

63 L. Mumford, 'The Skyline (Bay Region Style)', in Ockman, op. cit., p. 108

64 M. Nowicki, 'Origins and Trends in Modern Architecture, in ibid., p. 154

65 L. Kahn, 'Monumentality', in ibid., p. 48

66 Ockman, ibid., p. 47

67 Architectural Review, Sept. 1948, pp. 117–28. Giedion had delivered a lecture at the RIBA in September 1946 with the same title.

68 J. Sert, F. Leger, S. Giedion, 'Nine Points on Monumentality', in Ockman, op. cit., p. 29

69 Architectural Review, March 1947, pp. 101–5

70 E. Rogers, 'Pre–existing Conditions and Issues of Contemporary Building Practice', in Ockman, op. cit., p. 203
71 Ibid.
72 Ibid., p. 201
73 D. Jenkins, *Unité d'Habitation*.
74 J. Stirling, ' Garches to Jaoul: Le Corbusier as Domestic Architect in 1927 and 1953', *Architectural Review*, September 1955, p. 151
75 Joedicke, op. cit., pp. 116–17
76 Ibid., p. 109
77 Ibid.
78 Ibid.
79 Ibid., p. 146
80 Farmer, op. cit. See Joedicke, pp. 131–7
81 Joedicke, ibid., p. 109
82 Ibid., p. 146
83 Ibid.
84 Cited Frampton, *Modern Architecture*, op. cit., p. 271
85 Smithsons, cited ibid.
86 Smithsons, CIAM 9, 24 July 1953, cited ibid, p. 77
87 V. Walsh, *Nigel Henderson; Parallel of Life and Art*, p. 17
88 A. & P. Smithson, 'Uppercase', cited Smithson (ed.), pp. 96–7
89 Frampton, op. cit., p. 272
90 P. Smithson, cited D. van den Heuvel and M. Risselada (eds.), *Alison and Peter Smithson – From the House of the Future*, p. 16
91 Ibid.
92 A. van Eyck, 'The Interior of Time', in G. Baird and C. Jencks (eds.), *Meaning in Architecture*, pp. 178–213
93 A van Eyck, 'Otterlo Meeting' (1952), cited A. Smithson (ed.), op. cit., p. 20
94 Van Eyck, 'Dutch Forum or Children's House', cited ibid., p. 104
95 Van Eyck, cited ibid.
96 S. Goldhagen, *Louis Kahn's Situated Modernism*, p. 105
97 Cret, cited K. Frampton, 'Louis Kahn and the French Connection', in *Architecture, Labour, Work*, p. 170
98 Goldhagen, op. cit., p. 102
99 V. Scully, *Louis Kahn*, p. 11
100 Goldhagen, op. cit.
101 D.G. de Long, 'The Mind Opens to Realizations', in Brownlee and de Long (eds.), p. 51
102 Frampton, op. cit. p. 178
103 de Long, op. cit., p. 79
104 Kahn, cited ibid., p. 78
105 Kahn cited ibid., p. 59

106 Goldhagen, op. cit., p. 146
107 Kahn cited ibid., p. 108
108 Goldhagen, ibid.
109 Ibid., pp. 119–22
110 Ibid., p. 116
111 Ibid., p. 128
112 R. Wilhams, 'First Unitarian Church', in Brownlee and de Long (eds.), pp. 340–4
113 D.G. de Long, 'The Mind Opens to Realizations', in Brownlee and de Long (eds.), p. 98
114 Goldhagen, op. cit., pp. 122–5
115 J. Lobell, *Between Silence and Light*, p. 66
116 Kahn, cited ibid., p. 54
117 Ibid., p. 44
118 C. Norberg–Schulz, 'Kahn, Heidegger and the Language of Architecture', *Oppositions* 18, pp., 29–47
119 Kahn, cited ibid., p. 32
120 Frampton, op. cit., p. 181
121 Cited Goldhagen, op. cit., pp. 125–6
122 Lobell, op. cit., p. 67
123 Cited Frampton, op. cit., p. 183
124 D.G. de Long, op. cit., p. 46. The chair at Princeton was Jean Labatut who asserted that the 'past should be taken as a stimulant, not a refuge'.
125 Cited Goldhagen, op. cit., pp. 125–6
126 Norberg–Schulz, op. cit., p. 37

Chapter 11: From post-modernism to meaning in architecture

1   V. Scully, Introduction to R. Venturi, *Complexity and Contradiction in Architecture*, p. 11
2   A. Colquhoun, 'Sign and Substance etc.' in Colquhoun, op. cit. p. 140
3   V. Scully, 'Robert Venturi's "Gentle Architecture"', in *Modern Architecture and Other Essays*, p. 266
4   R. Venturi, *Complexity and Contradiction*, p. 18
5   Ibid.
6   T.S. Eliot, cited ibid., p. 19
7   Venturi, ibid., p. 22
8   Colquhoun, op. cit., p. 140
9   Venturi, op. cit., p. 88
10 R. Venturi, 'Learning the right lessons from the Beaux–Arts', in R. Venturi, *A View from the Campidoglia*, p. 74
11 Venturi, *Complexity and Contradiction*, op. cit., p. 117
12 Ibid., p. 102

13 Ibid.
14 Scully, op. cit., p. 262
15 Ibid.
16 Colquhoun, op. cit., p. 141
17 Ibid., p. 151
18 R. Venturi, *A View*, op. cit., p. 112
19 Colquhoun, op. cit., p. 150
20 Frampton, *Modern Architecture*, op. cit. p. 291
21 Ibid.
22 Ibid., p. 293
23 C. Jencks, 'Towards a radical eclecticism', in P. Portoghesi (ed.) *The Presence of the Past*, p. 30
24 C. Jencks, *Post–Modern Classicism, AD* 5/6 1980, p. 5
25 A. Colquhoun, 'Postmodernism and Structuralism: A Retrospective Glance', in Colquhoun, *Modernity and the Classical Tradition*, p. 243
26 Ibid.
27 J. Habermas, 'Modern and Postmodern Architecture' , p. 227
28 Thompson, op. cit., p. ix
29 G. Baird, in C. Jencks and G. Baird, *Meaning in Architecture*, p. 11
30 Colquhoun, 'Postmodern Critical Attitudes', in *Modernity and a Classical Tradition.*, p. 239
31 M. Bandini, 'Aldo Rossi', *Transitions*, March 1982, p. 9
32 A. Rossi, *The Architecture of the City*, p. 169
33 Bandini, op. cit.
34 Rossi, op. cit., p. 29
35 Ibid., p. 57
36 Ibid., p. 59
37 Ibid., pp. 59–61
38 Ibid., p. 29
39 Ibid., p. 48
40 Ibid., p. 47
41 C. Rowe and F. Koetter, *Collage City* pp. 68–9
42 Rossi, op. cit., pp. 99–101
43 Ibid., pp. 57–61
44 Ibid., p. 99
45 Ibid., p. 18
46 Ibid., p. 116
47 Ibid., p. 126
48 Ibid., p. 40
49 Ibid., p. 171
50 Ibid., p. 170
51 Ibid., p. 106
52 Ibid., pp. 130–1
53 Ibid., p. 116
54 Jung, cited in A. Rossi, 'An Analogical Architecture', *Aldo Rossi; Selected Writings and Projects*, p. 59
55 Ibid., p. 60
56 V. Scully, 'Postscript; Ideology

and Form', in A. Rossi, *A Scientific Autobiography*, p. 111

57 Ibid., p. 112
58 Rossi, op. cit., p. 61
59 Rossi, *The Architecture of the City*, op. cit., p 179
60 Ibid., p. 171
61 Ibid., p. 127
62 Ibid., p. 21
63 D. Veseley, *Architecture and Continuity*, p. 9
64 Ibid.
65 J. Rykwert, 'The 15th Trienalle', in Rykwert, *The Necessity of Artifice*, pp. 75–7
66 Ibid., p. 77
67 R. Moneo, in *Cruz/Ortiz*, p. 18
68 L. Krier, *Leon Krier; Drawings 1967–80*, p. xxv
69 M. Culot, in ibid., p. viii
70 L. Krier, 'The Reconstruction of the European City', in ibid.
71 Krier, 'Leon Krier talks to Colin Davies', in ibid., p. xx
72 Davies, ibid., p. xxii
73 Krier, ibid., xxi
74 Rowe and Koetter, op. cit.
75 Krier, 'Leon Krier talks to Colin Davies', in op. cit., p. xxi
76 E. Jones, 'A Country Villa and a City Plan', in *Figurative Architecture: The work of Five Dublin Architects,*. p. 3
77 P. Keogh, 'Aldo Rossi' in *Aldo Rossi; Selected Writings and Projects,*., p. 7
78 J.Rykwert, 'Meaning in Building', reprinted in *The Necessity of Artifice*, op. cit., p. 9
79 Ibid., p. 12
80 Ibid., p. 9
81 Ibid., p. 12
82 Ibid., p. 16
83 Ibid.
84 Ibid., p. 15
85 Ibid., p. 9
86 H. Mallgrave and D. Goodman, *An Introduction to Architectural Theory – 1968 to the present*. p. 39
87 Maldomado, cited ibid.
88 Rykwert, op. cit., p. 12
89 Ibid., p. 16
90 C. Jencks and G. Baird, *Meaning in Architecture*, p. 7
91 Mallgrave and Goodman, op. cit., p. 40
92 C. Jencks, , in Jencks and Baird (eds.), op. cit., p. 11
93 A. Colquhoun, 'Historicism and the Limits of Semiology', in, *Essays*

in *Architectural Criticism.*, p. 129
94 Ibid., p. 130
95 Ibid.
96 Ibid.
97 Ibid., p. 131
98 Ibid., p. 138
99 Ibid., p. 13
100 C. Norberg–Schulz, 'Meaning in Architecture', in Jencks and Baird (eds.), op. cit., p. 221
101 Ibid., p. 223
102 Ibid., p. 228
103 Ibid.
104 C. Norberg–Schulz, *Existence, Space and Architecture*, p. 17
105 Ibid., pp. 12–13
106 Piaget, cited ibid., p. 11
107 Norberg–Schulz, ibid., p. 17
108 Ibid.
109 C. Norberg–Schulz, *Genius Loci; Towards a Phenomenology of Architecture*, p. 5
110 Ibid.
111 Ibid.
112 C. Norberg–Schulz, *Existence, Space and Architecture*, op. cit.
113 Ibid.

Epilogue: History, tradition, memory

1 R. Moneo, 'End of the Century Paradigms', in *Harvard Design Magazine*, Summer 1998, pp. 71–5
2 Ibid.
3 R. Romanysyhn, *Technology as Symptom & Dream*, p. 19
4 Ibid., p. 13
5 H. Foster, *Postmodern Culture*, p. viii–ix
6 J. Habermas, 'Technology and Science as "Ideology"', pp. 82–5, and 'Technical Progress and the Social Life–World', p. 51, in *Toward a Rational Society*.
7 Habermas, 'Technology and Science as "Ideology"', ibid., p. 83. Habermas is quoting from Marcuse's *Freedom and Freud's Theory of the Instincts*.
8 Ibid., p. 98
9 Ibid., p. 114
10 Habermas, 'Technical Progress and the Social Life–World', op. cit., p. 55
11 M. Heidegger, *The Question Concerning Technology*, p. 14
12 Ibid., pp. 10–14
13 C. Guignon, *The Cambridge Companion to Heidegger*, p. 23
14 Hegel, *Introduction to the Lectures on Aesthetics*, p. 49

15 Ibid., p. 70
16 Ibid., p. 70
17 Ibid., p. 84
18 Ibid., p. 10
19 C. Keréyni, *The Gods of the Greeks*, p. 103
20 Heidegger, 'Building Dwelling Thinking', in *Poetry, Language, Thought*, p. 147
21 J. Macquarrie, *Existentialism*. p. 102
22 P. Ricouer, *History and Truth*, p. 28
23 H. Arendt, *Between Past and Future*', p. 25
24 H. Gadamer, *Truth and Method*, pp. 277–82. Specifically 'what has been handed down'.
25 Ibid., p. 282
26 Ibid., p. 283
27 Ibid., p. 150
28 Ibid.
29 Ibid., p. 278
30 K. Frampton, 'Towards a Critical Regionalism; Six Points for an Architecture of Resistance', in *Labour, Work and Architecture*, p. 78
31 Ricoeur, cited ibid., p. 77
32 Frampton, ibid., p. 78
33 Frampton, ibid., p. 95
34 Ibid.
35 Ibid., p. 86.
36 Frampton, Ibid., p. 85. T. Ando, cited Frampton 'Prospects for a Critical Regionalism', p. 158.
37 Frampton, 'Rappel à l'Ordre; The Case for the Tectonic', in *Labour, Work and Architecture*, p. 91
38 Frampton, 'Carlo Scarpa and the Adoration of the Joint', in J. Cava. (ed.), *Studies in Tectonic Culture*, pp. 300–10.
39 Ibid., p. 81
40 Frampton, 'Rappel à l'Ordre', in *Architecture, Labour and Work*, op. cit., p. 103
41 Ibid.
42 F. Yates, *The Art of Memory*, p. 18
43 Ibid., p. 20
44 Yates, 'Architecture and the Art of Memory', in *AAQ, Vol. 12, No. 4*, 1980. p. 11
45 Sitte, op. cit., p. 146
46 Ibid., p. 150
47 Heidegger, op. cit., p. 154
48 P. Zumthor, Interview on Verisagge TV.
49 G. Steiner, *On Difficulty*, p. 28
50 A. Vidler, *James Frazer Stirling; Notes from the Archive*, p. 179
51 Romanyshyn, op. cit., p. 24

Kris Ellam	9.9; 9.10; 10.9
Hilary French	7.7
Timothy Garnham	1.6; 2.2; 2.3; 2.5–7; 2.10; 2.11; 2.19; 3.1–6; 3.9; 3.12–15; 4.1; 4.5; 4.6; 4.19; 4.21; 6.1–13; 6.15–20; 6.23; 6.25; 7.6; 7.8–12; 8.1; 8.3; 8.4; 8.10; 8.11; 9.13; 9.14; 9.20; 9.21; 10.3; 10.4; 10.6; 10.7; 10.8; 11.5; 11.6; 12.14; 12.15
Trevor Garnham	1.4; 2.8; 2.14–18; 3.7; 3.8; 3.13; 3.20; 4.3; 4.4; 4.12–16; 4.20; 6.14; 6.21–24; 6.26; 7.1; 7.2; 7.5; 8.2; 8.5; 8.7–9; 8.14; 8.15; 9.1; 9.2–8; 9.15–17; 9.22; 9.23; 10.1;10.2; 10.5; 11.2; 11.7–17; 12.1–3; 12.6–9; 12.11–13
Tim Gough	9.11; 9.12
Tony Ingram	8.6
Peter Kohane	10.10–12
Werner Kreis	11.18; 11.19
Robert LaFrance	11.1
Skomark Associates	11.3
Tim Wilcockson	12.10
Richard Woolf	6.16
Brendan Woods	7.3; 7.4; 7.13; 7.14; 7.15; 11.4

Bibliography

Anderson, S., *Peter Behrens and a New Architecture for the 20th Century*, MIT, Cambridge, Mass. and London, 2000.

Arendt, H., *Between Past and Future*, Penguin Books, London, 1954.

Arendt, H., *The Human Condition*, University of Chicago Press, Chicago and London, 1958.

Arnold, D., Ergut, E.A., Ozkaya, B.T. (eds), *Rethinking Architectural Historiography*, Routledge, London and New York, 2006.

Arnold, D., *Reading Architectural History*, Routledge, London and New York, 2002.

Atterbury, P., *A.W.N. Pugin: Master of Gothic Revival*, Yale University Press, New Haven and London, 1995.

Aurenhammer, H., *J. B. Fischer von Erlach*, Allen Lane, London, 1973.

Bandyopadhyay, S., Lomholt, J., Temple, N. and Tobe, R., (eds), *The Humanities in Architectural Design: a Contemporary and Historical Perspective*, Routledge, London and New York, 2010.

Banham, R., *Theory and Design in the First Machine Age*, Architectural Press, London, 1980.

Barthes, *Mythologies*, Jonathan Cape, London, 1972.

Bergdoll, B., *European Architecture 1750–1890*, Oxford University Press, Oxford, 2000.

Braham, A., *The Architecture of the French Enlightenment*, Thames and Hudson, London, 1980.

Britton, K., *Auguste Perret*, Phaidon, London, 2001.

Brownlee, D. and De Long, D., (eds), *Louis Kahn, In the Realm of Architecture*, Rizzoli, New York, 1991.

Burrow, J., *A History of Histories*, Penguin, London and New York, 2003.

Caldenby, C. and Hultin, O., *Asplund*, Rizzoli, New York, 1985.

Campbell, J., *The Flight of the Wild Gander*, Harper Collins, New York, 1990.

Caponigri, A.R., *Time and Idea: The Theory of History in Giambattista Vico*, University of Notre Dame Press, London, 1953.

Carr, E.H., *What is History*, Penguin, London, 1961.

Cassirer, E., *An Essay on Man*, Yale University Press, New Haven and London, 1944.

Cassirer, F., *The Philosophy of the Enlightenment*, Princeton University Press, New Jersey, 1951.

Clark, K., *The Gothic Revival; An Essay in the History of Taste*, John Murray, London, 1982.

Coffin, D., *The Villa in the Life of Renaissance Rome*, Princeton University Press, New Jersey, 1979.

Collingwood, R.G., *The Idea of History*, Oxford University Press, Oxford, 1946.

Collins, P., *Changing Ideals in Modern Architecture*, Faber and Faber, London, 1965.

Collins, G. and Collins, C.G., *Camillo Sitte; The Birth of Modern City Planning*, Rizzoli, New York, 1986.

Colquhoun, A., *Essays in Architectural Criticism; Modern Architecture and Historical Change*, Opposition Books, MIT Press, Cambridge, Mass. and London, 1985.

Colquhoun, A., *Modernity and the Classical Tradition, Architectural Essays 1980–1987*, MIT Press, Cambridge, Mass. and London, 1989.

Conrads, U., *Programmes and manifestoes on 20th Century architecture*, Lund Humphries, London, 1970.

Coppleston, F., *A History of Philosophy*, Image Books, New York, 1990.

Danto, A., *Nietzsche: An Original Study*, Columbia University Press, New York, 1965.

Dilthey, W., *Pattern and Meaning in History: Thoughts on History and Society*, Harper and Row, New York, 1961.

Dray, W., *Philosophy of History*, Prentice Hall, Englewood Cliffs, N.J., 1964.

Drew, J., *The Architecture of Adolf Loos*, Arts Council, London, 1985.

Eitner, L. (ed), *Neoclassicism and Romanticism, 1750–1850; Sources and Documents*, Prentice-Hall International, London, 1971.

Eliade, M., *The Myth of the Eternal Return or, Cosmos and History*, Princeton University Press, New Jersey, 1974.

Eliade, M., *The Sacred and the Profane*, Harcourt Brace Jovanovich, New York and London, 1959.

Fischer von Erlach, J.B., *A Plan of Civil and Historical Architecture, in the Presentation of the Most noted Buildings of Foreign Nations, Both Ancient and Modern*, 2nd Edition, London: MDCCXXXVII.

Forty, A., *Words and Buildings: A Vocabulary of Modern Architecture*, Thames and Hudson, London, 2000.

Foster, H., (ed), *Postmodern Culture*, Pluto Press, London, 1983.

Foucault, M., *The Archaeology of Knowledge*, Tavistock Publications, London, 1972.

Frampton, K., *Labour, Work and Architecture*, Phaidon, London, 2002.

Frampton, K., *Le Corbusier*, Thames and Hudson, London, 2001.

Frampton, K., *Modern Architecture: A Critical History*, Thames and Hudson, London, 1980.

Francastel, P., *Art and Technology in the Nineteenth and Twentieth Centuries*, Zone Books, New York, 2003.

Gadamer, H-G., *The Relevance of the Beautiful*, Cambridge University Press, Cambridge, 1977.

Gadamer, H-G., *Truth and Method*, Continuum, London and New York, 1975.

Gaddis, J., *The Landscape of History*, Oxford University Press, Oxford, 2002.

Gagnon, S., *Man and His Past: The Nature and Role of Historiography*, Harvest House, Montreal, 1982.

Garnham, T., *Lines on the Landscape, Circles from the Sky*, Tempus, Stroud, 2004.

Garnham, T., *The Oxford Museum*, Phaidon, London, 1992.

Germann, G., *Gothic Revival in Europe and Britain*, Lund Humphries, London, 1972.

Giedion, S., *Space, Time and Architecture: Growth of a New Tradition*, Oxford University Press, London, 1967.

Goldhagen, S., *Louis Kahn's Situated Modernism*, Yale University Press, New Haven and London.

Gould, S.J., *Time's Arrow, Time's Cycle*, Penguin, London and New York, 1988.

Gropius, W., *The New Architecture and the Bauhaus*, Faber and Faber, London, 1935.

Guignon, C. (ed), *The Cambridge Companion to Heidegger*, Cambridge University Press, Cambridge, 1993.

Harries, K., *The Ethical Function of Architecture*, MIT Press, Massachusetts and London, 1998.

Harris, J., *The Palladian Revival; Lord Burlington, His Villa and Garden at Chiswick*, Yale University Press, New Haven and London, 1994.

Harvey, D., *The Condition of Postmodernity*, Blackwell, Oxford, 1990.

Hart, V., *Nicholas Hawksmoor; Rebuilding Ancient Wonders*, Yale University Press, New Haven and London, 2002.

Hegel, G.W.F., *Introduction to Aesthetics*, Oxford University Press, London, 1979.

Hegel, G.W.F., *On Art, Religion and the History of Philosophy: Introductory Lectures*, Hackett Publishing Company, Indianapolis/Cambridge, 1997.

Heidegger, M., *The Concept of Time: The First Draft of Being and Time*, Continuum, London and New York, 2011.

Heidegger, M., *Poetry, Language, Thought*, Harper and Row, New York, 1971.

Heidegger, M., *The Question Concerning Technology*, Harper Row, New York, 1977.

Herbert, R., (ed.), *Modern Artists on Art*, Prentice-Hall, New Jersey, 1964.

Herodotus, *Histories*, Penguin, London, 2003.

Hermann, W., (ed), *In What Style Should we Build?* The Getty Center/University of Chicago Press, Chicago, 1992.

Hermann, W., *Laugier and eighteenth century French Theory*, A. Zwemmer, London, 1982.

Hermann, W., *The Theory of Claude Perrault*, A. Zwemmer Ltd, London, 1973.

Heynen, H., *Architecture and Modernity; a Critique*, MIT Press, Cambridge, Mass. and London, 1999.

Hitchcock, H.R. and Johnson, P., *The International tyle; Architecture since 1992*, Museum of Modern Art, New York, 1932.

Hollingdale, R.J., *Nietzsche: The Man and his Philosophy*, Cambridge University Press, Cambridge, 1999.

Horkheimer, M., *Eclipse of Reason*, The Seabury Press, New York, 1947.

Horkheimer, M. and Adorno, T., *Dialectic of Enlihtenment; Philosophical Fragments*, Stanford University Press, Stanford, 2002.

Hunt, J.D., *Garden and Grove*, Princeton University Press, Princeton, New Jersey, 1986.

Hunt, J.D., *William Kent; Landscape Garden Designer*, A. Zwemmer, London, 1987.

Hussey, C., *The Picturesque; Studies in a Point of View*, Frank Cass, London, 1967.

Hvattum, M. and Hermansen, C. (eds), *Tracing Modernity: Manifestations of the Modern in Architecture and the City*, Routledge, London and New York, 2004.

Jencks, C. and Baird, G. (eds), *Meaning in Architecture*, The Cresset Press, London, 1969.

Jencks, C. and Kropt, K., *Theories and Manifestoes of Contemporary Architecture*, Academy Edition, London, 1997.

Joedicke, J., *Architecture Since 1945*, Pall Mall Press, London, 1969.

Kaufmann, E., *Architecture and the Age of Reason: Baroque and Post-Baroque in England, Italy, and France*, Dover Publications, New York, 1968.

Kaufmann, E., *Three Revolutionary Architects, Bouille, Ledoux and Lequeu*, Translations of the American Philosophical Society, Philadelphia, 1952.

Kaufmann, E, Jr., *The Rise of an American Architecture*, Pall Mall Press, London, 1970.

Kostka, A, and Wohlfarth, I., (eds), *Nietzsche and an 'Architecture of our Minds'*, The Getty Research Institute Publications, Los Angeles, 1999.

Krista Sykes, A., (ed), *Constructing a New Agenda: Architectural Theory 1993–2009*, Princeton Architectural Press, Princeton, 2010.

Laugier, A., *Essay on Architecture*, Hennessey & Ingalls, Los Angeles, 1985.

Leach, A., *What is Architectural History?* Politic Press, Cambridge, UK, Malden, USA, 2010.

Leatherbarrow, D., Character, 'Geometry and Perspective: the Third Earl of Shaftesbury's Principles of Garden Design', *Journal of Garden History*. Vol 4.

Le Corbusier, *Le Poème de l'Angle Droit*, Fondation Le Corbusier, Paris, 1989.

Lobell, J., *Between Silence and Light; Spirit in the Architecture of Louis I. Kahn*, Shambala Publications, Boulder, Colorado, 1979.

Löwy, M., *Fire Alarm: Reading Walter Benjamin's 'On the Concept of History'*, Verso, London and New York, 2005.

Macquarrie, J., *Existentialism: An introduction, guide and assessment*, Penguin Books, London, 1972.

Mallgrave, H. (ed), *Reflections on the Raiment of Modernity*, University of Chicago Press, Chicago, 1993.

Mallgrave, H., *Gottfried Semper; Architect of the nineteenth Century*, Yale University Press, New Haven and London, 1996.

Mallgrave, H.F. and Goodman, D., *An Introduction to Architectural Theory; 1968 to the Present*, Blackwell, Chichester, 2011.

Marsak, L.M., *The Nature of Historical Inquiry*, Holt, Rinehart and Winston, New York, 1970.

Middleton, R. (ed.) *The Beaux-Arts and Nineteenth-century Architecture*, MIT Press, Cambridge, Mass. and London, 1982.

Middleton, R. and Watkin, D., *Neoclassical and 19th Century Architecture*, Harry N. Abrams, New York, 1980.

Mostafavi, M. and Leatherbarrow, D., *On Weathering; The Life of Buildings in Time*, MIT Press, Cambridge, Mass and London, 1993.

Muthesius, H., *Style-Architecture and Building-Art: Transformations of Architecture in the Nineteenth Century and its Present Condition*, The Getty Centre, University of Chicago Press, Chicago, 1994.

Nietzsche, F., *Ecce Homo*, Penguin Books, London, 1979.

Nietzsche, F., *Human, All Too Human*, Penguin Books, London, 1994.

Nietzsche, F., *On the Genealogy of Morals*, Oxford University Press, Oxford, 1996.

Nietzsche, F., *Thus Spoke Zarathustra*, Penguin Books, London, 1961.

Nietzsche, F., *Untimely Meditations*, (ed.) Breazeale, D., Cambridge University Press, Cambridge, 1997.

Norberg-Schulz, C., *The Concept of Dwelling: On the Way to Figurative Architecture*, Rizzoli, New York, 1985.

Norberg-Schulz, C., *Existence, Space and Architecture*, Studio Vista, London, 1971.

Norberg-Schulz, C., *Genius Loci; Towards a Phenomenology of Architecture*, Academy Editions, London, 1980.

Norberg-Schulz, C., 'Kahn, Heidegger and the Language of Architecture', *Oppositions* Fall 1979:18 MIT Press, Cambridge, Mass.

Norberg-Schulz, C., *Meaning in Western Architecture*, Studio Vista, London, 1975.

Ockman, J., (ed) *Architecture Culture 1945-1960; A Documentary Anthology*, Columbian Books of Architecture/Rizzoli, New York, 1993.

Oppenheimer Dean, A., *Bruno Zevi on Modern Architecture*, Rizzoli, New York, 1983.

Ortega y Gasset, J., *The Dehumanization of Art*, Princeton University Press, Princeton, 1968.

Otero-Pailos, J., *Architecture's Historical Turn: Phenomenology and the Rise of the Postmodern*, University of Minnesota Press, Minneapolis and London, 2010.

Perez-Gomez, A., *Architecture and the Crisis of Modern Science*, The MIT Press, Cambridge, Mass. and London, 1983.

Pevsner, N., *Pioneers of Modern Design; From William Morris to Walter Gropius*, Penguin, London, 1964. .

L. Ploegaerts, 'Nietzsche and van de Velde', in Kostka, A and Wohlfarth, A, *A Nietzsche of our Minds*, pp. 233–55.

Polano, S., *Berlage: Complete Works*, Butterworth, London, 1988.

Popper, K., *The Poverty of Historicism*, Routledge and Kegan Paul, London, 1961.

Portoghesi, P., Scully, V., Jencks, C. and Norberg-Schulz, C., (eds), *The Presence of the Past*, Academy Editions, London and Milan, 1980.

Richardson, K. (ed.), *British Architecture in the Fifties*, Kingston University Press, Kingston, 1996.

Richardson, M., *John Soane Architect; Master of Space and Light*, Royal Academy of Arts, London, 1999.

Ricoeur, P., *History and Truth*, Northwestern University Press, Illinois, 2007.

Ricoeur, P., *Memory, History, Forgetting*, The University of Chicago Press, Chicago and London, 2006.

Bibliography

Ricoeur, P. *Time and Narrative: Volume 1*, The University of Chicago Press, Chicago and London, 1983.

Romanyshin, R.D., Routledge, *Technology as Symptom and Dream*, London, 1989.

Rosen, S., *The Mask of Enlightenment: Nietzsche's Zarathustra*, Cambridge University Press, Cambridge, 1995.

Rossi, A., *The Architecture of the City*, Opposition Books, MIT Press, Cambridge, Mass. and London: 1982.

Rowe, C. and Koetter, F., *Collage City*, MIT Press, Cambridge, Mass. and London, 1978.

Rowe, C., *The Mathematics of the Ideal Villa and Other Essays*, MIT Press, Cambridge, Mass. and London, 1976.

Rykwert, J., *The Necessity of Artifice*, Academy Editions, London, 1982.

Rykwert, J., *The First Moderns: The Architects of the Eighteenth Century*, The MIT Press, Massachusetts and London, 1980.

Schinkel, K., *Collected Architectural Designs*, Academy Editions, London, 1982.

Schildt, G., *Alvar Aalto in his own Words*, Rizzoli, New York, 1997.

Schorske, K., *Fin-de-Siecle Vienna: Politics and Culture*, Weidenfeld and Nicolson, London, 1980.

Schumacher, T., *Giuseppe Terragni,; Surface and Symbol*, Ernst and Sohn, Princeton University Press, Princeton and Oxford, 1991.

Scully, V., *Modern Architecture*, George Brazilier, New York, 1961.

Scully, V., *Modern Architecture and Other Essays*, Princeton University Press, Princeton and Oxford, 2003.

Scully, V., *Modern Architecture and Urbanism*, Henry Holt and Co., New York, 1998.

Schwarz, F., *The Werkbund; Design Theory and Culture before the First World War*, Yale University Press, New Haven and London, 1996.

Sennett, R., *The Craftsman*, Penguin Books, London and New York, 2008.

Sennett, R., *The Conscience of the Eye; the Design and Social Life of Cities*, Faber and Faber, London, 1991.

Shaftesbury, *Characteristicks of Men, Manners, Opinions, Times.*

Smithson, A. (ed), *Team 10 Primer*, Studio Vista, London, 1968.

Snodin, M., *Karl Friedrich Schinkel: A Universal Man*, Yale University Press, New Haven and London, 1991.

Spengler, O., *The Decline of the West*, George Allen and Unwin, London, 1980.

Stern, J.P., *Nietzsche*, Fontana Press, London, 1978.

Stroud, D., *Sir John Soane, Architect*, Faber and Faber, London and Boston, 1984.

Summerson, J., *Heavenly Mansions and other essays on Architecture*, The Norton Library, New York and London, 1963.

Summerson, J., *The Architecture of the Eighteenth Century*, Thames and Hudson, London, 1969.

Tafuri, M. and Dal Co, F., *Modern Architecture: Vol 2*, Faber and Faber/ Electa, London and New York, 1986.

Tafuri, M., *The Sphere and the Labyrinth: Avant-Gardes and Architecture from Piranesi to the 1970s*, The MIT Press, Massachusetts and London, 1987.

Taut, B., *Alpine Architecture; a Utopia*, Prestel, München, Berlin, London, New York, 2004.

Thompson, W., *What happened to History?* Pluto Press, London and Stirling, Virginia, 2000.

Toss, J., *The Pursuit of History*, Longman, London and New York, 1984.

Tournikiotis, P., *The Historiography of Modern Architecture*, MIT Press, Cambridge, Mass. and London, 1999.

Van den Heuvel, D. and Risselada,M. (eds), *Alison and Peter Smithson – from the House of the Future to a house of today*, 010 Publishers, Rotterdam, 2004.

Venturi, R., *Complexity and Contradiction in Architecture*, The Museum of Modern Art, New York, 1966.

Veseley, D., *Architecture and Continuity*, Architectural Association, London, 1982.

Vesely, D., *Architecture in the Age of Divided Representation*, MIT Press, Cambridge, Mass. and London, 2004.

Vico, G., *New Science*, Penguin Books, London and New York, 1999.

Vico, G., *The Autobiography of Giambattista Vico*, Cornell University Press, Ithaca and London, 1975.

Vidler, A., *Histories of the Immediate Present: Inventing Architectural Modernism*, The MIT Press, Massachusetts and London, 2008.

Vidler, A., *James Frazer Stirling: Notes from the Archive*, Yale University Press, New Haven and London, 2010.

Vidler, A., *The Writing of the Walls: Architectural Theory of the Late Enlightenment*, Princeton Architectural Press, Princeton, 1987.

Vitruvius, *The Ten Books on Architecture*, Dover, New York, 1960.

von Franz, M-L., *Time; Rhythm and Repose*, Thames and Hudson, London, 1978.

Wagner, O., *Modern Architecture*, The Getty Centre for the History of Art and the Humanities, Santa Monica, 1988.

Watkin, D., *The Rise of Architectural History*, Architectural Press, London, 1980.

Webster, H. (ed), *Modernism without Rhetoric: Essays on the work of Alison and Peter Smithson*, Academy Editions, London, 1997.

Weston, R., *Alvar Aalto*, Phaidon, London, 1996.

White, M., *De Stijl and Dutch Modernism*, Manchester University Press, Manchester and New York, 2003.

Whitrow, G.J., *Time in History: Views of Time in Prehistory to the Present day*, Oxford University Press, Oxford, 1988.

Wilson, C. St. J., *The Other Tradition of Modern Architecture: The Uncompleted Project*, Black Dog Publishing, London, 2007.

Wilson, C. St. J., Architectural Reflections: Studies in the Philosophy and Practice of Architecture, Butterworth, London, 1992.

Wilton-Ely, J., *Piranesi*, Arts Council of Great Britain, London, 1978.

Wittkower, R., *Architectural Principle in the Age of Humanism*, Alec Tiranti, London, 1962.

Wittkower, R., *Palladio and Palladianism*, George Brazilier, New York, 1974.

Wrede, S., *The Architecture of Erik Gunnar Asplund*, MIT Press, Cambridge, Mass. and London, 1980.

Yates, F., *The Art of Memory*, Penguin, London, 1966.

Zevi, B., *Giuseppe Terragni*, Triangle Architectural, London, 1980.

Index

Index

Index

Index